The Dismantling
of Time
in Contemporary
Poetry

The

Dismantling of

Time

in Contemporary

Poetry

Richard Jackson

The University of Alabama Press

Tuscaloosa and London

Library of Congress Cataloging-in-Publication Data

Jackson, Richard, 1946–
  The dismantling of time in contemporary poetry.

  Bibliography: p.
  1. American poetry—20th century—History and
criticism. 2. Time in literature. I. Title.
PS310.T56J33   1988   811'.5'09384   86-4338
ISBN 0-8173-0311-1

British Library Cataloguing-in-Publication Data is available.

For My Students

Contents

Acknowledgments

Parts of the Introduction appeared in *Southern Humanities Review, Prairie Schooner, Contemporary Literature, Poet and Critic, Poesis, Studies in Romanticism*, and *New England Review*. The essay on Warren appeared in *Boundary 2*, the essay on Hollander in *Poetry Miscellany*, the essay on Levertov in *Sagatrieb* (National Poetry Foundation), and the essay on Wright in *Chowder Review*. Several pages from the Hollander essay also appeared in *South Carolina Review*. I wish to thank the National Endowment for the Humanities for an independent research grant that helped me complete much of the secondary reading in philosophy for this project, and also the University of Chattanooga Foundation and Faculty Research Committee at the University of Tennessee at Chattanooga for several summer grants. I also want to thank Susan Barclift, who helped in the research and prepared the final copy of this manuscript, and Sandra Moore and Beth Riddlespurger for their help in proofreading the manuscript. My own teachers, especially John Murphy, Robert Pack, A. B. Giamatti, and Michael Cooke, taught wonderful lessons in how to read poems.

Acknowledgments

From *Shadow Train*, by John Ashbery, Copyright © 1980, 1981, by John Ashbery. Reprinted by permission of Viking Penguin, Inc. and Carcanet Press.

From *Houseboat Days*, by John Ashbery, Copyright © 1975, 1976, 1977 by John Ashbery. Reprinted by permission of Viking Penguin, Inc., and Richard Scott Simon, Ltd.

From *Self-Portrait in a Convex Mirror*, by John Ashbery, Copyright © 1972, 1973, 1974, 1975 by John Ashbery. Reprinted by permission of Viking Penguin, Inc. and Carcanet Press.

From *A Wave*, by John Ashbery, Copyright © 1981, 1982, 1983, 1984 by John Ashbery. Reprinted by permission of Viking Penguin, Inc., and Carcanet Press.

From *Our Ground Time Here Will Be Brief*, by Maxine Kumin, Copyright © 1977 by Maxine Kumin. Reprinted by permission of Viking Penguin, Inc.

Denise Levertov, *Collected Earlier Poems 1940–1960*, Copyright © 1946, 1957, 1958, 1959 by Denise Levertov Goodman. Reprinted by permission of New Directions Publishing Corporation.

Denise Levertov, *Life in the Forest*, Copyright © 1975, 1976, 1977, 1978 by Denise Levertov Goodman. Reprinted by permission of New Directions Publishing Corporation.

Denise Levertov, *Footprints*, Copyright © 1970, 1971 by Denise Levertov Goodman. "The Life Around Us" was first published in *Amphora* in 1971. "Novella" was first published in *Field*; "Hut" was first published in *OYEZ Summer Poems* in 1970; "By the Rail through . . ." was first published in *New Departures*. Reprinted by permission of New Directions Publishing Corporation.

Denise Levertov, *Relearning the Alphabet*, Copyright © 1968, 1970 by Denise Levertov Goodman. Reprinted by permission of New Directions Publishing Corporation.

Denise Levertov, *To Stay Alive*, Copyright © 1965, 1966, 1970, 1971 by Denise Levertov Goodman. "Prologue: An Interim" was first published in *Poetry* in 1968. Reprinted by permission of New Directions Publishing Corporation.

Denise Levertov, *Candles in Babylon*, Copyright © 1978, 1979, 1980, 1981, 1982 by Denise Levertov Goodman. Reprinted by permission of New Directions Publishing Corporation.

Denise Levertov, *Oblique Prayers*, Copyright © 1981, 1982, 1983, 1984 by Denise Levertov Goodman. Reprinted by permission of New Directions Publishing Corporation.

Denise Levertov, *The Freeing of the Dust*, Copyright © 1975 by Denise

Levertov Goodman. Reprinted by permission of New Directions Publishing Corporation.

Denise Levertov, *Poems 1960–1967*, Copyright © 1961, 1962, 1965, 1966 by Denise Levertov Goodman. The "Olga Poems" were first published in *Poetry* in 1965, and "Life at War" was first published in *Poetry* in 1966. Reprinted by permission of New Directions Publishing Corporation.

From *Summer Celestial* by Stanley Plumly, Copyright © 1983 by Stanley Plumly. Published in 1983 by The Ecco Press. Used by Permission.

From *Kicking the Leaves* by Donald Hall, Copyright © 1978 by Donald Hall. Reprinted by permission of Harper & Row, Publishers, Inc. and the author.

From *The Poems of Stanley Kunitz 1972–1978*, Atlantic-Little Brown, 1979, Copyright © 1979 by Stanley Kunitz. Used by permission of the author.

From *Blue Wine* by John Hollander, Copyright © 1979 by John Hollander. Reprinted by permission of the author and Johns Hopkins University Press.

From *Waking to My Name: New and Selected Poems*, by Robert Pack, Copyright © 1980 by Robert Pack. Reprinted by permission of the author and Johns Hopkins University Press.

From *The Palm at the End of the Mind* by Wallace Stevens, edited by Holly Stevens, Copyright © 1971 by Holly Stevens. Reprinted by permission of Holly Stevens and Alfred A. Knopf, Inc.

From *This Journey* by James Wright, Copyright © 1982 by Anne Wright. Used by permission of Anne Wright and Random House, Inc.

From *Collected Poems* by James Wright, Copyright © 1973 by James Wright. Reprinted with permission of Wesleyan University Press.

Excerpts from *To a Blossoming Pear Tree* by James Wright, Copyright © 1978 by James Wright. Reprinted by permission of Farrar, Straus and Giroux.

From *Two Citizens* by James Wright, Copyright © 1975 by James Wright. Used by permission of Anne Wright.

Excerpt from "Poem" from *The Complete Poems of Elizabeth Bishop*, Copyright 1949, renewed © 1976 by Elizabeth Bishop. Reprinted by permission of Farrar, Straus and Giroux.

From *Being Here: Poetry 1977–1980* by Robert Penn Warren, Copyright © 1980 by Robert Penn Warren. Used by permission of Robert Penn Warren and Random House, Inc.

From *Selected Poems, 1923–1975*, by Robert Penn Warren, Copyright © 1977 by Robert Penn Warren. Used by permission of Robert Penn Warren and Random House, Inc.

From *Chief Joseph of the Nez Perce* by Robert Penn Warren, Copyright ©

Acknowledgments

1980 by Robert Penn Warren. Used by permission of Robert Penn Warren and Random House, Inc.

From *Now and Then: Poems, 1976–1978* by Robert Penn Warren, Copyright © 1978 by Robert Penn Warren. Used by permission of Robert Penn Warren and Random House, Inc.

From *Rumor Verified: Poems, 1979–1980* by Robert Penn Warren, Copyright © 1981 by Robert Penn Warren. Used by permission of Robert Penn Warren and Random House, Inc.

From *Brother to Dragons* by Robert Penn Warren, Copyright © 1953, 1979 by Robert Penn Warren. Used by permission of Robert Penn Warren and Random House, Inc.

From *Selected Poems, 1923–1985* by Robert Penn Warren, Copyright © 1985 by Robert Penn Warren. Used by permission of Robert Penn Warren and Random House, Inc.

From *7 Years from Somewhere* by Philip Levine, Copyright © 1979 by Philip Levine; *Ashes* by Philip Levine, Copyright © 1979 by Philip Levine; *They Feed They Lion* by Philip Levine, Copyright © 1973 by Philip Levine. Used by permission of the author.

From "Until The Sea is Dead" in *The Shore* by David St. John, Copyright © 1980 by David St. John. Reprinted by permission of Houghton Mifflin Company.

From *Flood* by William Matthews, Copyright © 1982 by William Matthews. Used by permission of the author.

From *These Green-Going-to-Yellow* by Marvin Bell, Copyright © 1981 by Marvin Bell. Used by permission of the author.

From *Dismantling the Silence* by Charles Simic, Copyright © 1971 by Charles Simic; *Return to a Place Lit by a Glass of Milk* by Charles Simic, Copyright © 1974 by Charles Simic; *Charon's Cosmology* by Charles Simic, Copyright © 1977; *Austerities* by Charles Simic, Copyright © 1982 by Charles Simic; *Selected Poems* by Charles Simic, Copyright © 1985 by Charles Simic. Used by permission of the author.

From *Weather Report for Utopia and Vicinity,* by Charles Simic, Copyright © 1983 by Charles Simic. Reprinted with permission of Station Hill Press.

From *White: A New Version* by Charles Simic, Copyright © 1980 by Charles Simic. Used by permission of Logbridge-Rhodes.

From *Spectral Emanations* by John Hollander, Copyright © 1978 by John Hollander; *Powers of Thirteen* by John Hollander, Copyright © 1979 by John Hollander; *Reflections on Espionage* by John Hollander, Copyright © 1976 by John Hollander. Used by permission of John Hollander.

Acknowledgments

A special thanks to Dr. Charles Hyder, Associate Provost, UT-Chattanooga for his support and for his arranging for the funds to pay for these permission fees which could not otherwise have been met and without which the nature of this book would be changed dramatically or the book might have remained unpublished. Also thanks to Marg and Amy Jackson, and to Chuck Scott, for helping with the index.

Common Abbreviations

(Abbreviations for books by poets are given by main letters of titles and included parenthetically in the text.)

Acts	Jackson, *Acts of Mind*
AEM	Schiller, *On the Aesthetic Education of Man*
AK	Foucault, *The Archeology of Knowledge*
AWA	Howard, *Alone with America*
BA	*Beyond Amazement*
BBB	Wittgenstein, *Blue and Brown Books*
BL	Coleridge, *Biographia Literaria*
BN	Sartre, *Being and Nothingness*
BQ	Jabes, *The Book of Questions*
BT	Heidegger, *Being and Time*
CLC	*Collected Letters of Coleridge*
CP	*Collected Poems*, author identified in text
CPR	Kant, *Critique of Pure Reason*
D	Derrida, *Dissemination*
DL	Kristeva, *Desire in Language*
DT	Heidegger, *Discourse on Thinking*
E	Lacan, *Ecrits*
EB	Heidegger, *Existence and Being*
EO	Kierkegaard, *Either/Or*
FFC	Lacan, *Four Fundamental Concepts of Psycho-Analysis*
GR	*Georgia Review*
GM	Nietzsche, *Genealogy of Morals*
GS	Nietzsche, *The Gay Science*
HQ	Spanos, *Heidegger and the Question of Literature*
HTC	Hegel, *"Preface". . . Texts and Commentary*
ID	Heidegger, *Identity and Difference*

Abbreviations

IM	Heidegger, *Introduction to Metaphysics*
KPM	Heidegger, *Kant and the Problem of Metaphysics*
LCM	Foucault, *Language, Counter-Memory, Practice*
LF	Brisman in *Literary Freud*
LS	Lacan, *Language of the Self*
M	Derrida, *Margins*
MPR	*Modern Poetry Review*
N	Heidegger, *Nietzsche*
NC	*Notebooks of Coleridge*
NLH	*New Literary History*
NN	*The New Nietzsche*
OG	Derrida, *Of Grammatology*
OGM	Nietzsche, *On the Genealogy of Morals*
OWL	Heidegger, *On the Way to Language*
PHM	Hegel, *Phenomenology of Mind*
PLT	Heidegger, *Poetry Language Thought*
PM	*The Poetry Miscellany*
PP	Merleau-Ponty, *Phenomenology of Perception*
Problems	Heidegger, *Basic Problems of Metaphysics*
PS	Deleuze, *Proust and Signs*
REP	Kierkegaard, *Repetition*
RM	Ricoeur, *The Rule of Metaphor*
SC	*Structuralist Controversy*
SP	Riffaterre, *Semiotics of Poetry*
SPH	Derrida, *Speech and Phenomena*
TB	Heidegger, *Time and Being*
TFW	Bergson, *Time and Free Will*
TSZ	Nietzsche, *Thus Spake Zarathustra*
WC	*Collected Works of Coleridge*
WD	Derrida, *Writing and Difference*
WP	Nietzsche, *Will To Power*
WT	*Warren Talking*
YFS	*Yale French Studies*

Note: Abbreviations for texts of poetry refer to those texts cited in the Bibliography. Heidegger references use H numbers, not pages, and *The Will to Power* is given by section number.

Introduction

Time as Perspective

Introduction

For me, the firefly's quick, electric stroke
Ticks tediously the time of one more year.

—Stevens

In his *Essays on the Principles of Method*, Coleridge says that the man of "methodical industry" need not submit to time, for such a man can himself be the origin and creator of time:

> If the idle are described as killing time, he may be justly said to call it into life and moral being, while he makes it the distinct object not only of the consciousness, but of the conscience. He organizes the hours, and gives them a soul: and that, the very essence of which is to fleet away, and evermore *to have been*, he takes up into his own permanence, and communicates it to the imperishableness of a spiritual nature [*The Friend*, WC 430].

If the methodical man is the animator of time, one who, in traditional metaphysical terms, transforms time from lifeless matter to "spiritual" form, his transition from industrious pragmatic to essential idealist is perhaps less facile than Coleridge makes it sound. Yet that very transition reveals the crucial link which Coleridge, like the other Romantics, attempts to establish between history and metaphysics; and its problematic nature reveals the complex situation of the poet as founder of the link. The text, then, poses certain questions basic to the Romantic tradition. What is the constitution of the link that is posited here? By what *method* is it established? Where is it to be located?

Coleridge himself offers us some further clarification. In an 1811 letter to Henry Crabb Robinson, he describes Love as "always the abrupt creation of a moment," though it may be preceded by "years of *Dawning*." What follows, as he develops the analogy between

2

conventional linear time and the process of dawning, is a definition of the unique temporal structure of the moment: "between the brightest Hues of the Dawn and the first Rim of the Sun itself there is a *chasm*—all before were Differences of Degrees, passing and dissolving into each other—but there is a difference of *Kind*—a chasm of Kind in a continuity of Time." How is this chasm itself defined? "The sun calls up the vapour, attenuates, lifts it—it becomes a cloud—and now it is the Veil of the Divinity—the Divinity transpiercing it at once hides and declares his presence" (*CLC*, No. 814).

There is a tension in all Coleridge says, and indeed in nearly all Romantic and post-Romantic texts, between the moment of illumination and an analytic *progressus* towards that moment. We see it, for instance, in a title like "Lyrical Ballads," which combines the sense of lyric presence, of a continuous voice, with vagaries of narrative-ballad technique—a tension, really, between timelessness and time, or, as we already suggested, metaphysics and history. The moment of illumination—especially as we see it in, say, Blake's epics or Shelley's visions—is an attempt to stop time and order a coherent view of the world. Its great success is the tranquility or expansiveness, but its failure is simply that just as much as the world changes in time, the moment falsifies that change.

It is precisely such a paradox, for instance, that informs Maxine Kumin's "Caught," a poem clearly in the Wordsworthian tradition. After mentioning how her "goats keep leaving Eden," how time always seems to seep away, she ends with a gesture that tries literally to paddock time, to fence it in, even as her staccato syntax acknowledges time's push:

> Late August. Truce, this instant, with what's to come.
> Everything Caught. This moment caught. My horse
> at the paddock fence making that soft
> ingratiating nicker that asks for supper.
> No older and no riper than was planned
> the sun straining the west. My matching hands.
>
> [*GT* 77]

What she achieves, a "truce," suggests how creatively failed all such attempts finally are, and the passage ends with a rather passive stance,

3

acknowledging time's "plan," a sort of fate. And this is, in fact, the fate of all poetry that attempts to overcome a traditional view of time, especially poems in the Wordsworthian mode. This is not to criticize this mode at all, only to outline the terms of its temporal encounters. It sees time as external to the self, spatialized (here, literally held in the paddock); in that way it can be viewed, analyzed, even re-structured.

A perfect example of the desire to spatialize time occurs in Robert Pack's "Rondo of the Familiar," where the speaker situates himself in an enclosure, a threshold between past and future. What the speaker hopes for is an extended duration, a reprieve from time. The "Rondo" itself, with its opening "text" of four lines and consequent phrasal modulations of those lines, provides a subtle vehicle for a further deferral of the opening moment of the "pause." The poem begins as the speaker addresses his wife:

> Beside the waterfall,
> by the lichen face of rock,
> you pause in pine shade to remember blue
> for drawing back, green
> for trust, replenishing yourself
> among familiar leaves
> with scattered sunlight.
>
> [WN 12]

As the poem progresses, an Hegelian dialectic between motion and rest emerges through the Romantic emblems of waterfall and stubborn lichen. That is, Time is seen not simply as a measure of changes or in idealistic attempts to ignore it, but rather as a dialectic of the desire to hold the moment still, what any poetic form attempts, and the knowledge that the form itself marks an incremental progression through time. The pause gradually expands to include the couple's own past and the future lives, and eventually their children's lives "beyond the trees in time not ours." The speaker's hope is that the children might "hold for an instant in the pause," and more, that he might "enter that pause / though the waterfall spills on." As the modulations of the opening phrases continue, though, it becomes apparent that the pause must dissolve. Yet the poem ends triumphantly by

4

returning fully to its beginnings when the speaker anticipates his children's repeating the opening scene. Pack's, finally, is a modulated time, defined as a moment of repeating beginnings, repeated expansions.

The key to the spatialized moment's success, then, is precisely this sort of expansiveness. Yet this also begins to involve a certain kind of interiorizing, a certain acknowledgment of the self as the source for time, of poetry as the generator of the self's time. In a recent interview, for example, Stanley Kunitz says that "poetry has its source, deep under the layers of a life, in the primordial self" (*AM* 116). It is the task of the poet, he goes on, to "fold back these layers" in order to recover that self. On the one hand, these layers are what he some-times calls "masks," a multiplicity of selves we manifest in our lives and which obscure something more permanent. In the title poem of the section of new poems, "The Layers," in this latest collection, for example, he exclaims:

> I have walked through many lives,
> some of them my own,
> and I am not who I was,
> though some principle of being
> abides, from which I struggle
> not to stray.
>
> [*PSK* 35]

On the other hand, there are also "layers" of historical time. So, for example, Kunitz stands upon a "seven-layered world" in "The Mound Builders" (II) and defines his own moment by his relation to various archeological periods, to "a manifold tissue of events, connected with different epochs." What Kunitz manages to do by his interpenetration of personal and historical time is establish these various layers as "different aspects of the eternal present." Time becomes fully spa-tialized, and ever expanding. The result is an encompassing vision that strains against the tight but fluid lines. The vision is something like that described in the powerful "Robin Redbreast" where the speaker peers through the "whistle-clean," perfectly centered bullet hole in the head of a robin he has found: "I caught the cold flash of the blue / unappeasable sky."

Introduction

Perhaps the most difficult problem facing any vision of an endlessly proliferating, expanding moment is simply, as Jacques Derrida points out, that it must eventually be punctuated by time—it ends, the poem ends (*SP*). This sort of expansiveness, balanced against the discontinuity of time that is ultimately recognized, goes a long way towards explaining the sectioning in so many modern poems. It is the sort of discontinuous expansion Byron called "piecemeal"—a linking of potentially eternal moments. The process of piecemeal expansion contains what Friedrich Schiller calls two simultaneous movements: a deployment of the self's temporal structures throughout the world (a process of *actualization*, of producing history from one's possibilities), and an incorporation of the world's diversity in time under the temporal structures of the self (a process of creating forms that consolidate the self's possibilities in art). In the first case, the poet creates a new time for the world, and in the second he "annuls" traditional time: the poet, says Schiller, "realizes form when he creates time, and opposes constancy with alteration, the eternal unity of his ego with the diversity of the world; he gives form to matter when he proceeds to annul time, affirms persistence in change, and subjects the diversity of the world to the unity of his ego" (*AEM* 63). The play between these two movements is of course endless; for a metaphysics of time creation, Being is subsumed under Becoming. "Hence even in dreams of Sleep the Soul never *is*," says Coleridge in a *Notebook* entry, "because it cannot or dare not be any (ONE) THING; but lives in approaches" (*NC* #3215). According to Schiller, the poet who lives always on the "horizon's verge" achieves "the highest expansion of being," where "all barriers disappear." Through the piecemeal process of expansion, the time-creating impulse we have described, "we are no more in time but time, with its complete and infinite succession, is in us" (*AEM* 67).

With time fully internalized, the poet's choices become more complex. One solution is to suggest that the poem itself is only a catalyst, that time goes on, the self goes on, beyond the lines of the poem. In "Stone Walls," the final poem in Donald Hall's *Kicking the Leaves*, the poet, remembering his grandfather, tells how "riding home from the hayfields, he handed me the past." It is just such a "handing over" that Hall repeats and extends in this flawless and moving book. And that past, as he suggests later in "Stone Walls," is a complex arrange-

6

ment of perspectives—social, personal, and geological perspectives—
Allende, the Shah of Iran, Tiberius, a slain grocer; his own family
history; the "Jamming plates" of the Appalachian range which formed
the White Mountains of New Hampshire where he now lives, and the
retreat of glaciers even as there were "Siberian eyes / tracking bear
ten thousand years ago / on Kearsage." Now the basis of this handing
over of the past is what Hall calls a "return" to the very origins of the
conscious self:

<blockquote>
I am wild
with the joy of leaves falling, of stone walls
emerging, of return to the countryside
where I lay as a boy
in the valley of noon heat, in the village
of little sounds; where I floated
out of myself, into the world that lives in the air.

[*KL* 51]
</blockquote>

The counterpointing of past and present which constitutes the
"return" provides the basis for a system of balances that is gradually
modulated—between floating and falling; by the movement into the
past self, then out of that self, then into past imaginings; between
these dynamics of motion and the stasis of the reclining boy; between
that solitary boy in the countryside and his "village / of little sounds,"
and so on. These balances are sustained, here and throughout the
book, by the repetition and variation of vowel sounds, the easy con-
traction and expansion of line lengths (one remembers Hall's definition of form in the conclusion to his recent *Remembering Poets*:
"minute resolutions of vowel and metaphor, consonant and idea, by
which the poem finds its requisite wholeness"). These balances, inherent in the "return," also suggest a pattern of compensations—the
very barrenness of autumn allows the old stone walls to be seen, and
the stone walls themselves, "emerging" each autumn, are man's counterpart to the "unperishing hills," to the cyclic nature of the seasons.
The impulse to "return" to the "world that lives in the air," then, is
not finally a metaphysical or transcendental one; the aim, and the
difficulty Hall confronts in this book, is both to "float out of the self"
and yet "walk on the earth of the present."

The way to the "return" is opened by a realization of how all things, on a very physical level, interpenetrate. Thus the drama of the opening poem, "Eating the Pig," resides in the poet's carefully establishing distinctions and links between the present "now" and all time. After describing how he and his friends "forage" the pig like an army, Hall, after digressing into a description of some army's activities, pulls back to the simple present: "No, we are here, eating the pig together." Yet the military metaphors and similes keep *emerging*—the pig's skin is like a "parchment bag," and like a "contour map of a defeated country." These metaphors are then replaced by references to pre-historic life along the Tigris and Euphrates, to Hannibal, to ancient China, to Abraham, to Achilles. But the lines of descent always remain physical; he addresses the pig at the end, telling how he and his friends "tore your body apart, and took it, / into our bodies." In "Maple Syrup," a quart of syrup made twenty-five years ago by Hall's now dead grandfather, and now recently discovered, serves as a vehicle for this physical transcendence:

> taste
> the sweetness, you for the first time,
> the sweetness preserved, of a dead man
> in his own kitchen,
> giving us
> from his lost grave the gift of sweetness.
>
> [*KL* 27]

In a sense, the "return" (note here the returns of "sweetness" and the counterpointing of the long vowel sound in that word with the short-*i* sounds), as an *emergence* of new relations, is always a beginning, a "first time," an enterprise for the future.

The solution William Matthews finds in "Rosewood, Ohio" is at once more trancendental and more subjective (*F* 16). He begins to think about how "time goes one way only but we / go two: We disappear into the past / And into the future at once." And if the past, when he was young, could be forgotten so that he "wouldn't know, even / how to name its loss," the future has become the present now, ambiguous because it, too, has forgotten part of the past. It is, finally, this poetic doubleness ("The truth is that I slept well / And that I was awake all night") that allows the narrator to make presence of absence,

8

to reinscribe loss with the mythic texture of fullness, to touch the surface of his own words, so that he can "drowse," Keats-like, in the "Care" of his "dreams"—

> their sheltering, flamboyant wings
> stretched over us, one in the past
> and one in the future—and in care
> of whatever slow hum the body
> sleeps by when it will not dream
> about itself, Rosewood, or anywhere.

The dream strategy is a way to subvert the spatiability of time, and yet achieve a sort of transcendental, spatialized vision. This sort of poem is in the Stevensian tradition. Stevens' "The Pure Good of Theory," for example, relies on a certain doubleness to criticize the spatialization of time and move towards a more authentic sense of time as the self's soul making—a Coleridgean and a Heidegerrian account. The poem begins conventionally, as the self, in its first canto, is overwhelmed by an exterior clock "time / That Batters against the mind" (*PEM* 265). To combat this sense of time, the speaker suggests that "we propose / A large-sculptured, Platonic person," free from time, who would offer a logical, coherent vision of time as a hopeful alternative. "Time," he says, "is the hooded enemy." But this solution fails in Canto II, when the "Platonic person" detaches himself in his "holiday hotel" from the enemy time, from the green "simmering" world around him, and becomes an "invalid in that green glade." He becomes as powerless, as passive in his understanding of time, as the speaker is in the opening. He is looking for a final, static, spatialized temporality. Thus the question still remains, "On what does the present rest?" The solution proposed by the last two cantos is that the present does not rest at all. We wake, Stevens says, "in a meta-phor," in a language system, and we soon sense that it is a "paradise malformed" in relation to any static, Platonic world of eternal ideas. We must recognize the inadequacies of any metaphor, any language, and attend not to its literal claims for an immobile truth, but rather to its variations, its music—what Derrida calls its "force" and "play"—

Introduction

> Now, closely the ear attends the varying
> Of this precarious music, the change of key
> Not quite detected at the moment of change
> And, now, it attends the difficult difference.

The "difficult difference"—uncannily, the very term Derrida uses—
is the erased moment between the two "nows" that straddle and
dissolve the "Moment." This moment marks the vanishing trace, the
"change of key / Not quite detected." This difference that we must
attend to "is never the thing but the version of the thing," Stevens
says in the last section. It is a structure of metaphors that continually
defers any sense of finality by always moving down Lacan's "endless
chain of signifiers" from idea to metaphor to word to pure sound:

> The day in its color not perpending time,
> Time in its weather, our most sovereign lord,
> The weather in words and words in sounds of sound.

Language, then, provides deconstructions, what Stevens calls "dev-
astations" of the conventional moment and its spatialized time. The
moment, or time, he suggests, must be seen as the fictions we make
and remake in our "malformed" language. Any moment must be "a
moment in which we read and repeat / the eloquencies of light's
faculties."

If, as Stevens goes on to say, we are to "inscribe" our "ferocious
alphabets" for this radical time upon the conventional understanding
of the moment, we must be ready to sing, as he says in "The Owl in
the Sarcophagus" (*PEM* 302), the "abysmal melody" of endlessly vanishing certainties and meanings. Paradoxically, we must be willing to
create for ourselves, as Stevens does in "Description without Place,"
a temporality that always evades us, or what Stevens calls in "Description," referring to Nietzsche's texts, the ever moving, "much
mottled motion of black time." In "Prologues to What Is Possible,"
Stevens' speaker (*PEM* 377) "creates" time when he follows out the
routes and traces of his metaphor of the self as a questing boat towards
what he hopes will be "a point of central arrival, an instant moment"—only to find that "the object with which he was compared /
Was beyond his recognizing." His language carries him playfully

beyond the referentiality of time so that he questions, "What self, for example, did he contain that had not yet been loosed, / Snarling in him for discovery as his attentions spread." And yet, we see in the word "spread" that the spatial metaphor can never be fully abandoned. Stevens, though, creates a fictive time which the self creates by uttering "a name" in a momentary "flick which added to what was real and its vocabulary."

There is, in all this, considerable risk for the persona-narrator, a risk that the loss of certainty and meaning will mean a fall into selflessness, into nothingness. This is precisely the problem that Wordsworth faces crossing the Alps in Book VI of *The Prelude*, the problem that Keats faces in *The Fall of Hyperion*, and Shelley in "Mont Blanc." Shelley asks of the cloud-covered, source of time that is the peak of that mountain—a peak, a time, and history he cannot see but can only trust—"And what were thou, and earth, and stars, and sea, / If to the human mind's imaginings / Silence and solitude were vacancy?" In contemporary poetry, this question is taken up by, among others, Philip Levine in 7 *Years from Somewhere*—the title itself suggests something of the isolated wanderer who speaks Levine's poems, something of the lost origin he proceeds from (we should recall the title of an earlier book, *Names of the Lost*), and perhaps something of the blind teleology of his quest (which is yet conscious of a progress through time) towards what he calls the "here and now" that can mean something, provisionally, like "home." But the acknowledgment of such indefiniteness should not suggest that Levine's is a poetics of surrender. Quite to the contrary, Levine constructs his "homes," or what Stevens calls "supreme fictions," precisely as Stevens' "Old Philosopher in Rome"—by sensing "The extreme of the known in the presence of the extreme / Of the unknown." So, for example, in the title poem which ends this book, Levine exclaims that we "waken / in the world we made / and will never call / ours," for ours is a world always separate from us, a radical otherness that remains finally unknowable. In this world, he ends the poem, there is no one to

> smile and say something
> that means nothing, that

> means you are, you
> are, and you are home.
>
> [7 Y 77]

What is so striking here is the Stevensian way in which the negative meaning is deconstructed by the positive force of the rhetoric, so that the lines seem to assert Being, a being-home, the fact that "you are you," as the line break underscores. Levine, that is, connects this positive "nothing" not only with the nothingness that is the empty and abandoned position he finds himself in, but with the "nothing" that is the only thing he can speak. It would be difficult to overlook the parallels with "Notes towards a Supreme Fiction" (*PEM* 207) here. Stevens says in the first section of that poem: "From this the poem springs: that we live in a place / That is not our own and, much more, not ourselves." Later, in the last section, a positive reality emerges from a subjunctive rhetoric said so forcibly it seems to become, as in Levine's lines, a positive imperative:

> Out of nothing to have come on major weather,
>
> It is possible, possible, possible. It must
> Be possible. It must be that in time
> The real will from its crude compoundings come.

Out of the "evasive" rhetoric of the poem—to use Stevens' term, a rhetoric that blurs the possible and the impossible, nothing and all— one creates a positive world, and indefinite everything, "created from nothingness."

Just this sort of double strategy informs Levine's poem, "Everything" (from *Ashes* 38). This poem—which counterpoints "nothing," "anything" and "everything," a disembodied voice, and the relation (or lack of it) between what we say and what is—ends:

> I must wait and be still
> and say nothing I don't know,
> nothing I haven't lived
> over and over,
> and that's everything.

One of the senses of the second line here—to say the "nothing" one doesn't know—recalls the task of Stevens' snowman who, "nothing himself, beholds / Nothing that is not there and the nothing that is." Nothing, then, is not nothing; it is. To reduce ourselves to this Stevensian first idea is to glimpse a nothingness that underlies all existence, that links it. Stevens learns this from Whitman and Nietzsche, as Harold Bloom and J. Hillis Miller have shown. The will to nothingness is the will to a dynamic eternity, as Maurice Blanchot has suggested with respect to Nietzsche. Levine's version is a kind of Nietzschean dithyramb that expresses a will to nothingness that is also a will to power, an openness of the self to and as the world. Thus in "Dark Head" (7 Y) he would address a lover he is about to leave by offering this version of nothingness as a means to make presence of absence:

> tomorrow I shall be fire,
> then ashes, then a hint
> of something animal
> moving out of the corners
> of the wind, and then at last
> I shall be nothing, not
> even the echo of someone's
> voice, and then I'll be
> ourselves once more,
> this world, opening
> in each eye and damp fist
> for those who would have her.
>
> [7 Y 57]

This "opening" of self, of Being, of nothingness, is thus predicated upon a metamorphic impulse, a faith that, as Stevens says, "Alpha continues to begin. / Omega is refreshed at every end." In "Lost and Found," which ends *Ashes* (65), Levine acknowledges that "certain losses are final," but then, as the "night that seems so final" ends and dawn approaches, he begins to understand something of the eternal return of things, the unendingness of everything, even nothing, and can exclaim triumphantly, "for now / the lost are found" in the imaginative processes of language itself.

13

Introduction

The unique problematics of Levine's poetry rest precisely with the nature of this "for now." The moment, for Levine, is never a fixed or static moment of timelessness, as, say, we encounter in *Four Quartets* or "Byzantium." It is never the moment of "pure presence," as it is sometimes called, which symbolically spatializes past and future into a "meaning" for the "everything" of life. Levine's moment is the postmodernist moment described by Jacques Derrida, a moment that is always infused by time, always evaporating, always "opening" possibilities rather than symbolically closing them, always a moment in which we repeatedly discover that we exist "not knowing / the answers to anything" ("Let Me Be," 7Y 66). But then, we must ask, in the light of our discussion so far, what does this moment of nothingness, of meaninglessness, demand of us? How are we to read these poems? In an earlier book, *They Feed They Lion*, Levine has said— "The words become, / like prayer, a kind of nonsense / which becomes the thought of our lives" (47). How, then, are we to think this "thought" which is "nonsense" but which is so basic to "our lives," this evanescent or indefinite thought of the moment, the "for now"? Or perhaps the question should be: How are we to avoid the thematic packaging, the no-nonsense of a symbolic, static presence that a more conventional reading might lead us into?

The "meaning" of a Levine poem is always the dramatic process— the rhythm, the pace it goes through in undercutting, deconstructing, its own momentary assumptions, in opening up those assumptions to free new possibilities. For example, in "Red Dust" (*Ashes*, 24), Levine is situated on a mountaintop "Above the tree line," where "the pines / crowd below like moments of the past." But then he imagines eagles soaring below him, seemingly timeless, but in fact linking him to time, undercutting the timelessness that seemed to define his privileged perspective:

> I can hear
> their wings lifting them down, the feathers
> tipped with red dust, that dust which
> even here I taste, having eaten it
> all these years.

One of the most powerful poems in *Ashes,* "Any Night" (31), is a meditation which begins in a moment of pause where the speaker bemoans lost time. But he begins to learn that his assumptions about time and about the melancholy detachment of such privileged moments are false. In thus welcoming an undercutting sense of nothingness, here by a Nietzschean "forgetfulness," he exclaims: "I will have to forget / my name, my childhood, the years / under the cold duration of the clock." His awakened "voice" would then sing a moment, a time that "could be any night," and the poem turns to a "prayer" of eternal re-beginnings ("that life follows death") for some wandering boy who just now passes. The gesture of Levine's voice is almost always this opening out; here the moment becomes a shared one, becomes finally the boy's and whatever changing, expanding gestures he will assign to it. For Levine, what replaces the closed signification of the symbol is what he calls the "mark" (a Derridian "trace") in "Each Time Is Different" (7 Y 42), the title itself suggesting a lack of closure:

> I will look up and hear nothing
> or feel a certain kinship with
> a place so old, the cross still
> carving a blackened sky, not
> as a symbol of power or belief
> but as a mark beneath which
> something we made once lived and died.

The moment, then, includes the absent, the other, the unknown, the radical nothing within the "certain" "something" that is "for now" only a trace.

One way to combat the seemingly disembodied nature of time that often seems to result from such contexts is to make the poem itself a sort of promise, to hand it over, hand it down. In order to combat a potential lack of referentiality, that is, the poem becomes self-referential and, following the paradoxical gesture traced by Levine, expands. Here, for example, is Stanley Plumly's "Promising the Air" (*SC* 21):

15

Introduction

A woman I loved talked in her sleep to children.
She would start her half of the conversation,
her half of asking, of answering the need to bring
the boy up the path from some dream-lake, some

wandering source, water, a river, or a road along
the tree-line of a river, she would say his small name,
then silence, privacy, the drift back to the center.
The child was the tenderness in her voice.

I can remember waking myself up talking, saying nothing
that mattered but loud enough for someone else to hear.
No one was there. It was like coming alive, suddenly,
in a body. I was afraid, as in the dark we are each time

new. I was afraid, word of mouth, out of breath.
Waking is the first loneliness—
but sleep can be anything you want, the path
to the summerhouse, silence, or a call across water.

I am taught, and believe, that even in light the mind
wanders, speaks before thinking. This piece of a poem
is for her who wept without waking, who, word for word,
kept her promise to the air. And for the boy.

The speaker is an outsider, an Other, denied presence on two counts: first, he is denied her dream; then, the setting is the past—she is denied him. But as he remembers listening he also begins to re-connect to her world. In the end, the best way to attach himself to her time is to enter her dream world—to give, as a sort of wistful fantasy, the poem to her and the boy. It is the boy who is crucial here, the representative of that inaccessible time and world. To give him the poem is to assert and confirm the very connection that can't actually be made—except in poems.

That's exactly what David St. John is doing in his poem "Until the Sea Is Dead" (*S* 43). It begins with an embracing gesture—"What the night prepares, / Day gives"—then goes on to describe a scene for his absent lover, and says:

> I watch the wild oats
> Leaning with the wind, as I try
> To imagine what I could
> Write to you beyond these few
> Details of a scene, or promises
> You already know. Perhaps
> I'll draw myself into the landscape,
> To hold you closer to it
> Than I could alone.

He continues, remembering the story of a Russian trader, the story of Abraham, then back to the scene, then to the memory of dreams, the Russian again. All times begin to connect so that he can speak, in the end, of the future, his hopes, as a kind of past, as history fulfilled—

> If you had been beside me, sleepless
> Or chilled by the sudden violence
> Of the winds, maybe you'd have walked
> Here with me, or come after
> To see what kept me standing in the night—
> You'd see nothing. Only, what
> Dissolves: dark to dawn, shore to wave,
> Wings to fog, a branch to light:
> The vague design that doesn't come
> From me, yet holds me
> To it, just as you might, another time.

What more can we ask our language to do than turn supposition into proposition, desire into history, to presence the far and the future?

A more elaborate version of the proleptic giving over of the past occurs in Marvin Bell's "The Hedgeapple" (*TGGY* 3)—

> I
> I wish we'd gone back—
> you didn't tell me she came off her porch
> and ran through the green yards
> waving us back as we drove away

but all the time in our blind spot.
That heavy fruit, the hedgeapple,
had made us stop. Then when she came waving
to the screen we flinched
a foot down on the gas pedal not to be
pinned for having intentions
on her hedgeapple tree.
She knew us,
she told you later,
but still we had the fear of correspondence,
and the guilt that comes from watching
someone else's treasure
in the open,
and also the fear of letting things be
more than they seem and ourselves less.
We should have gone back.

Do the trees really laugh?
Can we smell the light?
Is there smoke inside the cornstalk
and a light inside the tree,
a light that will not find where it came from?
What they call a hedgeapple—
it is one more perversion of the apple,
one more story like unto the ancient
unwilling airs and dances.
I am sure that we could have stolen one
and taken a bite apiece
and made ourselves crazy from the ground up.
We should have gone back.
We should have beckoned the wind
back into the hedgeapples
and her back in through the screen.

2
In spring, when the trees laugh,
like men and women who have been breathing
deeply and are also thirsty,
and the light
increases and increases

its waxy luxury so that a stand of bush
might seem an artist's wash,
we forget
what we were told.

First, the hedgeapple
is the giant birthing of a tree,
not a hedge, and second,
is no apple. A lemon grapefruit, maybe.
Like a grapefruit, but green.
Like an apple, but lemony.

We were lucky,
three in a car, the language we spoke
seeming to make light everywhere
because we stopped to look.
For a moment then, we forgot
what we were told.
And we didn't think.
Without us, the hedgeapple is perfect—
means nothing.
We should have gone back.
I am sure now she was watching us
from the beginning,
and the whole time too.
We thought we didn't take her hedgeapple.
We should have given it back.

So: here.

What's so intriguing here, as in all his poems, is the way he seems
to be talking to each of us, in his study sitting in his favorite easy
chair. He begins by assuming we know the past, which captivates us,
then gives it to us, in a carefully paced way—through the pace of his
sentences and paragraphs—so he won't lose us. And we get a sense
of being right there in the scene because of the specific details, but
also that there's something beyond, which helps us feel the expansiveness—sky, divinity, mortality. Look, for instance, at the second
stanza, with its references to the light, real and metaphoric, in the

tree, and to the larger references to spring, to seasons, in part 2. Look at the sort of scientific account of the tree in the second paragraph of part 2, and to the sense of language, in the next paragraph, that gave substance to the scene, then and now. Notice that the language seems to "make light everywhere." To make light—to make a joke of, but to carry that hidden tree light of the first part, its moment of illumination. The uncertainty revealed in the questions, the sense of regret, the idea of stories, myths around apples, the hazy description of what constitutes a hedgeapple, the emotions of the woman, the age of the boys—all these, connected, demand a mixture of levity and seriousness, of self-satire mixed with revelation, of past and present. And that mix is Bell's way of escaping the thing as thing, of moving beyond the level of conventional time. He accomplishes it because he is willing to talk, to go back, but through his language. He can give the apple back in the end because it, in a real sense, transubstantiates the object as the text of the poem.

We have progressed a great deal from the original, Coleridgean question about managing time, discovering along the way that the question of time is a question of the play between presence and absence, origin and end, eternity and temporality, metaphysics and history, thing and representation—a never ending proliferation of terms, viewpoints, perspectives. The situation is like that described in Frost's "For Once, Then, Something," where the speaker leans over to gaze into a well and for a moment thinks he sees, beyond the surface glitter, "a something white, uncertain" (*CP* 225). Almost immediately, a water drop hits and the surface ripples—"Blurred it, blotted it out. What was that Whiteness / Truth? A pebble of quartz? For once, then, something." The white, indistinguishable, and fading trace leads us not to answers, to the presence of "Truth," but to questions—questions that found any "Truth" in the fading, the blurred, the momentary. Poetic Time is, in effect, the self-questioning of presences; it is, in the end, a matter of perspective.

This is certainly the truth of Elizabeth Bishop's view of time. In "Poem" (Bishop, *CP* 176), for example, she describes a picture, suddenly realizing in the middle—"Heavens, I recognize the place, I know it!" Though she and the artist lived there years apart, there is a link through the time of the poem: "art 'copying from life' and life itself, / life and the memory of it so compressed / they're turned into each other. Which is which?" There is, of course, no answer, for to answer it is to stand in a static, timeless realm—not to live in the world.

Time is a perspective, then, a concept which brings us back to our opening comments, and to the rest of this book. Rather than attempt to consider the question of time thematically through a myriad of authors, I have focused on six perspectives, six poets whose visions are radically different. Obviously, a greater number of poets could be chosen, including most of the ones I have mentioned in this chapter, but I have chosen six who seem to me not only to develop different strategies for dealing with time, but have time itself as a central and directly treated theme.

Robert Penn Warren is probably closest, in his treatment, to some of the ideas already discussed. His poems can be seen as gradually expanding moments that, especially later in his career, confront the eternal, the transcendental. Yet Warren's metaphysics is always deeply rooted in the physical, in a radical realism. John Hollander extends some of Warren's ideas, writing more of a symbolic history which takes the movement and flow of language itself as its subject; for Hollander, time is a style, and styles or language hold within them whole other worlds. The notion of the Other is developed in James Wright's work as a sort of flight out of the self, a desire to attach the self to Other selves, other times. There is an incredible sympathy and understanding in Wright, an incredible sense of the historicism of Others that always interrupts yet defines his poems, which are always, in some way, addresses to the Other. In the end, this sense of fullness and otherness provides Wright with a sort of reserve of time, a sort of transcendental storehouse. For John Ashbery, on the other hand, time becomes a sort of floating opera, to use John Barth's term; in Warren, Hollander, and Wright, even as we move from Warren's full presence to Wright's concern with the absent Other, there is still the stable self and the sense of a conventionally referential world. With Ashbery, everything deconstructs, is about to break apart; even his own language cannot compass it, symbolize it, or transcend it. These very categories, in fact, are denied—time becomes language in a truly linguistic, figurative way. The Otherness of Wright becomes a radical sense of parallel times and worlds, intersecting by chance, deconstructing its own temporal structures. Ashbery's solution for time's passing, we might say, is to have the passage of the poem keep up with, parallel to, time itself.

The last two poets, Denise Levertov and Charles Simic, look for structures to circumscribe the time of their own poems, and so, in a way, invent an extra-textual time. Levertov's concern is with political, social, and historical forces, with using her poems to explore and discover coherent forms of time in order to deal, in a practical way, with its effects. The poem thus becomes an indicator of a communal time. Simic develops this idea indirectly by returning to the notion of myth. For him, our histories and our myths reside in our language— not the symbolic language of Hollander or the disruptive language of Ashbery, but in the images, figures of speech, clichés we use to describe the world. Time and myth thus become literalizations of language.

This book describes, then, six different strategies for dealing with six different visions of time in contemporary poetry: Warren's metaphysics, Hollander's symbolics, Wright's Other, Ashbery's deconstructions, Levertov's politics, Simic's mythologies. The book also attempts to place these poets in the context of several major philosophies of time, especially those of Heidegger and Derrida. Even when the poets themselves have not known these various philosophies (though Hollander, for example, is steeped in Kierkegaard, Simic in Heidegger), there is an indirect influence through popular culture and poetics. In this context, perhaps we can find, to paraphrase Stevens, poems of the mind in the act of finding what time will suffice.

1

The Generous Time

Robert Penn Warren and the

Phenomenology of the Moment

I

The Moment of Arriving

Yet permanence and perpetuity only appear when
what persists and is present begins to shine. But
that happens in the moment when time opens out
and extends. After man has placed himself in the
presence of something perpetual, then only can he
expose himself to the changeable, to that which
comes and goes; for only the persistent is
changeable.

> —Heidegger, "Holderlin and the Essence of Poetry"

In Robert Penn Warren's recent poem, "Snowshoeing
Back to Camp in Gloaming," the speaker confronts an
"alabaster" landscape above which the sun

> Unmoving, hung
> Clear yet of the peak snagged horizon.
> The shadow of spruces, magenta,
> Bled at me in motionlessness
> Across unmarred white of the morning.
>
> And Time seemed to die in my heart.
>
> [*BH* 27]

By situating himself, as Heidegger says in the headnote above, "in
the presence of something perpetual," which is also, therefore, a
"moment when time opens out and extends" towards the eternal—
that is, the timeless and epiphanic moment the Romantics so val-

ued—Warren can begin to understand something of his own life. In describing Faulkner's work in an interview in 1957, Warren stresses the importance of such moments of consciousness: "That's the frozen moment. Freeze time. Somewhere, almost in a kind of pun, Faulkner himself uses the image of a frieze for such a moment of frozen action. . . . Some of these moments harden up an event, give it meaning by holding it fixed" (*WT* 41). And yet, for Warren, perhaps the most overtly time-conscious poet of this century, such a moment only becomes significant as it reveals the "changeable" in our lives, as it returns us to time. Thus the speaker in "Snowshoeing" continues:

> So I stood on that knife edge frontier
> Of timelessness, knowing that yonder
> Ahead was the life I might yet live
> Could I but move.

This act of projection occurs simultaneously with an act of remembrance as he realizes how his "past flowed backward" from that stilled moment. The moment is Janus-like; the absent past and future are modulated into the present *now* to create a sense of the presence of the three extascs of time. So the poem ends as the speaker reinserts himself into this structure of time that has emerged:

> Remembering, too, that when a door upon dark
> Opens, and I, fur-prickled with frost,
> Against that dark stand, one gaze
> Will lift and smile with sudden sheen
> Of a source far other than firelight—or even
>
> Imagined star-glint.

This new understanding of the self is coincident with a new understanding of time as what Heidegger calls a "presencing." The trick is that the poet must "convert what now is *was* / Back into what was *is*" (*SP* 141). Such a presencing of the past, in turn, establishes a teleological ground that is the source of the self's hope—"This / Is the process whereby pain of the past in its pastness / May be converted into the future tense / / Of joy."

Now this "retrieve" of the past, as Heidegger calls it, is not a simple nostalgic return, but rather a presencing that uncovers lost possibilities, a going back to go forward. The *"moment of vision"* for Heidegger is characterized by "anticipatory resoluteness." That is, Dasein hands down to itself its own pastness in order to "throw" itself upon the world in an essentially futural manner. Its resoluteness about its own finite situation, its "heritage," is given purpose by anticipating or projecting itself, by attempting to understand and structure its own direction in history (*BT* H385). Thus, ironically, "Its own past . . . is not something which *follows along after* Dasein, but something which goes already ahead of it" (*BT* H20). History and the future, inextricably bound, become the responsibility of Dasein; they do not constitute a passive field to be entered, but rather a structure always yet to be determined. In fact, the *moment of vision*, says Heidegger, simply cannot be clarified in terms of the simple "now," as a simple "making present," but rather temporalizes itself in terms of a future, the emerging structure of the moment that cannot be summed up in any single instant (*BT* H337–38). The focus, for both Heidegger and Warren, is always upon potential, possibility; the moment is always futural, always a function of will and conscience.

It is through such responsible "presencing" of Time that one situates and defines oneself. This is perhaps the central discovery in Warren's *A Place to Come To*. At one point, Jed Tewksbury, facing, as he often does, the sense of himself as a mysterious other living in a pre-conscious and timeless state, is suddenly made aware of the pressure of time and, through that, of himself. What is learned, and here Warren's philosophy of time both resembles and is as emphatic as Heidegger's, is the notion that one's "authentic" being is a temporal "dwelling" or "abiding"—

> I knew that I myself was very strange to me. I thrust forth a hand to regard it. I did not, in the deepest sense, know whose hand it was. I stood in the middle of timelessness, lit by the brilliance of snow, and carefully drew in each breath slow and deep, trying to live in this new medium, in which there was no past and no future, only the strange present that existed only breath by breath.
>
> But, suddenly, I did know that the past and the future did exist, and I must live in them, too. For from the old weight-clock in the hall came the tiny whir and bong announcing that it was one o'clock [*APC* 189].

Warren's texts typically present such homecomings in which the home is not simply a physical place, but the more elusive temporal "sheen" comprised of mortal "firelight" and eternal "starglint," what Heidegger calls the "shining forth" of Being. As Heidegger suggests in "What Are Poets For?" the poet's role is to "unveil" to us "a presence grounded in a temporality whose essential time, together with essential space, forms the original unity of that time-space by which even Being itself presences" (*PLT* 129). And so, Heidegger would say, the experience of Being, of the self's essence, is an experience of an authentic, poetic, and inner temporality. Obviously, then, it is not clock time which is at stake here, though a relationship between inner and clock times is always implicit. "But Time is not time," as Warren's Valéry understands when he observes a gull glide through clock time from the privileged and governing position of a moment which has its own Time ("Paul Valéry Stood on the Cliff and Confronted the Furious Energies of Nature"; *SP* 107). So, Heidegger remarks in *Time and Being*, "time itself is nothing temporal" (*TB* 14), but rather a means of presencing times. There is always the difference, Warren says in an interview, between "chronological time and history," passage and coherent structure (*WT* 40). Man's duty, Heidegger says in the *Introduction to Metaphysics*, is to "transform the being that discloses itself to him into history and bring himself to stand in it" (143). One must learn to live, that is, in a structure that provides a more complete experience than in sensations that follow "breath by breath" in some sequence of unrelated, pure presences, a more coherent structure than the ticks of a clock.

The great tragedy of Warren's *Chief Joseph* is that the eternal and the historical cannot be merged, that a mindless push of history overwhelms the order and ideals of the eternal. Joseph "strove to think of things outside / Of Time, in some / Great swirling sphere, like truth unnamable." Time is always "triumphant" because like a "prism" it deflects a singular, eternal unity. It becomes a simple change—"There is only / Process, which is one name for history." Even if, later, his own being "would shine" through history, the inadequacy of a vision that does not combine both dimensions becomes all too apparent. The only hope is in the word "process"—a sense that order can be imposed on the structures of time, that a shift from metaphysics to the physical facts of the world is coherently possible.

But how is this transformation from metaphysics and timelessness into history and time effected? We can refer to Heidegger's teacher, Edmund Husserl, who describes in *The Phenomenology of Internal Time-Consciousness* a more dynamic version of the proleptic moment of memory we have encountered thus far in Warren:

> Recollection is not expectation; its horizon, which is a posited one, is, however, oriented on the future, that is, the future of the recollected. As the recollective process advances, this horizon is continually opened up anew and becomes richer and more vivid. In view of this, the horizon is filled with recollected events which are always new. Events which formerly were only foreshadowed are now quasi-present, seemingly in the mode of the embodied present [76].

The moment, that is, always redefines itself, always transforms itself in an ever expanding movement; prophetic history and historical prophecy merge as the "horizon" is always dissolving. This is what Chief Joseph finally understands when he decides to "fight no more, forever," absorbing his people's history like the seasonal movement of time that provides provisional order and direction. The "truth" of a moment is dependent upon this structure. For example, Heidegger says in his analysis of Nietzsche: "In order for the real [the living creature] to *be* real, it must on the one hand ensconce itself within a particular horizon, thus perduring the illusion of truth. But in order for the real to *remain* real, it must on the other hand simultaneously transfigure itself by going beyond itself, surpassing itself in the scintillation of what is created in art—and that means it has to advance against the truth" (*N* 217). Truth, as Heidegger explains in the *Introduction to Metaphysics*, is based upon *physis* and involves the self's "placing-itself-in-the-limit" to achieve a sense of ever-emergence which alone authenticates it (*IM* 60, 109). The truth of the moment, then, resides in its dynamic process of appearing, emerging, expanding its horizons. This transformation of the moment as such, then, is also a transformation of, emergence of, the self. It is consciousness, the self, then, that not only creates but *is* Time. As Coleridge long ago realized, "an act of consciousness is indeed identical with time considered in its essence" (*BL* 47).

The relation of self and Time goes back at least as far as Kant. For him, the operation of "opening up" through futural recollection that Husserl describes, and which Heidegger and Warren in turn adapt, is based upon a "categorical" structure of thought that imposes its own temporality. So Kant, in describing the workings of human consciousness, writes of "the generation of time itself in the successive apprehension of an object" and, more specifically, of "my generating time itself in the apprehension of the intuition" (*CPR* B184). Thus, Heidegger says of Kant: "Pure imagination, thus termed because it forms its images spontaneously, must, since it is itself relative to time, constitute time originally" (*KPM* 180). Time as the structure of intuition, then, and its content, are not an indifferent field in which things are enacted, but rather a complex of forces originating in the self. Time and the "I think," as Heidegger interprets Kant's innovative yoking, become one. Imagination forms images of the present, reproduces them from the past, and anticipates those of the future in a constant flux as an ever changing but unified world structure is produced. These syntheses, as Kant calls them, provide continuity for the self: they "form" time in that they intuit and order images so that we can perceive them, and it is this intuiting and ordering which is the essence of time formation. Thus, for example, in the mode of the present, "This pure synthesis of apprehension does not first take place within the horizon of time; rather, it is this synthesis itself which first forms the *now* and the *now*-sequence." And so for Kant, "the self originally and in its innermost essence is time itself" (*KPM* 185, 201).

A good example of this time-generating power of the self occurs in "Tires on Wet Asphalt at Night" (*BH* 68). In the first part of the poem, the narrator remembers the way a car's highlight would light up the darkness of his room years ago, and then, imagining the car's occupants, remembers the way it "hisses / On rain-wet asphalt." The time is described as if it were a present ("They do not know / / That I am thinking of them"), yet is also "different / From here and now, leaving me / To lie and wonder what is left." That memory invokes another through the association of the sound of the tires on the pavement, an association with a time when he lay by the ocean at night, perhaps "Embracing the world." The result of these associations is ambiguous, except that the present moment, combining the two, creates a third whose meaning must be deferred: the poem ends—"I wish I could think what makes them come together now." A further synthesis is called for.

It is in such a Kantian tradition that Henri Bergson writes in *Time and Free Will:* "Within myself a process of organization or interpretation of conscious states is going on, which constitutes time duration" (*TFW* 108). The moment of duration, then, is a hermeneutic one, a moment of deployment and organization of the self. It is not a quantity but a quality; it suggests, as Bergson says, a question of valuation. And so, too, for Warren, in "Heat Wave Breaks" (*N&T* 73):

> In the gasp of silence that follows your new heartbeat
> Do you catch the echo of one only just now spent?
> Or does Time itself, in that timeless and crystalline heat,
> Hang transparent, a concept bleached of all content?
> At this moment can you recall what your own life has meant?

For Kant and Bergson, too, Time is the result of seeing oneself, as Jed Tewksbury does, as a detached (metaphysical) "object" that must "retrieve" itself by creating its own history. Behind every object and event, Warren says in "History During Nocturnal Snow(A)" (*NSP* 71), is a history, a life, a "buried narrative." This does not mean that one simply deciphers or decodes a past, for, as Husserl and Heidegger have shown us, the past is always seen in relation to a teleology. To recall what a life has meant is to create that life as an act of Bergsonian will. It is in this context that Heidegger writes in his essay on Holderlin's originating imagination, "Poetry is the foundation which supports history," and, more specifically,

> The essence of poetry belongs to a determined time. But not in such a way that it merely conforms to this time, as to one which is already in existence. It is that Holderlin, in the act of establishing the essence of poetry, first determines a new time [*EB* 283].

And it is in this context of the self which embodies time that Warren's "Saul" exclaims:

30

I am the past time, am old, but
Am, too, the time to come, for I,
In my knowledge, close my eyes, and am
The membrane between the past and the future, am thin, and
That thinness is the present time, the membrane
Is only my anguish, through which
The past seeps, penetrates, is absorbed into
The future, through which
The future bleeds into, becomes, the past even before
It ceases to be
The future. Am also

The knife edge that divides.

[*SP* 174]

Apart from us, Kant had written, the past, all time, is nothing; it is a "purely subjective condition" (*CPR* B51).

Such knife-edge moments, through which an historical future can be "appropriated," are a signature in Warren's work. Heidegger often calls such threshold pauses moments of "betweenness" (*BT* H409). For Warren, these moments are always eventually narrative ones. Thus in "Tale of Time" (*SP* 141) he exclaims:

the future is always unpredictable.
But so is the past, therefore

At wood's edge I stand, and,
Over the black horizon, heat lightning
Ripples the black sky.

Now the developing narrative of this poem, as in so many of his poems or sequences of poems, is predicated on the vision that repetitions, re-beginnings, "thrusts" or "heat lightning" supply to the dark horizons of past and future. The narrative emerges as the duration created by the stillness, the deferral of ends, the temporal expansiveness we have seen characterizes such threshold moments. Such a deferred Time, for example, provides the occasion for "Forever

O'Clock" (*SP* 43): "The clock is taking time to make up its mind and that is why I have time / To think of some things that are not important but simply are." The kind of spacing that Warren evokes here is not of the Derridian variety that suggests the "nonpresent" and the "nonconscious," the absence of the subject. On the contrary, this spacing denotes an internal presence and a Bergsonian duration, for the sound the clock "Makes trying to make up its mind is purely metaphysical. / The sound is one you hear in your bloodstream and not your ear." It is during spacing that the narrative moment of the poem emerges, a storied portrait of a black girl sitting in the dust of a farm. It is a story in which the speaker presences himself as the central consciousness of the moment at the same time he attempts to re-define himself as a possible absence from it, pressing towards the horizon. Thus at one point the girl watches the car, and the speaker meditates: "I watch the car that I know I am the man driving as it recedes into distance and approaches the horizon."

This "doubleness," manifest in the speaker's simultaneous presence and departure, detachment and participation, is a defining characteristic of the "between," and we should briefly explore it. On an ontological level, the narrative "between" is Heidegger's mode of "abiding," not only in the sense of the "homecoming" discussed above, but also as a "waiting," a "lasting." This "lasting" is not a simple extension and coagulation of "nows," but an expansiveness inherent in the structure of the moment itself. That is, if Being's "destiny," as Heidegger explains it, "lies in the extending of time" as an act of appropriation or presencing, that extending or "opening" is also a "withholding." Presencing is a "constant abiding that approaches man," but to sustain this approach is to realize that it is never completed (*TB* 12–22). The clock never strikes, the waited-for moment never arrives, and the deferred "now" never ends, except arbitrarily in the last line, in "Forever O'Clock." The final lines of "Sunset Scrupulously Observed" (*RV* 31) are: "The evening slowly, soundlessly, closes. Like / an eyelid." Yet the poem has literally filled its lines with minute observations that seem not only to fill the moment, but overflow it, leaving, in spite of the last few lines, a sense of lingering presence, time given and withheld. The experience of

Being is of a continual "nearness," but the "nearing of nearness keeps the approach coming from the future by withholding the present as it approaches" (*TB* 15).

Thus in the Heideggerian *moment of vision*, "When such a moment makes the Situation authentically present, this making-present does not itself take the lead, but is *held* in that future which is in the process of having-been. One's existence in the moment of vision temporalizes itself as something that has been stretched along in a way which is fatefully whole in the sense of the authentic historical *constancy* of the Self" (*BT* H410). Now the relationship between the ontological and the narrative levels of a text is a complex but important one. The *moment of vision* manifests itself as a "span," a "stretching along" of "historical temporality." But the two levels are not simply identical. So, for example, Heidegger defines the ontological moment of the opening and withholding of presence as an "epoch." Now an "epoch" "appears" as a result of the "retrieve" I described earlier, that is, as an "emerging," constantly qualified structure. "Epoch does not mean here a span of time in occurrence, but rather the fundamental characteristic of sending, the actual holding back in favor of the discernibility of the gift, that is, of Being with regard to the grounding of beings" (*TB* 9). And we might add, of Time with regard to the grounding of time. The ontological moment of Being is "articulated," as the difference between Being and beings, Time and time, in the form of "perdurance" (*ID* 67). The ontological structure determines an historical existence, determines the structure of events and discoveries, the structure of "retrieves" manifest in a poem. This structure, a "span," is the structure of the poem itself as a process of "articulation" and "interpretation" which make up the "between," and which are the poetical means for expanding its horizon (*BT* H409).

I return now to "Tale of Time" in the context of this move from ontology to history. The poem or moment, really a sequence of poems or "epochs" as so many of Warren's texts are, moves from a sense of mere seasonal time—October, the depression, night—towards a more "authentic" time. The actual occasion is the death of the speaker's mother. Immediately following her burial is a duration of utter emptiness—

> What
> Was there in the interim
> To do, the time being the time
> Between the clod's *chunk* and
> The full realization, which commonly comes only after
> Midnight?

That "interim" becomes the text of Time's Tale, the poem itself as it defers its own end, comprehending an expanding moment—from the particular life of speaker and mother to the very span of Being itself. The expansion occurs as the speaker attempts to "retrieve" his mother's past as a set of new possibilities; "I come back to try to remember the faces she saw everyday," he says, and later, "What were you thinking, a child, when you lay, / At the whippoorwill hour?" The speaker, then, would, "Pacing the cold hypothesis of Time, enter / Those recesses." The solution, when memory fails, is thus to imagine her in his own terms, to appropriate her past as his own. Thus he can remember at least how he himself, "A child, in the grass of the same spot, lay, / And the whippoorwill called, beyond the dark cedars." The moment, focused always upon that dark horizon, upon the mother's possible pasts and what the son might make of them for himself, always approaching the mysteries of that horizon yet finally withholding them, produces a questioning of time:

> Whom we now sought was old. Was
> Sick. Was dying. Was
> Black. Was.
> *Was:* and was that enough? Is
> Existence the adequate and only target
> For the total reverence of the heart?

The question here is Bergson's qualitative one, and its dynamic nature is underscored by the line break patterns around the copulatives. The beginning of this questioning is the beginning of the realization of a more authentic time. In fact, Heidegger says, this inquisitiveness about Being is itself a basis for creating one's history: "The asking of this question is historical in the fundamental sense that this questioning first creates history" (*IM* 143). The withholding of a final

34

presence of the mystery of Being provides the "span" in which the narrative of the speaker's approach becomes articulated, in which the Time of the poem is generated, in which the text is produced.

This authentic time transcends particular circumstance. The "between" occurs as "span" in which the question of Being articulates the question of the self.

> Between the clod and the midnight
> The time was.
> There had been the public ritual and there would be
> The private realization,
> And now the time was, and
> In that time the heart cries out for coherence.
> Between the beginning and the end, we must learn
> The nature of being, in order
> In the end to be.

And so the speaker would, in "Pacing the cold hypothesis of Time, enter / Those recesses" of his mother's past to "Reach out" and "offer" the possibility of protection to her, at the same time he imagines her hand reciprocally "reaching" to his cheek. The gesture brings not simply a knowledge of her, but, as he says, "The hand has brought me the gift of myself." That "gift" of Being, as Heidegger too calls it, is the gift of one's "heritage" that becomes transformed into the self's history (*BT* H383–386). What began as a nostalgic moment ends as an appropriation of Being and the discovery of an authentic, historical self in the emerging narrative. The poem ends with an affirmation of presence, even under the guise of the absent presence of the heat lightning on the far horizon. Thus, says Heidegger: "The vast reach of presencing shows itself most oppressively when we consider that absence, too, indeed absence most particularly, remains determined by a presencing which at times reaches uncanny proportions" (*TB* 7).

Now what provides a "presence" to absence, what sustains continuity, is this sense of "heritage," as Heidegger calls it, which is given by the poem. The *moment of vision* involves a "handing down to itself the possibility it has inherited" (*BT* H385). That is, any "retrieve" is in a sense a "repetition," but repetition with a difference—that is, the difference of having an anticipatory structure, a desire to question, to transform, to make one's own. This structure is the very theme of Warren's *Brother To Dragons.* In that poem, the setting begins as "No Place" and the time "No Time," but a more authentic Time and Place emerge—the Heideggerian "site" of Being or "opening" of a region. The characters trace or repeat their own pasts, but in doing so they come to such realizations—for example, Jefferson's of his pessimism, Isham of the scope of guilt—that they in effect create another history in their metaphoric languages of discovery. While the participants seem under the burden of a chronological and fated historical time throughout, the possibility of making a personal Time becomes most strong towards the end in another climatic "touch" scene. Jefferson exclaims:

> Touch him—touch him—yes?

> Yes, look! I've touched. Oh, may we hope to find—
> No, thus create—

The repetition of words here suggests something of the larger pattern of creative repetitions or "retrieves" in the poem itself—in all of Warren's poems. The result is the sort of "suspending" structure J. Hillis Miller sees in any narrative repetition. Not content to simply repeat without difference, the structure of repetition tends to organize itself into links, chains, strands, figures, configurations—for example, the sectioned or chaptered poems Warren is so fond of writing. That is, repetition itself erects a superstructure that "retrieves" or presences what is absent; "recollection," as Husserl describes it in the passage cited earlier, expands the horizon of the moment as a futural enterprise.

II

The Abyss in the Mirror

> The time is destitute because it lacks the uncon-
> cealedness of the nature of pain, death, and love.
> This destitution is itself destitute because that realm
> of being withdraws within which pain and death
> and love belong together. Concealedness exists inas-
> much as the realm in which they belong together is
> the abyss of Being.
> —Heidegger, "What Are Poets For?"

In the midst of the deferred moment that is Warren's "Tale of Time," a problematic of presence as such briefly emerges. The Kant-ian coalescence of perceiving self and its intuitive form, Time, is challenged by the very structure of history it creates:

> The sound of water flowing is
> An image of Time, and therefore
> Truth is all and
> Must be respected, and
> On the other side of the mirror into which
> At morning, you will stare, History
> Gathers, condenses, crouches, breathes, waits. History
> Stares forth at you through the eyes which
> You think are the reflections of
> Your own eyes in the mirror.
> Ah, Monsieur du Mirror!
>
> Your whole position must be reconsidered.

The poet's vision of Time begins to gain an authority that threatens the self—Frankenstein's monster, as the Romantics well knew, lurks in our own texts. Now in "Tale of Time" a pure presence later reasserts itself in the "cold hypothesis" that Time has, like the soul, many faces, or as Heidegger says, "veils" which simply "mask" pure presence. But the question arises with increasing force in Warren's career. *Or Else* (*SP* 21), for example, re-introduces the mirror image in its opening poems. In "The Nature of the Mirror," Warren describes the ennui of a summer solstice with the sun slowly sagging, and ends by realizing once again that the time of an outer landscape and the Time of consciousness are implicitly connected—"Time / / Is the mirror into which you stare." But that poem, in turn, is followed by the brief "Introjection" (such "Introjections" questioningly punctuate the text of *Or Else*, undercutting its assertions):

> *Is it really me?* Of course not, for Time
> Is only a mirror in the fun-house.
>
> You must re-evaluate the whole question.

This re-evaluation of the nature of Time, then, is a re-evaluation of the status of the self. This reevaluation, or questioning as we called it in the previous section, itself constitutes a form of historicizing which we must follow here. What abyss lurks here beneath the distorting mirror of simple presence, and even in absence, that the referentiality of presence seems to veil? What does this calling into question mean for the structure of the moment of presence I have sketched in the first section of this chapter? What does it mean for the self whose stability seems so bound with the continuity of Time?

In his essay on Heidegger, Jacques Derrida deconstructs the structure of Time and Being that is based upon the "now." For Derrida, Heidegger's "now" as "pure presence" and as "present" is always slipping away, yet always relying on the spatialized metaphor of the horizon to provide it with continuous extension. In Warren's scheme, the resulting "presence" of past, present, and future within the horizon of the moment provides a referential structure through which the self can define its own history. But ironically, the very structure of "links" and "chains," which establishes presence in so many of Warren's poems, also produces gaps between sections where absence opens up. This whole referential structure of presence is most vulnerable, then, when the continuity of the "now" is broken. Thus Derrida calls into question the self's continuous horizon in his essay "Violence and Metaphysics"—"The present of presence and the presence of the present suppose the horizon, the precomprehending anticipation of Being as time. If the meaning of Being always has been determined by philosophy as presence, then the *question of* Being, posed on the basis of the transcendental horizon of time . . . is the first tremor of philosophical security, as it is of self-confident presence" (*WD* 134).

Such a tremor occurs, for example, in "Youth Stares at Minoan Sunset" (*N&T* 25). In this poem Warren describes an horizon line upon which the sun seems to rest suspended—but, unlike in "Snowshoeing Back to Camp in Gloaming" (*BH* 27), the moment here dissolves, the defining limit of the horizon turns blank:

> On that line, one instant, one only,
> The great coin, flame-massy and with
> The frail human figure thereon minted black,
> Balances. Suddenly is gone. A gull
> Defiles at last the emptiness of air.

The abyss here is the darkening world that escapes the structuring categories of any self, of any Time or "instant" that would provide a continuous order. There are two textual strategies that attempt to veil this abyss. The first is the referential "human figure" on the metaphoric coin, but that is, after all, only a symbol for a presence; and besides, it, too, lasts only "one instant." The second is the gull which "Defiles at last the emptiness of air." Despite the fact that "Defiles" seems to suggest a confusing admiration for the purity of "nothingness," the gull becomes by the end of the poem an anthropomorphic symbol of consciousness—"He spreads his arms to the sky as though he loves it—and us." The conditional "as though" is asserted so forcibly by the incantatory rhythms that the absence of an actual, full presence in nature is overlooked. The figure and the strategy recall Stevens' "pensive man" who "sees that eagle float / For which the intricate Alps are a single nest" (*CP,* Stevens 216), and who thus assumes by mere force of faith an order of presence in the midst of the chaos of absence. That is, the eagle and the gull are symbols for a presence which is itself given only as a possibility; the referentiality of the pure presence is at once called into question by the thematic of the poem and also supported by the rhetoric of the poem. The youth thus defines his own position in the broken moment with a certainty that defies the actual situation and which restores continuity to the moment itself.

Being Here perhaps presents the most intense dramatization of the dangers of the abyss. It is a book that can be read like a novel, describing early, in "Speleology," a daydream about being beyond time: "Light out, unmoving, I lay / / Lulled as by song in a dream, knowing / I dared not move into a darkness so absolute." The narrator has been slowly slipping through Jungian recollections of "Ages back," sinking "deeper" into a darkness, cave-like, until "I cut off the light. Knew darkness and depth and no Time." He is on the verge here of losing his identity—"I thought: *This is me.* Thought: *Me—who am I?*" The abyss here is a timeless origin, a problem we will come back to several times in this book, but it soon becomes apparent, as in the title of the book, that it is not "Then" (as in *Now and Then*) but "being here" and now which is the chief concern. The problem is that the *here,* seen as timeless, as an abyss, hides the benevolent structures of natural time. Another dream poem, "Boyhood in Tobacco Country" (*BH* 11), contains numerous time markers ("evening," "autumn," the "first star," the "harvest moon," etc.) that tend to combat the dark groves' "bronze blackened / To timelessness." The problem is that from where he is, a "dark roof hides the sky," hides the forces of time, and leaves him, as in "Speleology," about "To forget my own name and be part of the world." He would blend into non-entity, and there is a dangerous but seductive desire to lose the self in this way—"Oh, grief! Oh, joy!" he exclaims.

A little later in the book, in "August Moon," the dangers of the abyss are more easily recognizable. Most of the first part of the poem discusses the differences between understanding the world, dreaming for some "inward means of / Communication" and simply keeping track of time like children at birthday parties, or worse, "unexpectedly, / At random, like / A half-wit pulling both triggers / Of a ten-gauge with no target." In the end, the sky and natural time markers hidden, he remembers childhood, "A hand on your head," and closes with the following advice:

> The moon is lost in tree-darkness.
> Stars show now only
> In the pale path between treetops.
> The track of white gravel leads forward in darkness.
>
> I advise you to hold hands as you walk,
> And speak not a word.

The touch here provides the sort of contact with others, with history, as the touch we saw in *Brother to Dragons*, and the gesture of embrace in "Youth Stares at Minoan Sunset," and it is at least as tenuous, given as a hope, a piece of advice. The closing lines, with their sense of finality, and thus of command, parallel the move from subjunctive to actual.

When the abysses in *Being Here* become more expansive and more encompassing, the solutions become more complex. The problem is that the expanding moment opens suddenly to infinity, threatening to dissolve everything. In "Snowshoeing Back to Gloaming" the solution was the narrator's perception of a black crow against the faceless expanse of snow, a speck that ignited, as we saw earlier, a memory and a projection from which to expand the self in a parallel manner to meet the threat of the infinite. In "Acquaintance With Time in Early Autumn" it is a falling leaf, described in over twenty lines in the middle, that prolongs a moment, infusing it with time, as a sort of counter to "the timeless instant hanging / At arc-height" in the dark pool where the narrator swims. What is required of the narrator in both these cases is a sort of double vision, a focus on the threat of the infinite and a focus on the gradual expansion of a moment through time. The infinite is a threat not because of itself, but because of its suddenness, and the poems must gradually, temporally, begin to make the kinds of associations we saw in "Tires on Wet Asphalt," combining associations from several times. Otherwise, the infinite becomes an absolute discontinuity, a gap between the self and the world.

That situation is most dramatically portrayed in "Antinomy: Time and Identity" (*BH* 47), which begins: "Alone, alone, I lie. The canoe / On blackness floats." In the first section, the narrator tries to distinguish, in a sort of dream state, what "must / Be so," what is "time," what is the "illusion I'd once / Thought I lived by," in a series of memories and perceptions. The problem quickly becomes one of deciding "what new dimension" he now occupies. In the second section, the distant and near sounds, memories and sensations, define this new dimension as all combine—

> To a tangle of senses beyond windless fact or logical choices,
> While out of Time, Timelessness brims
> Like oil on black water, to coil out and spread
> On the time that seems past and the time that may come,
> And both the same under
> The present's darkening dome.

In the characteristic darkness of timelessness, the sameness of the abyss, the narrator attempts to find and focus upon one distinguishing item from which to build out a moment. He does so first by fragmenting the form; the entire third section reads—

> A dog, in the silence, is barking a county away.
> It is long yet till day.

It is almost as if the time consciousness surfaces because of the rhyme, and the perception itself is not a perception but rather an imagining, a projection. What happens next, once this projective ability has been established, is that "as consciousness outward seeps, the dark seeps in"—timelessness becomes internalized as something able to be dealt with. And while the "self dissolves," a new "fictionality" emerges—sky and lake exchange places ("the lake's blue parodic sky"), the stillness of eternity takes on the slightest of motions, an "unrippling drift." Now the sense of time as process, as progress, can reassert itself gradually. Section 5 is simply a repetition, with the slightest difference, a sort of draft—"It is not long till day." The poem then ends:

> Dawn bursts like the birth pangs of your, and the world's, existence.
> The future creeps into the blueness of distance.

Far back, scraps of memory hang, rag-rotten, on a rusting
barb-wire fence.

(7)
One crow, caw lost in the sky-peak's lucent trance,
Will gleam, sun-purpled, in its magnificence.

The key words here, besides the obvious ones of time's re-appearance, are "like" and "will," a movement from the "as if" to the region between hope and confirmation, the force of the "will" being somewhat ambiguous. Here, then, the formal fragmentation, the gradual associations, the keying in on a particular image produce the movement from the realm of wish and hypothesis to at least a Stevensian fiction. In a sense, the poem has asserted its own abysses, its own discontinuities, in order to overcome them.

This rhetorical overcoming of the conditional or subjunctive does not always work so smoothly, however. In "Chain Saw at Dawn in Vermont in Time of Drouth" (*SP* 39), the poet wakes to the song of a saw in the far-off woods; the saw

Sings: *now*! Sings:
Now, now, now, in the
Lash and blood-lust of an eternal present, the present
Murders the past, the nerve shrieks, the saw

Sings *Now,* and I wake, rising
From that darkness of sleep which
Is the past, and is
The self. It is
Myself, and I know how,
Now far off,
New light gilds the spruce tops.
The saw, for a moment, ceases, and under
Arm-pits of the blue-shirted sawyer sweat
Beads cold, and
In the obscene silence of the saw's cessation,
A crow, somewhere, calls.

When the "now" ceases there is an utter absence of Time that must be "supplemented," to use Derrida's term, by the sound of the crow, the call of the presencing voice. It is this voice, like the projected visions of eagle and gull, that attempts to veil the discontinuity of the "nows," the impossible irony of a temporary "eternal present." The voice of the crow provides what Derrida would call the "trace" of whatever lost past the self emerges from and which has not been retrieved as yet. The trace, which is a notion I will return to later, provides no referential basis for reconstituting the self's history, but only the basis for the question, "Have I learned how to live?" The answer is couched again in the deceptively confident "must" and "may," but in the end the poem slips back into what Heidegger calls the "ordinary conception of time" when it subordinates its hope to the clock:

> I must endeavor to learn what
> I must learn before I must learn
> The other thing. If
> I learn even a little, I may,
> By evening, be able
> To tell the man something.
>
> Or he himself may have learned by then.

The function of the other man here, a dying neighbor, is similar to that of the birds; he provides another consciousness, a supplement to the poet's own point of view, who might, in turn, provide the answers that the poet's failed, discontinuous vision cannot. Thus the man functions like what Jacques Lacan calls the Other, as a symbolic link to the referential world of time from the frozen, Timeless abyss within which the poet finds his moment frozen. A similar function is maintained by the generalized "you" in Warren's poems that always serves as both an indicator and supplement for the abyss the poems articulate (*Ecrits;* Strandberg, 18).

These discontinuities that are supplemented in poems like "Youth," "August Moon," "Antinomy," and "Chain Saw" occur between Time and what Warren often names "no-Time." In "There's a Grandfather's Clock in the Hall" (*SP* 65), he writes: "The minute hand stands still, then it jumps, and in between jumps there is no-Time." The empty abyss of the Timeless is, after all, only a form of clock time which

44

can be restructured by the self's Time: "Hold your breath and wait. / / Nothing happens, nothing happens, then suddenly, quick as a wink, and slick as a mink's prick, Time thrusts through the time of no-Time." Time becomes a kind of comically procreative act that supplements the gaps opened by a series of discontinuous "nows"— Time replaces time as the "time of no-Time." The repetition, through negative beginnings and re-beginnings where "nothing happens, nothing happens" thus establishes a structure of consciousness, a veil, across the abyss.

The problem that Warren faces here, and throughout *Or Else*, is that although "we must think of the / world as continuous" in order to establish a coherent order,

> only, oh, on-
> ly in discontinuity, do we
> know that we exist, or that, in that deep-
> est sense, the existence of anything
> signifies more than the fact that it is
> continuous with the world.
>
> ["Interjection #2: Caveat"]

Derrida has explored how this "difference," founded upon a kind of Nietzschean forgetfulness of the past, marks the relation between Being and beings, presence and absence, act and potential, center and horizon, authentic Time and everyday time—the whole system of oppositions that founds Heidegger's thought. It is forgetfulness, then, of authentic Time, a "falling" back into everyday time (*KPM* 241–45; *BT* H410). It is this difference which allows *Dasein* to repeatedly recenter its world in the face of its dissolving moments. Later in this poem, for example, Warren directs the reader to focus his eyes upon a single piece of gravel on a highway under construction:

> Then, remarkably, the bright sun
> jerks like a spastic, and all things seem to
> be spinning away from the univer-
> sal center that the single fragment of
> crushed rock has ineluctably become.

45

What will result, eventually, is "the moment when, at last, the object screams // in an ecstasy of // being." The aim of such an intense consciousness of difference is what Heidegger calls the "rescue of things from mere objectness." It creates what Gaston Bachelard refers to as "intimate immensity," the sense we get of an eternity opening inside us, especially when we contemplate objects such as the crushed rock, or the cry of the crow in "Antinomy." The inner imaginative moment opens to meet the expanse of the world (*PLT* 130).

In his essay, "Language," Heidegger describes "difference" as that which "stills the thing, as thing, into the world" (*PLT* 206). It isolates the thing as stilled center—Warren's gravel—and yet that center sets in motion a world—Warren's "spinning away"—so that "the stilling of stillness, rest, conceived strictly, is always more in motion than all motion and always more restlessly active than any agitation" (206–7). The aim here is to convert stasis into action, the broken moment into a new beginning. The roots of this notion go back, in modern times, to Hegel's moment of difference as both a "whirl" and a "repose," which forms the basis of all Truth—"The appearance [reality, being] is the coming to be and passing away that itself does not come to be and pass away; it is in itself and constitutes the actuality and the movement of the life of the truth. The true is thus the bacchanalian whirl in which no member is not drunken; and because each, as soon as it detaches itself, dissolves immediately—the whirl is just as much transparent and simple repose" (*HTC* 22). The problem in "Chain Saw at Dawn" and "There's a Grandfather Clock" (*SP*), for example, is that these two phases are not one; the stillness of the frozen moment has not been integrated with the passage of time.

Now the whirl and the repose, difference itself, is manifest only in language. In "Brotherhood in Pain" (*SP* 3), Warren again asks us to focus upon an object: "You will suddenly observe an object in the obscene moment of birth." But here, coming to birth is a function of how we "name" the object, for we ourselves "exist only in the delirious illusion of language." Ultimately, then, it is language which overcomes the abyss, which fills it; in any work of art, Being itself is brought into, made manifest, in the "cleft" or "rift," as Heidegger calls it. Language, he says, "calls" us, suggests to us something of the nature of Being as the process of "homecoming" described earlier, and the "place of arrival which is also called in the calling, is a presence sheltered in absence" (*PLT* 63). In *An Introduction to Meta-physics* Heidegger describes in detail how Being, Time, and language are intertwined; "the question of being will involve us deeply in the question of language," he says (*IM* 51). As he analyzes the situation, "logos" meant originally a "gathering," and then, in relation to speech, the way things gradually, temporally appear in language's "calling." Precisely such a calling occurs in "The True Nature of Time" (*SP* 57). Here Warren describes the constantly deferred approach of a lover towards his beloved and the suspended time of a remembered past which they shared when "a gull, in the last light, hung." Called by the sound of gulls, he senses Time again coming to a stillness. At the end of the poem he asks—

> How
> May I know the true nature of Time, if
> Deep now in darkness that glittering enclave
> I dream, hangs? It shines. Another
> Wind blows there, the sea-cliffs,
> Far in that blue wind, swing. Wind
>
> Lifts the brightening of hair.

The distant wind of Time stirs almost imperceptibly at the heart of timeless Being; but the center and the absent, invisible horizon, are related by the language of the poem:

> Out of the silence, the saying. Into
> The silence, the said. Thus
> Silence, in timelessness, gives forth
> Time, and receives it again.

It is in the breaking out of the abyss of silence through language that Time is created as the supplement of that abyss. It is in silence that one drowns in timelessness, as Warren says in "Timeless, Twinned" (*BH* 70), in which it seems that one has "forgot all other nights and days, / Anxiety of the future's snore, or nag of history."

It is for this reason that language, as Heidegger says in "Holderlin and the Essence of Poetry," is the foundation of Being:

It is only language that affords the very possibility of standing in the openness of the existent. Only where there is language, is there world, i.e. the perpetually altering circuit of decision and production, but also of commotion and arbitrariness, of decay and confusion. Only where world predominates, is there history. Language is a possession in a . . . fundamental sense. It is good for the fact that . . . man can *exist* historically. [*EB* 276]

It is the poet who manipulates language best, who makes of it the "span" which crosses the abyss. For Heidegger, all works of art create and fill this abyss; the poem itself is its own "cleft," marking the difference between Time and "no-Time," engaging the utter emptiness of that abyss, its utter loss of referentiality, loss of relation to the self—but also remaking that self, that Time, in recentering the moment (*PLT* 220,63). In this way, all art is a beginning, a re-founding, a futural projection, a "leap." Thus he writes: "A genuine beginning, as a leap, is always a head start, in which everything to come is already leaped over. . . . The beginning already contains the end latent within itself" (*PLT* 76). It is in this way, he goes on to say, that history, as a "grounding" of the self, begins. The "leap," in fact, is related to the "retrieve" we saw in the first section, in that the aim of the "retrieve" is to "transform" the past "into a new beginning." But, says Heidegger, "we do not repeat a beginning by reducing it to something past and now known, which need merely be imitated; no, the beginning must be begun again, more radically, with all the strangeness, darkness, insecurity that attend a true beginning" (*IM* 39). The insecurity, the "tremor" of any leap stems from a consciousness of the abyss, the knowledge that a profound absence hollows at the presences we make for ourselves.

One of the clearest examples of such a Heideggerian leap, and a poem which also charts the progress of the moment as I have given it thus far, is "Sunset Walk in Thaw Time in Vermont" (*SP* 76). The poem, which is divided into four parts, begins with a sudden loss. The poet confronts the sudden *"Rip, whoosh, wing-whistle"* of a partridge who "plunges" towards the sky and suddenly "Is / Gone." Now, "In the ensuing / Silence, abrupt," the poet stares at the western horizon, emptied, and hears, "In my chest, as from a dark cave of / No-Time, the heart / Beat." The sense of loss and absence, of timelessness, is overcome as the poet "begins to hear," in the second section, a "stream, thaw-flooding." The sound provides the sort of "calling" I described just above and it leads the poet to "see," in his "imagination," the water itself. The call, that is, provides the basis upon which the horizon is expanded and the repose again infused with the whirl; the darkening frozen landscape is counterpointed against the beginning sounds of movement, of whirl, under the ice.

Yet, by the third section, the integrated movement of the moment of vision again breaks down and a radically new discontinuity opens:

> On the same spot in summer, at thrush hour, I,
> As the last light fails, have heard that full
> Shadow-shimmered and deep glinting liquidity, and
> Again will, but not now.

Even the hope of future repetition becomes thwarted, though. For, as he continues to stare westward, hearing only a vague sound of ice-locked water, and trying to discover "Whatever depth of being I am" and whatever "soul-stillness" he still has, he confronts again the frozen landscape that seems to overcome him. As darkness "coagulates," he finds himself lost in an abyss, surrounded by an impersonal, "massive geometry," a deathly repose. The solution emerges as suddenly as the problem and constitutes the leap itself. The poet projects ahead fifty years, to when his son is an old man, and with the hope

> That some time, in thaw-season, at dusk, standing
> At woodside and staring
> Red-westward, with the sound of moving water
> In his ears, he
> Should thus, in that future moment, bless,
> Forward into that future's future,
> An old man who, as he is mine, had once
> Been his small son.
>
> For what blessing may a man hope for but
> An immortality in
> The loving vigilance of death?

In this sudden futural expansion of the moment from out of the abyss of the previous section, a new beginning is made, a new history for the self is written in the Wordsworthian language of the blessing. The blessing provides what Heidegger calls a "saying" in which occurs a "projecting of the clearing, in which announcement is made of what it is that beings come into the Open *as*" (*PLT* 73).

This projecting-clearing is the expansion of horizons, the creation of Time. The blessing is a "saying" in a distinctly Heideggerian sense; it both calls and is called by Being (*BT* H163–65, 273–75). It is, Heidegger says, a "listening," what he sees as analogous to the "holding back" or resoluteness in the "anticipatory resoluteness" that we saw define the moment of vision (*PLT* 209–10). That is, it is a "voice" that establishes presence by both inserting itself and recognizing itself as a Time structure in the world. Saying is the means by which possibility is appropriated, what is anticipated is brought near, and the silence of the abyss filled. The burden, then, is upon the imagination to generate "nows," however discontinuously they seem to be brought into consciousness. In "Identity and Argument for Prayer" Warren writes, for example:

> Thinking now that at least you are *you*,
> Saying *now,* saying *now,* for
> Now *now* is all, and you *you*.
>
> At least, for a minute.

The saying is always provisional, always preparing for its own unsaying, its own silence, the abyss that lurks within the voice, the falling towards inauthentic time that the voice cannot avoid.

III

The Earliness of the Moment

> Saying, as the way-making movement of the world's
> fourfold, gathers all things up into the nearness of
> face-to-face encounter, and does so soundlessly, as
> quietly as time times, space spaces, as quietly as the
> play of time-space is enacted.
> —Heidegger, "The Nature of Language"

In his essay, "The Way to Language," Heidegger distinguishes between two functions of language—"stipulation," which designates the way in which we are directed from one object to another—and "showing," which "makes something come to light" (*OWL* 115). It is this second function which Heidegger evokes in his analyses of "Saying," but as useful as the notion is, it is not without its difficulties. In *Kant and the Problem of Metaphysics* he had associated the full presence of the moment of time-formation with the representational power of language and of mind. Indeed, it is this representational power which allows Warren, in "Sunset Walk," to conjure up the picture of the river, and a new horizon from its slight sound, and then to leap towards, to presence, to represent the "now" fifty years hence. This "showing" power of language to represent presence is evident, Heidegger says, in the old German word *sagan*, which meant both an allowing to be seen and to say (142)—it acts to construct a referential theory of art. But, if beneath the language of the moment the abyss still lurks, if the moment itself, moreover, is hollowed by absence, how is representation grounded? How can there be a referential art? How can a poem then mean? The problem is faced in "Two Poems about Suddenly and a Rose" (*SP* 141), when Warren once again describes a sudden discontinuity:

> Suddenly, Is. Now not what was *not*,
> But what is. From nothing of *not*
> Now all of *is*. All is. Is light, and suddenly
> Dawn—and the world, in blaze of *is*.

Later, he tries to provide the discontinuity with meaning—"suddenly, everything / Happens / / . . . suddenly / Life takes on a new dimension"—but then he undercuts himself: "Christ, believe that / And you'll believe anything." He finally ends by exclaiming "Suddenly is too sudden to tell," thus acknowledging a failure at least of "stipulative" language. Yet the poem does "tell" something, "shows" a sense of the Being of the moment.

If, as Warren says, we "exist only in the delirious illusion of language" ("Brotherhood in Pain," *SP* 11), it is this language of "showing" that we need to explore further. Heidegger writes: "The nature of language does not exhaust itself in signifying, nor is it merely something that has the character of sign or cipher" (*PLT* 132). What we must give attention to, Heidegger says in several essays, is rather the "path of saying." Thus his "teacher" says in a dialogue: "A word does not and never can re-present anything; but signifies something, that is, shows something as abiding into the range of its expressibility" (*DT* 69). For Heidegger, language is a form of *energia*, a "force" (as Derrida would call it), that motivates and reveals Being as a temporal activity: "Language speaks in that it, as showing, reaching into all regions of presences, summons from them whatever is present to appear and to fade. We, accordingly, listen to language in this way, that we let it say its Saying to us" (*OWL* 124). What we experience in this saying is a "nearness" which "manifests itself as the motion," the path, "in which the world's regions face each other" (*OWL* 106–7). It is, in fact, this very motion, the trace of the path itself, which constitutes authentic Time. This is something, for instance, of what Warren is trying to express at the end of *Audubon*, where he hears geese passing north:

> Tell me a story.
>
> In this century, and moment, of mania,
> Tell me a story.
>
> Make it a story of great distances, and starlight.
> The name of the story will be Time,
> But you must not pronounce its name.
>
> Tell me a story of a deep delight.

For Heidegger, such an evocation reveals the "design" of language as the unity of Time and Being; it is the metaphoric impulse at the heart of all language. The "design" cannot be known outright, is always veiled like Warren's geese; it is a "trace" cut out of or into a larger ground (*OWL* 121).

More specifically, then, Being and Time are given metonymically in poetry. They must always be talked around, traced, recentered. It is the poet's task, Heidegger says in "What Are Poets For?" to recover some of the "traces" from the abyss. Rather than a statically centered, purely referential moment, a moment of clear origins, there is instead the moment of traces, of re-beginnings in the shadows of the abyss (*PLT* 93–94). In fact, instead of continuing to think of the moment in terms of the "horizon," Heidegger increasingly thinks in terms of the more evasive "releasement," something akin to the "opening up" we saw earlier. The Heideggerian trace can be understood as a concealment or denial of Being by the historical self, the sort of withholding I described earlier that produces the "lasting" quality of authentic Time:

> Never—yes, never—before these months just past
> Had I known the nature of Time and felt its strong heart
> Pulse, stroke by stroke, against my own, like love,
> But love without face or shape or history:
> Pure Being that, by being, Being denies.

The trace suggests something of the repose of Being and Time amidst our historical experience of being and time. The voice of the trace becomes like that of the murdered slave in *Brother to Dragons*, who speaks only three lines. Warren says of him in an interview: "I wanted him to be there all the time. I wanted his presence to speak, his experience to speak" (*WT* 45).

Yet if, as Warren echoes in *Audubon*, "For everything there is a season," there is also "the dream / Of a season past all seasons," a dream of pure, stable communication, pure referentiality. But such a dream is only that, and impossible—in fact, it becomes a part of Time's language itself. To fully and purely secure such a dream, anyway, would be to simply fall into the abyss. The abyss of the origin is simply the incapacitating entanglement of endless nostalgias. This is the problem in "Heart of the Backlog" (*N&T* 63). The poem is addressed to someone who simply measures the past as it literally burns in the old logs of a fire, and who wonders with the speaker, "What, oh, is Time!" but who remains passive, a victim of nostalgia. Warren prescribes instead a going forth, the radical new beginning, the new "listening," which I described at the end of the previous section:

> Has the thought ever struck you to rise and go forth—
>   yes, lost
> In the whiteness—to never look upward, or back,
>   only on,
> And no sound but the snow-crunch, and breath
> Gone crisp like the crumpling of paper? Listen!
> Could that be the creak of a wing-joint gigantic
>   in distance?
>
> No, no—just a tree, far off, when ice inward bites.
> No, no, don't look back—oh, I beg you!.
>
> I beg you not to look back, in God's name.

Yet the temptation persists, as it has through the history of poetry, that we might conjure with our words some pure origin, untouched by our ambiguities, revealing some absolute, eternal truth beyond language:

54

> If only
> I could say just the first word with breath
> As sweet as a Babe's and with no history—but, Christ,
> If there is no history there is no story.
> And no Time, no word.
> For then there is nothing for a word to be about,
>   a word.
>
> Being frozen time only.
>
> ["How to Tell a Love Story," *N&T* 54]

But to achieve an absolute origin would be to arrive at a moment when nothing has happened, a time "bleached of all content." In addition, the meaning of an origin, the past, can only be known, can only be verbalized, in retrospect, in time. So the origin, as Heidegger suggests, continually withdraws as the poet's language attempts to approach it. Warren asks:

> If only the story could begin when Time truly
>   began
> White surf and a storm of sunlight, you running ahead
>   and a smile
> Back-flung—but then, how go on? For what would it
>   mean?
>
> Perhaps I can't say the first word till I know what it
>   all means.
> Perhaps I can't know till finally the doctor comes in and leans.

The coincidence of founding word and original time never occurs; we cannot arrive "when Time truly began," even in language, for there is always an echo, a trace, a "ghost," sounding from farther back. But because of this labyrinthian structure of time created by language, the moment can be understood not as a vanishing point in a regressive sequence, but as part of a vast, ever emerging architecture. Rather than positing an origin, Heidegger writes, "True time is the arrival of that which has been. This is not what is past, but rather the gathering of essential being, which precedes all arrival in gathering itself into the shelter of what it was earlier before the given moment" (*OWL* 176). Rather than positing an origin, the moment appropriates the trace of a past, even a history, in its own futural enterprise, its own re-beginning as a form of what Heidegger calls "earliness." And so, as Warren says, "Moments not quite ready to be shaped are already there, waiting, and we feel their presence" (*WT* 41).

We should note that the temptation to reside in a timeless realm is always great in Warren, and is the result of a latent neo-Platonism in his thought. It is a tendency that seems to increase in his work and results, for instance, in two recent books, *Being Here*, which confronts the problem and works its solutions in time, and *Rumor Verified*, a more formal book whose strategy is verification of what is beyond the horizon, the moment, beyond time itself. In "Another Dimension" (*RV* 70), a Shelleyan poem, the narrator assumes the song of a lark "at an altitude where only / God's ear may hear." He remembers how

> Once I lay on the grass and looked upward
> To feel myself redeemed into
> That world which had no meaning but itself,
> As I, lying there, had only the present, no future or past.

And the poem goes on: "Who knows that history is another name for death?" But, then, meditating on the epistemology of what he is trying to describe, he gradually shifts towards the subjunctive in a tense that really combines the ideal and the earthly—"I have felt earth beneath my shoulder blades. / I have strained to hear, sun high, that Platonic song. / / It may be that some men, dying, have heard it." The subjunctive here undercuts the Platonism and unwittingly thrusts the narrator back into history. The poem that follows this, "Glimpses of Seasons," questions whether the "no-Time" is "but Time fulfilled," before finally realizing that the heart, the way we live, gives us "gray seeds of Time" however abstractly we would like to think of things. *Rumor Verified*, then, confronts, as one poem's title suggests, the "Paradox of Time," that, in the abstract, we can believe we live in an eternal, timeless realm, but that thinking itself takes place within time, and defines us as temporal. Not surprisingly the spatial axis for time metaphors shifts in this book to inner/outer, a confrontation between desire and hope for "fulfillment." It may be that the spatial metaphor of the expanded moment is what leads Warren to these considerations in the first place. The most complex and compelling moments, in fact, are those where inner and outer become blurred, where the inner of one thing becomes the outer of another:

> Three friends and I, we sat
> With no conversation, watching
> The bud of the century plant
> That was straining against the weight
> Of years, slow, slow, in silence,
> To offer its inwardness.
>
> ["Paradox of Time," 62]

One of the ironies here is that the silence must be broken, of course, for the scene to be rendered in the poem—and the timeless moment ends up being, in human consciousness, only the "weight / Of years, slow, slow."

Perhaps we should pause to suggest further the danger of attempting to simply "repose" in the nostalgia of a static origin. "American Portrait: Old Style," the opening poem of *Now and Then* (3), relates something of the lifelong relation between the narrator and "K," beginning in a time, years earlier, when they were unable to see the Civil War's legacy and history in the land around them and so "had to invent it all" in their play. Imagination thus becomes their supreme fiction, a means to mold and alter time—

> Yes, a day is merely forever
> In memory's shiningness,
> And a year but a gust or a gasp
> In the summer's heat of Time, and in that last summer
> I was almost ready to learn
> What imagination is—it is only
> The lie we must learn to live by, if ever
> We mean to live at all.

The danger is that the fiction, the "lie," become merely solipsistic, nostalgic, and that the sectioned form of the narrative wander in its own nostalgias, hence that time not be given direction. K, an aimless drunk later in his life, lives lost in a lost past; even the poet nearly succumbs to a return to his native past: "How the late summer's thinned-out sky moves, / Drifting on, drifting on, like forever, / From *where* on to *where*, and I wonder / What it would be like to die." But the very consciousness of the mortality of his life reinvests the moment in time, and the poet simply begins, moves on: "But why should I lie here long? / I am not dead yet." It is the poet's meditation on his present and past language for grasping the world that leads to his rebeginning; he effects what Heideggar calls a "destruction" (Bové, *DP*) of his old metaphors, and in the abyss that is left, and which almost entraps him, he finds a "clearing" through which he will propose new metaphors—the poems, in fact, that constitute the rest of *Now and Then*. As Heidegger says in his analysis of Nietzsche's destructions, "meditation on language and its historical dimension is always the action which gives shape to Dasein itself" (*N* 145).

The language of poetry, then, is a language of silences—is itself constituted by traces, by words that cannot fully embrace the dynamics of being. In "Code Book Lost" (*N&T* 43) the speaker wonders what a veery says: "There must be some meaning, or why should your heart stop, / / As though, in the dark depth of water, Time held its breath." Later in the poem he explains: "The whole world pours at us. But the code book, somehow, is lost." Even when the poet can stand where the present "landscape now reduplicates" the old one where he "once stood," there is an "immense distance" across which he glimpses, "without being able / To make adequate communication" ("Mountain Plateau," *N&T* 22). Thus not only the moment but the whole structure of time remains evasive:

> Yes, I once stood there, and now have
> Just dreamed, in painful vividness, of standing
> Again *there*, but if
> I should, I have it on good authority, that
> *There* is not there any more,
> Having dropped through Time into otherness.

> But what did happen *there* is—just now
> In its new ectoplasmic context—
> Happening again even if
> The companion who smiled in that dusk long ago, and
> Smiles now again—ah, new innocence,
> For now freed from Time—
> Is long dead, and I
> Am not always readily certain
> Of the name now.
>
> ["Identity and Argument for Prayer," *N&T* 66]

The amorphous structure of time is revealed by the play between a vague "earliness" and forgetfulness, perception and anticipation in the dream context. Such doublings of time become more insistent as Warren's career progresses. In "Doubleness in Time" (*NSP* 27), Warren remembers a scene from the past so vividly it seems to be present: "*Then* / Uncoils like *Now* / Like Then." The memory/presentation becomes something that "Roofs all Time." The process of reconstruction, of retrieval, is a slow one, for it takes "a long time for truth to become true." A similar inventive confusion of times occurs in "Old Photo of the Future" (*NSP* 55), a proleptic elegy. The structure in these poems recalls Freud's analysis of the temporality of fantasy—a "current" impression "wanders" back towards a past in a way that recalls the structure of the moment in Husserl and Bergson: "Then it creates for itself a situation which is to emerge in the future, representing the fulfillment of the wish—this is the day-dream or phantasy, which now carries in it traces both of the occasion which engendered it and of some past memory. So past, present and future are threaded, as it were, on the string of the wish that runs through them all" (*OCU* 48). This evasiveness of the trace, the unnamable essence of being, is owing to the difficult connection between language and dream, the unconscious. In *Audubon*, the speaker listens: "The world declares itself. That voice / Is vaulted in—oh, arch on arch-redundancy of joy." But he also asks: "Why / Therefore, is truth the only thing that cannot / Be spoken?" The answer, he goes on to speak, is that truth "can only be enacted, and that in dream." There is a distinction implicit here between language as "enactment"— Jacques Lacan has demonstrated how the unconscious is structured *like* a language—and language as communication of facts, a distinction along the lines of Heidegger's "showing" and "designating" functions of language (*E*, 18). Warren ends the poem, for example, by once again appealing to the primacy of language in determining and receiving Time—"Tell us, dear God—tell us the sign / Whereby we may know the time has come." What he is after, as he says in speaking of Ransom's work, "is a very intense reality which exists in the language, created in the language" (*WT* 17).

How, then, is a sense of the depth of Being uncovered in a Warren poem, where "adequate communication" is impossible? How, in the realm of our own language, are signs told to us? How can we say them? It is helpful to refer to Paul Ricoeur's discussion of poetic referentiality. Using Ramon Jakobson's notion of "split reference," of the priority of the "poetic function" over any "referential function," Ricoeur suggests that "the meaning of a metaphorical statement rises up from the blockage of any literal interpretation of the statement. . . . The entire strategy of poetic discourse plays upon this point: it seeks the abolition of reference by means of self-destruction of the meaning of metaphorical statements, the self-destruction being made manifest by an impossible literal interpretation" (*RM* 230). But what this blockage or self-destruction of the "referential" in favor of the "poetic" accomplishes is "the negative condition of the appearance of a more fundamental mode of reference." This mode of reference is broader than the word or even the sentence; it involves a "suspension" of a primary "meaning" in order to allow the physical, *iconic* nature of language to form the basis of a "reality" that is difficult to penetrate:

> Language takes on the thickness of a material or a *Medium*. The sensible, sensual plenitude of the poem is like that of painted or sculptured forms. The combination of sensual and logical ensures that expression and impression coalesce within the poetic thing. Poetic signification fused thus with its sensible vehicle becomes that particular and "thingy" reality we call a poem [*RM* 225].

Now for Ricoeur, as for Jakobson, the poetic "meaning" is ambiguous—and there is always an hermeneutics that can uncover it; for

Warren, as we saw in *Audubon,* the name must not be pronounced.

Thus, Heidegger says, "Poetry's spoken words shelter the poetic statement as that which by its essential nature remains unspoken" (*OWL* 188; Quinn, *SLJ*). What, we must finally ask in the face of this suspension of meaning, and the role of the unconscious, is the status of the self and the moment it creates? In "Dream" (*N&T* 29), Warren writes:

> Waters, hypnotic, long after moonset, murmur
> Under your window, and Time
> Is only a shade on the underside of the beech-leaf
> Which, upward, reflects a tiny refulgence of stars.
>
> What can you dream to make Time real again?

The dream of time, though, is not a passive one, not purely unconscious, for it involves active struggle, an almost Hegelian fight for self-definition:

> Yes, grapple—or else the Morning Star
> Westward will pale, and leave
> Your ghost without history even, to wander
> A desert trackless in sun-glare.
>
> For the dream is only a self of yourself—and Jacob
> Once wrestled, nightlong, his angel and, though
> With wrenched thigh, had blackmailed a blessing, by dawn.

And of course this blessing lasts only until the next night, the hypnotic moment we saw Jed Tewksbury trapped in earlier, until the dream and struggling birth into time again. More problematic is the teleology of the whole process—of the self, too—for "Dream" is followed in *Now and Then* by "Dream of a Dream."

In "Dream of a Dream" Time becomes not a matter of logical meaning or presences, but the random "flux" of absences, of the "nothing" that "glimmers," the unconscious that undermines consciousness:

The Generous Time

> Moonlight stumbles with bright heel
> In the stream, and the stones sing.
> What they sing is nothing, nothing,
> But the joy Time plies to feel
> In fraternal flux and glimmer
> With the stream that does not know
> Its destination and knows no
> Truth but its own moonlit shimmer.
> In my dream Time and water interflow,
> And bubbles of consciousness glimmer ghostly as they go.

What we encounter is the imagination's, language's, labyrinth of end-less referentiality—"deferred" by the traces, the "nothing" that is sung. Symbols, signifiers, times, mean *other* symbols, signifiers, times: "From what dream to what dream do we / Awake." Even to-wards the end of this poem, when the poet seems finally on the threshold of finding "what moon / Defines the glimmer and froth of self before it is gone," he must concede that "this, of course, belongs to the dream of another dream." Time becomes known by the differ-ences established between discontinuous moments, experienced by a central self which yet finds "definition" in that very experience. Even the self, then, must be understood as a "trace," a "ghost" that must always be marked over once again, that dissolves and is created in the process of generating its own history. This is not to suggest, in the end, that Warren's view of the self and its time is simply incoherent, especially in the light of the way his characters rest their being in empirical experience; it is only that he recognizes, with Heidegger in *Introduction to Metaphysics*, that "the understanding of being resides first and foremost in a vague, indefinite meaning, and yet remains certain and definite" (*IM* 83) as a temporal experience.

Warren's vision of Time, finally, is one of "generosity," a "handing over," as Heidegger calls it, of the self through the language of the poem, a handing over of the history the self generates through its own verbal presences. Time is a presencing of the self to and for the world; it is a "saying" that includes but goes beyond words—that goes be-yond, finally, the abyss of the isolated moment itself—for in the end all moments become part of the dissolving and solidifying. In "Cari-bou" (*NSP* 8), for instance, the narrator spots a herd from a plane,

turns away, then looks back: "I have lost the spot. I find only blank-
ness," he says in the second-last line. But yet, the whole poem, from
the moment he turns the binoculars over to another passenger to the
moment he gets them back, is a conjectural history, a conjectural
presencing.

> The heads heave and sway. It must be with spittle
> That jaws are ice bearded. The shoulders
> Lumber on forward, as though only the bones could, inwardly,
> Guess destination. The antlers
> Blunted and awkward, are carved by some primitive craftsman.

As a result of this imaginative thrust, built on the traces and hints
he has seen, and because of his own admissions in the middle of the
poem that there are things about them "we do not know," the narrator
can comfortably, in an eased way, end the poem with an expression
of faith: "But / they must have been going somewhere." Increasingly,
Warren's poems express such a faith in what is beyond—"God / loves
the world. For what it is," he ends "Three Darknesses" (*NSP* 3), a
sequence both optimistic and pessimistic, forward looking and nostalgic, a sequence, typically, of doublings.

I want to conclude this chapter by referring to "Night Walking"
(*BH* 108), a poem which is like a companion piece to "Sunset Walk
in Thaw Time" but which provides, despite its abysses, a more continuous sense of re-beginning (*MPR*, 8 No. 4, 48). In the poem, Warren
describes his son, "breeched but bare / From waist," rising one night
and climbing a hill to face the moon, and the poet too watches,
remembering a past far away, turning his attention to the horizon of
mountains and then to the movement of his son disappearing over a
ridge. Then, at the end of the poem, Warren himself pauses, remembers one of his own moments of vision and resulting experience of
Being too intense to name, but a moment, nonetheless, that can be
"said" in the "path" the poem takes. It leads him finally to address
the now absent son, to presence him (and us), to gather the son, along
with the two moments of vision, into the moment of the poem itself,
to gather, in a sense, the whole vision of Time I have been describing.

The Generous Time

The abysses within and between these moments are filled so generously by the last lines. What is recognized there, what is spoken, is not a static meaning, but the drama of our existence in a Time we must always make, always remain open to, even as we always fail to name it:

> I stop
> As one paralyzed at a sudden brink opened up,
> For a recollection, sudden, has come from long back—
> Moon-walking on sea cliffs, I
> Had once dreamed to a wisdom I could not name,
> I heard no voice in the heat, just the hum of the wires.
>
> But that is my luck. Not yours.
>
> At any rate, you must swear never,
> Not even in secret, the utmost, to be ashamed
> To have lifted arms up to that icy
> Blaze and transforming light of the world.

2

The Most Transparent Time

John Hollander and the Moment

of Erasure

I
_____

The Question of the Middle

To communicate a state, an inward tension of pa-
thos, by means of signs, including the tempo of these
signs—that is the meaning of every style.
                              —Nietzsche, *Ecce Homo*

T he Ninth of July," the fourth poem in John Hollander's *Visions from the Ramble*, begins as a
memory collage that recites fragments which
include a love affair from 1952, intimations of World War II from
1939, and boys' pranks at a lake camp. But then Hollander pauses,
after some forty lines; the tempo slows to a meditative pace, and the
"streaking" memories are contrasted with the historical "moment"
out of which he writes, through which he compasses and structures
the self's time:

> This is the time most real: for unreeling time there are no
> Moments, there are no points, but only the lines of memory
> Streaking across the black film of the mind's night.
> But here in the darkness between two great explosions of light,
> Midway between the fourth of July and the fourteenth,
> Suspended somewhere in summer between the ceremonies
> Remembered from childhood and the historical conflagrations
> Imagined in sad, learned youth—somewhere there always hangs
> The American moment.

[*SE* 153]

The contrast between the two times is instructive. "Unreeling time" is a fading of memory traces, an unintelligible experience of loss, of time as unreal. The "time most real," on the other hand, is a still point, the "American Moment" around which events become significant; thus this real time is a time of interpretation. This "suspended" or still movement is not simply a static one; indeed, it has no fixed center, lying as it does "somewhere" between ceremony and history, or the "deed" and the "dream," as Hollander explains a few lines further on. And more—its opposite terms, the fictive and the factual, are in a dialectic relation that provides an optimistic structure to the meaning of the self's time: "world and I, in making each other / As always, make fewer mistakes." The time of interpretation is a dynamic one, the "*tempo* of these signs."

What Hollander is playing with here, in other words, is a variation upon Hegel's notion that the moment of repose is also a ceaseless whirl, that self and the world define each other in moments of pause that are always incomplete, always emerging, always failing to pause. The moment, then, is always undecidable, its text, to use DeMan's term, "unreadable." To emphasize the suspension, the stillness of repose, is to emphasize an order beyond mere "streaking across the black film of the mind's night." Thus, in the last poem from *Visions*, "framing our world in a vast / Moment of stillness," the lovers can make "a cycle of months spin on a frail / Wheel of language and touch." It is language, then, that is the origin of the world, the self, the poem—and of the "moment," the "heartbeat in the moonlight" that contains them:

> Burning, restless, between the deed
> And the dream is the life remembered: the sparks of Concord were mine
> As I lit a cherry-bomb once in a glow of myth
> And hurled it over the hedge. The complexities of the Terror
> Were mine as poring eyes got burned in the fury of Europe
> Discovered in nineteen forty-two. On the ninth of July
> I have been most alive; world and I, in making each other
> As always, make fewer mistakes.
> The gibbous, historical moon
> Records our nights with an eye neither narrowed against the brightness
> Of nature, nor widened with awe at the clouds of the life of the mind.

Crescent and full, knowledge and touch commingled here
On this dark bed, window flung wide to the cry of the city night,
We lie still, making the poem of the world that emerges from shadows.

Doing and then having done is having ruled and commanded
A world, a self, a poem, a heartbeat in the moonlight.

To imagine a language means to imagine a form of life.

We should note that the sexual metaphor which pervades these lines
serves to underscore not only the obvious links between procreation
and artistic creativity, but the very "fragility" and brevity of any
human enterprise, whether it be the emergent moment of the poem
or the lover's touch, "language," or a "form of life."

This fragility is manifest in the history of Hollander's poetry, for it
is a history of failed attempts to found a poetic upon a metaphysics
of presence, as Penn Warren does, but also a history of recoveries that
discover for Hollander a rich poetic in a metaphysics of absence. Thus,
even in this early sequence, the passage we have been discussing
makes a gesture towards an inclusive and "still" moment of presence
as a completed event beyond time. It is a gesture that deconstructs
itself. Indeed, the next poem, "Humming," gathers a number of related, cicada-like sounds within its moment: "The humming of human time is loud / And crowded with single, unbearable voices, that,
hour by hour, / Blend more into timeless buzzing." This blending,
however, of a sort of background noise we suppress, is never complete,
is always defined in relation to the dialectic whirl of the moment
always emerging and always fading. Hollander avoids the spatialization of time Warren is always tempted with. Thus "Ninth of July"
opens: "This is the business of being. To have heard / These undying
cicadas, immortal while yet they live, is to burn / For a time in the
moment itself."

It is instructive to refer here to Derrida's critique, in *Speech and
Phenomena*, of Husserl's timeless moment, the "blink of the eye."
Just as Husserl's moment of pure presence is compounded with a non-
presence (the recollections, after images, "protensions" the mind senses), so are Hollander's "timeless" moments compounded by inclusive
references to all that time is beyond. There is always a duration to

the timeless moment, and, as Derrida says, "it closes the eye" (*SPH* 65). The result, in Hollander's work, is a moment founded upon fading traces and provisional anticipations.

This moment, for instance, defines what we usually think of as the static "moment" captured by a piece of sculpture, according to Hollander's recent "August Carving" (*Blue Wine*). Here the sculpture is a presence founded upon absence, "a knowledge as of / Distant light composed here." The figures of lovers represented "will pass among / Moments of astonishing shadow, then enter the dark, / Coldly, invisible, forms fractured from their radiance." The prose poems that open and close *Spectral Emanations* present this process as an allegory of reading and writing. Here is the last half of "Crossing Water," the opening piece, a diminutive quest romance:

> All of this went on and on, finally growing pale seemingly at the same rate at which all the motion slowed eventually, colors, fading into a glowing dimness against the dark, until, at a moment that could have come along almost anywhere during the period of five minutes it marked the middle of, a long slow streak of white meteor shot through the pallor above, a gasp of luminosity, a revision of wonder and a reduction of what had been seen to be a sign. Ironic, clear, distinct; vector of agency against a scene; short, pointed, a stretch of high path heading downward. . . . Well, I was young and foolish and unable to know—as with everything else I had ever been given—the nature of the gift. The bright track of the Perseid was short, but long enough to lead into the vast space of darkness between sky and sea. It has taken me thirty years to remember the mockery of its accidence, thirty years to recompose the prior light.

Here the faded moment, now a trace lost in darkness, is seemingly recomposed. But the companion piece, "Building the Tower," suggests, even after all the discoveries of the volume between, something quite different—whenever we seem to have arrived and ended, we find ourselves "amid what has always been, and will be, beyond."

To be amid what is always already beyond; to find the "moment that . . . marked the middle" reduced to a sign, a trace; to have the moment of stillness where "motion slowed" defined by the "short track" of the meteor—all these provide us with echoes of the deconstructed moment of presence we have been describing in these pages.

We are facing Heidegger's moment of "betweenness," where the poem is ever approaching and dissolving the temporal boundaries it defines for itself through language. But the "betweenness" of any moment or sequence of moments poses Hollander's problem, in terms proposed by "Crossing Water," of a temporal "vectoring," a problem of direction. So Hollander has said of the sequences of moments in long poems: "The problem of middles is very important, isn't it? How do you know when you are at the middle? Beginnings and endings are easy—they are the first things we learn. The question of the middle is a question of pace, of timing, of rhythm" (*Acts* 200).

Such concerns are always at the heart of Hollander's thinking. In his book-length sequence, *The Powers of Thirteen*, for instance, the three middle poems create a section of "long moments of pause" where one can feel "a general pulse." The exact center is still:

> But at its most contracted state the center stands
> (Everything lies around it, it is about nothing),
> Center of origin, equidistant, silent rest,
> And pointlessness. For only in the meddling schoolboys'
> Destructions of certainty do areas arise,
> Dim, jagged of bound, unexplored, in which one might roam
> Ever dangerously, yet safe in the dark knowledge
> That mapping these places means covering everything.
>
> [#85]

What begins to happen is a gradual expansion from the center that we saw in Penn Warren, but with a difference. The movement is guided not by a particular external reference, but by the example, the schoolboys, who were mentioned earlier in the poem; metaphor or symbol and referent are always being blurred in Hollander's poems, as if the particular and the general were equal. What we have then is a complex rhythmical movement, pace: between symbol and reference, center and circumference, and along the steady measure of the sequence of thirteen-line poems.

The whole sequence of poems is itself a quest romance for someone or something left ambiguous, though it is perhaps for the woman whose statue is described as an "archaic maiden who has lost / Her head over time" (62), a plot which thus adds its own pacing as a sort of overlay of subplots, "Of quests for the nature of the quests" (#1). And of course it begins, as all epics do, *in medias res,* but with its epic rhythm placed upon the everyday rhythms of even our most mundane lives:

> In the midst of things that have gone on awhile.
> Thus we need not undergo the old delusion that
> Comes from entering the day soon after all the great
> Goings on, feeling that morning has been warned by our
> Work. Thus we need not add our own weariness to that
> Of afternoon; and as far as endings are concerned
> One does not begin feasting at dawn, but at sundown.
>
> [#2]

What is crucial for Hollander, then, is not the subject of the quest (there are mock echoes from Milton, Wordsworth, Pope, Spenser, the Bible, etc. which give it a sense of "weight," however ironic), but the ways the various echoes and overlays, each with its own rhythm of beginning, middle, and end, all interact. The concern is with "a kind of drawing of breath, murmuring of pulse," with "the mind's caress which shapes and loves at once" (#28). Thus, at times there can be an idyllic pause in the quest—"So with me conversing you forget / All time" (#42), the Miltonic echo here conjuring Eden's eternity, but also its inevitable fall. At other times, his vision of the whole spectrum of time can be clear, even though ironically undercut by the metaphoric terms of his vision: "How charming—magical, fragile both, I mean—the time / When Past was like a dungeon, Present a wide fore-court / Looking further out at open, sunny future fields" (#46).

What is crucial, for Hollander, is what we might call a rhythm of discourses, a tempo of saying—

> The clock rings in your arrival, making room in time
> For our dear discourse in all its hidden silences,
> Room in time among the hurried hours that shoulder
> Each other into the cold, dim valley at the end
> Of day and night where they shall ever stand shuddering.
>
> [#167]

But it is not clock time which measures, but the time of language itself; the time of the poem does not recount "Moments totally contiguous in the clocked world," but rather

> This black gap between days is no place for us: should you
> Creep into my bed then you would find me shuddering
> As at the opening of a secret whose shadowed
> Power unbroken lay in coupling day to day.
>
> [#168]

The middle of things seems always a "black gap," an endless quest, a tangle of rhythms—but it is only in the addition of a further rhythm, the comic lovemaking, that the quest may be furthered and so fulfilled. The sequence ends tenuously, with a sense that we have been left near where we began, in the middle, among the various resonances that accumulate there, the various paces,

> Moving toward the mirror's surface each through the magic
> Space that the other's world must needs transform in order
> To comprehend: when our voices have surrounded one
> Another, each like some penumbra of resonance.
> So that you have the last word now I give it to you.

The last word, the "you," continues, in the midst, combining, as the poem has, various time frames, from the mundane to the exotic, and various kinds and rhythms of language, from the curt, to the streetwise, to the highly literary, each with its own temporality.

Pace, timing, and rhythm were precisely the issues that had surfaced in our discussion of the interrupted moment in "Ninth of July." The whirling narrative movement is interrupted by a moment of repose that yet fades, and the two deconstruct each other as conflicting "tempos" of a style. When we recognize the movement of this style, its tempo, its force, the question of vectoring dissolves into the movement of language itself. Time becomes a question of this tempo, this force. "Force," as Derrida uses it in "Force and Signification," suggests "the other of language without which language would not be what it is" (*WD* 27). That is, force reflects the trace structure of language, the otherness beyond the mythic presence of the moment; it is reflected in the movement between "humming" and "buzzing," the continual interruption of presence by absence, the undermining of the certainty of final meanings by the provisional play of language. A randomness thus enters time. Hollander says: "A very important experience for me was my youthful love for a contemplation of 'lap dissolves' in films. A fading in would occur contrapuntally with a fading out so that you would not set a cruder ironic montage, not, say, where a clock on the wall dissolves into a prisoner's face as he waits to be executed, but more subtle and random ones" (*Acts* 200).

In Hollander's poetry, then, this random and transitional quality of the moment constitutes its "tempo" or force of style. Perhaps the most direct treatment of this random vectoring of time occurs in "Just for the Ride" (*BW*), which describes a ride on a "bus with its destination / Rolled up out of sight" and which ends when the narrator disembarks at a place which provisionally feels like home. The pace of the poem is partly a function of the occasionally falling four- and eight-syllable lines (the bus stops at each "fourth or eighth corner"). What lies behind that pace are the arbitrary links between the outside "meaningless fields" that seem to flow by the muddy window in a sign rhythm of their own, and the "inside" of the bus where "there is a motion, / If only of noticing." Time is neither objective nor subjective, but rather a play of rhythms based upon an arbitrary tempo of ever emerging and ever fading relations. Nietzsche summarizes in the *Will to Power* this sense of time that occurs in Hollander's poetry: "Duration, identity with itself, being are inherent neither in that which is called subject nor in that which is called object: they are complexes of events apparently durable in comparison with other complexes—e.g., through the difference in tempo of the event" (*WP*, 298). All questions about the between, the middle, the transitional blurring, the random lap dissolve, the interrupted moment—and these are questions we must pursue further—all these questions are ultimately questions about style. Time is not a concept for Hollander, or even a form for a content, but rather time is a style.

II

Regions of Erased Shapes in the Air

> That is the purpose of active forgetfulness, which is
> like a doorkeeper, a preserver of psychic order, re-
> pose, and etiquette: . . . there could be no happiness,
> no *present* without forgetfulness.
> —Nietzsche, *Genealogy of Morals*

"Perhaps there is something about my memory that tries to defeat continuity," Hollander has commented. "To remember fully and perfectly would be to unreel a long stretch of time, and perhaps the implication is a movement towards an end, towards death" (*Acts* 199). What Hollander reveals here is the importance of repression, of the tempo of the play between consciousness and unconsciousness, as an element of time as style. We can for a moment turn to Jacques Lacan in order to place the issue in an illuminating context. In "Function and Field of Speech and Language," Lacan discusses the tempo of analytic sessions, emphasizing the importance not only of what is said but the timing of the saying—the way a session breaks, for instance. Because for Lacan the unconscious is structured like a language, the question of time is a question of the *tempo* of this "language"—the "pace" at which the unconscious reveals itself. The "language" of the unconscious, however, is a language of pure signifiers, of images not tied to specific meanings. Now the movement from the unconscious to the consciousness is a movement from the "Imaginary" to the "Symbolic," from a realm of pure signifiers to a realm of gradually achieved meanings, from a pre-verbal language to a verbal one. For Lacan, there is a continual shifting between these two realms, and some degree of interpenetration. In this scheme, he says, objective time is meaningless—"Perhaps we might get a somewhat better idea of time by comparing the time required for the creation of a symbolic object with the moment of inattention when we let it fall" (*E* 98).

Hollander himself turns to Kierkegaard's "The Rotation Method" (as he suggests in the note to his poem "Rotation of Crops" *SE*), in order to link memory and forgetting, the consciousness and the unconsciousness, with time and style (*Acts* 197). For both writers, a "rotation method" is a means of countering any simple synchronic vision by emphasizing the temporality of style: one rotates unusual poetic strategies, views objects from skewed angles, speculates, defers, undercuts—in short, varies his poetic tempo. The farmer in "Rotation of Crops," for example, facing the "tedium of the soil," dreams "after dark, the night itself / Shifted her ground" while he "gleaned / Mindfulls from outside the mills of light." The farmer escapes the tedious repetitions of objective, seasonal time by forgetting the daylight world as he dreams: he dreams another time. Kierkegaard, then, also explores the relationships between the creation of a symbolic world and the forgotten or unconscious world from whose ashes the symbolic arises: "The more poetically one remembers, the more easily one forgets: for remembering poetically is really only another expression for forgetting. In poetic memory the experience has undergone a transformation, by which it has lost all its painful aspects" (*EO* 289). To forget, in the poem, is to re-begin, to be caught in the metamorphic impulse of style, to submit to the play of the unconscious, to dream one's own time.

Now it is just such a double process of building and letting fall, of remembering and forgetting, that informs Hollander's "The Head of the Bed." The poem begins with an enigmatic prose commentary describing a mythical, indeed dream-like mountain region that contains an ambiguous border, "marked by an occasional sign," between two countries. As it turns out, the spatial division is superseded by a temporal one, created by the sounds of a "Trumpeter" that "divide the air as the border divides the land. It can be heard at no fixed intervals, and yet with a regularity which we accept, but cannot calculate. No one knows whether the trumpeter is theirs or ours."

The relation of this prologue to the poem that follows becomes clearer when we realize that "The Head of the Bed" deals with the blurring of the boundaries between sleep and waking, dream and actuality, and with the undecidability about which realm the main consciousness of the poem occupies at any given moment. The poem enacts a simple process of waking, of moving between the Imaginary to the Symbolic; the pace of this movement is erratic, but within the certain "regularity" which the fifteen-part structure of the poem posits.

Before proceeding with this poem, though, we can turn briefly to Lacan's description of the "temporal pulsation" of the unconscious to suggest a structural pattern for this tempo (*FFC* 143). For Lacan, something emerges from the unconscious, "is for a moment brought into the light of day—a moment because the second stage, which is one of closing up, gives this apprehension a vanishing aspect" (31). We perceive this pulsing of the unconscious through "slits" that are themselves revealed in language at certain temporary "points" (or "sutures") that mark a progression in understanding by the mind. The "temporal structure" that "circumscribes" this process constitutes what Lacan calls a "Logical Time." This time consists of three "moments"—one of immediate perception, one of understanding, and a terminal moment that, in effect, never terminates, for there is also something that "eludes" the logic of this time:

> The appearance/disappearance takes place between two points, the initial and the terminal of this logical time—between the instant of seeing, when something of the intuition itself is always elided, not to say lost, and that elusive moment when the apprehension of the unconscious is not, in fact, concluded, when it is always a question of an "absorption" fraught with false trails [*FFC* 32].

Lacan is describing both a psychic process and the conduct of an analytic session. And as we shall see, a very similar structure and result define the movement of Hollander's poem.

"The Head of the Bed" (*SE*) begins with a description of the first stirrings of language, of consciousness, from within the Imaginary realm, here a deep unconscious characterized by "a dream of forests far inside such sleep." The tempo of this stirring is crucial; it is not with "a shore rhythm," the regular beat of waves, that language can begin to emerge, but

with the pulsings of dark groves—as if
A bird of hunting swept over hooded
Places, fled, and at intervals returned—
Clocked by the broken aspirates roaring

Along their own wind, heard within their wood,
Their own deep wood, where, fluttering, first words
Emerge, wrapped in slowly unfolding leaves.

The beginning of a consciousness of the word is also the beginning
of time consciousness. But paradoxically, in the second part of the
poem a desire to close the gap between the beginning and the end of
the process of emergence leads to a desire for timelessness—"where
there are no gaps / Between the seeding and the gathering," a desire
for a "seasonless land." This represents a shift back towards the
unconscious, a becoming lost in the synchronic world of the Imaginary: "Dreaming of intervals lost—stretched out on / Wastes not of
snow, nor sand, nor loud, he tossed, / And knew not why, in that
undying noon." The time that finally emerges in the poem is an
equivocal one, for when the character fully wakes, it is to a darkened
room where he seems to see "distant stars whistling through darkness," a "momentary Jupiter / Passing at night"; he wakes to see the
"night dawn." The moment of waking, then, reveals, as do the decayed
constellations the character spies, "the mark missed, by the unsting-
ing tail, / The moment that was: the time of this dark / Light beyond,
that seemed to be light above." The moment of waking becomes a
moment of loss; the time of consciousness is a time always receding
towards the unconscious. It is this double movement that constitutes
the pulsation of the slit that Lacan describes. The time of language,
of a Symbolic and stylistic time, always reveals what Derrida calls
the "trace" of something anterior, the false trail, the Imaginary.

What this leads us to is an acknowledgment that time, even considered as a style, is always incomplete. The trace always remains
elusive: "The concepts of *present, past,* and *future,* everything in the
concepts of time and history which implies evidence of them—the
metaphysical concept of time in general—cannot adequately describe
the structure of the trace" (*OG* 67). Because this trace of the unconscious cannot be known but remains "beyond" language, because it
in effect constitutes a separate "time" (a synchronic time, Lacan

would say) that leaves its trace in style, we have begun to open up another problem—the referentiality of time as style. The exploration of this problem is one of the tasks that Hollander's "Tales Told of the Fathers" sets for itself.

The sequence opens with a poem, "The Moment," in which the central character has stood "waiting, withholding his gaze," detached as "he felt the moment pass." Within the duration of this passing he has dreamt "Regions of erased shapes in the air" that transport him from the very physical world in which he has stood. The aim of the moment, of the sequence, is to move away from a simple presence given by the physical senses and towards a time of the Fathers, an anterior time. However, all the tales that can be told of these Fathers are erasures, traces. "The dead," Hollander says, "are not even / Things"—they disappear into "part of night." What we are faced with, then, is "the dark / Opening into further / Dark"—traces of traces. The apparent meaninglessness that threatens here is redeemed later in the sequence, in "Signs," where the central character spies "a skull floating / On the face of the waters" that seems to signify something beyond merely "a cup of life emptied." But what this signification might be, precisely, remains undeciphered:

> —And seeing it just at noon,
> Bobbing on bright water at
> The most transparent time, when
> He could look back over his
> Shoulder and see a clear field,
> When his long ever-vengeful
> Shadow vanishes and stops,
> For a moment, following:
> This was most dreadful of all.

Now the precise "meaning" here is evaded. As Derrida suggests, the trace is "understood" by a "temporalizing"—"namely, the action of postponing until later, . . . the taking account of time and forces in an operation that implies an economic reckoning, a detour, a respite, a delay, a reserve, a representation." The tempo of the lines, then, which could but don't quite connect the skull and the speaker's sense of his own mortality, "resort(s), consciously or unconsciously, to the temporal and temporalizing mediation or a detour that suspends the accomplishment or fulfillment of 'desire' or 'will,' or carries desire or will out in a way that annuls or tempers their effect" (*SPH* 136). This description of the dynamics of the trace provides us with a fine description of the special quality of Hollander's poetry; we are presented with a "transparent time," a style that presents "erased shapes in the air." Such is the vision that the gardener in the last poem of the sequence accomplishes. An "Edenist of the mid-air," he has pruned what he'd like to think has always been a timeless or synchronic garden where "there was nothing to lose." But his seemingly bracketed world is traced by another time of distant but brilliant sunsets, of decay. The desire, posited at the beginning of the sequence, to move away from the present becomes manifest in this strange temporality of the trace.

The world of Hollander's poems, then, is a world where "shadows / Are insubstantial and always full of motion." What we encounter is "a broken / Circle of representations dancing in the sunlight, / Given a common substance by their chorus of shadows" ("A Statue of Something," *BW* 12). What is represented by the representations, what binds them together, finally, is the "chorus of shadows" itself, a chorus of traces, of lost representationality. Hollander himself has acknowledged the importance of Kierkegaard for his thinking about shadows. In *Either/Or* the narrator describes the unreadibility of his "shadowgraph" method; for him, "outward appearance has significance, it is true, but not as an expression of the inward, but rather as a telegraphic communication which tells us that there is something hidden deep within" (*EO* 173). The signs lead to an unexpressable, a knot, the hidden that presents itself as absent. He goes on to describe the experience of seeming to see the trace of one face in another, with the result that there is produced "an ambiguity that resists artistic production." This resistance, or ambiguity, is at the core of every one of Hollander's poems. For Hollander, the concern of a poem is with this process, this tempo—with rhetoric and style; it is with shadows, transparencies, and symbols rather than with things, as, say, in Penn Warren's poems. His concern is more with the symbolic and general world than the material and particular; this world is, for both Hollander and Kierkegaard, the product of an "instant," of a "fleeting moment" that resists a simple presence.

The poem "Monuments" (*BW* 9), set in a cemetery, further examines the problem of traces. In fact, the monuments themselves are traces: "something has exhaled this marble and moved / On, itself a kind of wind." Now, however, there is only a vague "remembrance" of a connection—these trace stones "whose inscriptions keep being sure of what was / Not, by way of hedging about what was." The line break here seems to shadow the very meaning of the lines. The scene, in short, presents Hollander, with a "chorus of shadows"—

We bump against
Knowing that it was not in pursuit of solid
Pictures that we wandered in among all this, but
That there need be no seeking that which sleeps away
In stone for which the living butterfly is but
An image, as of its own fluttering shadow;
That the tombstones were there wherever we were then,
Where we are now, wherever there is wandering.

The poem ends with an acknowledgment that the stones can represent nothing of the past or future of the inscribed lives. The stones provide "closed doorways out into the sky, the grass." But Hollander does not slip into a facile silence. The poem, any art, he hedges, may provide "a monument of eternal crystal" that is yet temporally structured by a play of traces, the unending, evasive "reflections on and in it." The result, finally, is that the poem would become "empty of itself, and bright with what was meant." But what is ever *meant*? How do the poem's pulsations *mean*?

In "The Viewer" (*BW* 59) Hollander suggests that our basic desire is to dwell in the kind of "transparent / Fiction" that occurs in a dream world (seen in our unconscious by the mythical "viewer"). That is, "In our time we have come to see / Through the glass, to want to enter / The bright ball whose bottom is deep." This center is the knot, the trace, the unreadable, the resistance the poem offers. But on the other hand we find ourselves too often "Stranded on the shore of meanings" that is our conscious life. Meaning, in other words, "hardens" and freezes a text as if it were an object; it attempts to spatialize a certain structure out of time rather than set it in motion as play of Time. Any "meaning" of a poem must be its Time, the desire for what is always deferred. We must return, then, to the tempo of the unconscious.

The unconscious progresses, we might say, like the dream of the two lovers in "The Train" (*BW* 18), a poem that plays upon the sexual suggestions in trains coupling, straightening out after curves, passing into tunnels, and the like. Within a labyrinth of dreams, the lovers "dream the epic of gleaming and distant / Vanishing, the diminution of time." But the dream of timelessness, of synchronized rhythms and "endless lines," becomes disrupted by the tempo of the poem (seven- and eleven-syllable lines, numbers of chance) so that signs and meanings never quite fit. There is always what Lacan calls the "sliding of signifiers" (*E* 146 ff). That is, there is always a sense not only that meanings cannot be finalized, but that metaphors and referents are never quite aligned, that there is always a "remainder," even at the points of "suture," the openings of the "slit." In the sexual metaphor of the poem, the train gets blocked by a tunnel wall and cannot penetrate (a metaphor, by the way, which Lacan would heartily endorse).

> One needed to live by was always missing
> The satisfying cardinal verticals
> And could only read seven
> Or eleven o'clock, too soon or too late.
> It was the dark place of loss.

For Lacan, the unconscious, which is structured like a language, is the locus of an Other. The pulsation of the unconscious, in fact, serves "to mark that time by which, from the fact of being born with a signifier, the subject is born divided" (*FFC* 199). That is, its signifier, its meaning, always evades it, splits away from it, is creatively forgotten. The result of the dialectic between the two is repetition—what Lacan calls the "appointment always missed," a rhythm of absences, the creation of a new time. The referent of time as style thus becomes the unconscious, the trace of the Other, and Hollander's poem marks, in a sense, the play between time as style and time as Other in the sexual play between the mismatched rhythms of lover and beloved. We might call the logical time of this interplay, after Lacan, an "intersubjective time," a concept we can explore in *Reflections on Espionage*.

III

An Enciphered Time

The eternal hourglass of existence is turned upside
down again and again, and you with it, speck of
dust!
> —Nietzsche, *The Gay Science*

According to Nietzsche, all writing is inherently metaphoric, and
his theory of metaphor is based on the subversion of the self: "To
transpose, one must be able to transpose oneself, to have conquered
the limits of individuality; the same must partake of the other, it
must become the other" (*NN* 206). In other words, "the 'self' and the
individual are fictions concealing a complexity, a plurality of forces
in conflict" (*NN* 18). It is this line of thinking that both Hollander
and Lacan inherit: the self is always in conflict with unconscious
forces (in addition to events), with the Other whose setting is language.
The play of forces is what supplants the traditional notion of "Being"
for Nietzsche, and it constitutes a text that must be interpreted—not
by a synthesizing, unifying subject, but by a "subject" who radically
changes and transforms both himself and his text:

> Ultimately, the individual derives the value of his acts from himself;
> because he has to interpret in a quite individual way even the words he
> has inherited. His interpretation of a formula at least is personal, even if
> he does not create a formula: as an interpreter he is still creative [*WP*
> 403].

In Hollander's *Reflections on Espionage* the discovery and burden of
this vision constitutes the central drama. For him in this text, the

time of style, intersubjective time, must be understood as the time of the transformation of the self in the Other.

This process of self-transformation that occurs in interpretive acts is described in Lacan's poetics, especially "The Function and Field of Speech and Language in Psychoanalysis," and it will be useful to use Lacan as a guide through Hollander's *Reflections*. Lacan writes, for instance, that

> I identify myself in language, but only by losing myself in it like an object. What is realized in my history is not the past definite of what was, since it is no more, or even the present perfect of what has been in what I am, but the future anterior of what I shall have been for what I am in the process of becoming [E 86].

The desire that motivates Lacan's poetics is a desire to find the subject, the self, as a lost, a forgotten other—to explore the temporality of language in which loss and gain, or at least our experience of them, occur. It is precisely such a desire that motivates John Hollander's master spy, Cupcake, as he works through the "ciphers" and "codes" of his history, the specialized language of his profession in *Reflections*. Thus, in the second decoded "message" of the book Cupcake wonders: "What kind of work is this / For which if we were to touch in the darkness / It would be without feeling the other there?" (1/15, the entries are dated). This desire for interaction with the Other constitutes what Lacan calls an "Intersubjective time" whose rules are given by a sort of "theory of games" of the unconscious, for it is in the unconscious, in the shiftings and play of language, that the Other is situated. The concerns of Hollander and Lacan, then, are with

> the temporal sources through which human action, in so far as it orders itself according to the action of the other, finds in the scansions of its hesitations the advent of its certainty; and in the decision that concludes it, this action given to that of the other—which it includes from that point on—together with its consequences deriving from the past, its meaning-to-come [E 75].

Now this "meaning-to-come," pointed towards by the pulsations, the tempo, the "scansion" of hesitations, is quite complex. Ultimately, as Lacan points out, it concerns the death instinct, not simply in the Freudian sense, but in the Heideggerian sense of a finite horizon: "so does the death instinct essentially express the limit of the historical function of the subject. This limit is death . . . as Heidegger's formula puts it, as that possibility which is one's ownmost, unconditional, unsupersedable, certain and as such indeterminable" (*E* 103). Cupcake himself faces this horizon, as an implication of the finitude of language, when he projects a self fully "lost," in Lacan's sense, within his code: he would become "an agent / Whose only life was a part of the work. / He would be a pure null." However, this linguistic limit does establish a certain ontological existence in that the "Others" which help define the self in *Reflections* are "Notional characters, thinner than fictions, / Yet fully formed on these pages they dwell in" (5/12). The "text of life" and the text of *Reflections* intersect in the ironic realization that the world of the poem may contain more "truth" than the world of objects and "facts," so that the "false self reflects back a real image" (1/31). The negation and transformation of the self as a "null" in language becomes the basis for creating supreme fictions, versions of the self as processes of becoming, progressive encipherments of self and Other.

It is a knowledge of the language code as both a finite limit and the source of fictive transformations that structures the self's creation of its own past:

> This limit represents the past in its real form, that is to say, not the physical past whose existence is abolished, nor the epic past as it has become perfected in the work of memory, nor the historic past in which man finds the guarantor of his future, but the past which reveals itself reversed in repetition [*E* 103].

In order to understand this sense of "repetition," Lacan turns us to Kierkegaard's *Repetition* which distinguishes between "recollection," a melancholy remembering backwards, and Repetition, a joyous "remembering forward" (*REP* 33, *E* 103). As Lacan says, "Repetition demands the new"—there is no mindless repeating for the focus is always on the future anterior. We could turn to Nietzsche's "Eternal Return" as another variation upon this theme. Now in *Reflections* this sort of repetition is accomplished by the various 'reflections' that are not only stages in Cupcake's self-analysis, but the plethora of *mirror* images, of "Others," of Cupcake's "routine" (nightly decoding), and of the mirroring of Cupcake, the editor-narrator whose notes reveal his puzzlement, his otherness, and of Hollander himself (who actually sent some of these as transmissions to friends while in the middle of "Spectral Emanations") (*Acts* 201).

What all this mirroring or reflecting does, in effect, is defer meaning, make the process of enciphering and deciphering a seemingly "eternal" one. The "resonances" and "insinuations" of the code are never quite captured within the code itself, within its eleven-syllable line:

> For instance, this eleven by eleven
> Grid I am using seems to dictate to me
> Messages it might most lovingly encode,
> As an eternal form of water-jar might
> Whisper to some monk in a cold, white room the
> Secrets of size, color of glaze. More later.
>
> [1/19]

Always the Derridian deferral, always "More later." In fact,

> one would want to be
> Able to look upon his literal world
> Half-forgetting what it enciphered; one would
> Want to walk one's gaze among the cool columns
> Of letter groups, through the shades of averted
> Signification. That would be the one world
> Where letter itself was all the spirit that
> Was.
>
> [4/18]

Ultimately, then, Cupcake is not concerned with the coding and decoding of messages, meanings ("boring transmissions"), but with "the actvity they provide a Fabric for: our little thoughts on the nature / Of Code" (2/27). The life of the self, then, becomes defined in this playful self-referentiality of the code, not in meanings but in the play of meanings, in the deferral of meaning and teleology. Thus, Cupcake explains: "We must keep asking for / Ciphers more difficult, each month, to use lest / Our care and hope vanish into the message" (4/3). To finish, to end, is to deny the self. Thus, at the end of *Reflections*, Cupcake refuses to finish a message sent by Lyrebird, his chief (muse). Its pieces lie upon the table: "whatever the promise of / Their scatter might suggest washed away by the / Grossness of finishing" (9/17). And as Cupcake says early in the book, in a parody of Valéry, "No case is ever / Finished, but only abandoned" (2/4).

The complex pulsation of *Reflections*, built upon the processes of negation, repetition, and deferral we have been exploring, actually receives a provisional teleology in the notion of what Cupcake calls the "Final Cipher." The Final Cipher would produce a static, final poem, "a poem whose form was of the world itself," a poem in which one "would walk in rhythms / Of transposition, in its modes of shifting"—a poem of pure "tempo" (5/10). But the Final Cipher also poses a problem, for it betrays a desire for rest, a desire to temporalize. The business of poetry, as we have seen, is to work within the "Finite Cipher" that consists of "Building and unbuilding" (5/11), to watch the fictive Final Cipher "gradually taking shape" (5/10) but never being realized. Cupcake's final transmission suggests just how much he has learned this unlearnable (because never completed) lesson—

> Squibs snap from the logs. Outside,
> Paeans of meaningless wind rush past trees, shutters, *et*
> *Ainsi de suite.* But how do you know that encoded
> In those cycles of whining, the rise and fall of a sigh,
> There is not some message of mine—not of the work we
> Are agents of, nor cover lives, but of breath itself.
> Emphasis of breath; a hushed study in the decay
> Of our material timber into its embers.
> Echo of wind? Burletta of its urgency? Breath
> Enwraps no messages, but of its aeromancy
> There are no need of forms which, enciphered in twilight,
> Are decoded in the blue morning air. The outside
> Wind is an agency of breath. The low fire inside
> Is an agency of rhyming death. Where is my breath?
> Eeee wheezes the respiring wind despairingly, Eeee!

[9/30]

It is both the utter simplicity and increasing "difficulty" of "breath" in its relation to wind, sighs, words, the word, flames, and the nullity of the rhyme word "death" that provide Cupcake with a new time in which to transform himself. Cupcake, abandoning his profession, dissolves like wind as "an agency of breath" into his own text, becomes endless forms. And yet a *trace* of the old self remains, erased, even its rhymes—"Material timber into embers"—creating a continuing dialectic of breath and death. No longer is a linear, clock time, measured by the calendar dates that head each transmission, adequate to account for Cupcake's progress. We are faced here with a time that wavers "enciphered in twilight," that echoes back and forth, that links inside and outside, self and other, word and cry—a time, in short, that is always reversed in the repetitions of language.

This dissolving into one's own unreadable text is reminiscent of Kierkegaard's passage where the character receives a letter of great importance concerning matters in his life but cannot make out the "pale" and "illegible" script, who hopes to decipher one word and so deduce the whole text, whose tears of frustration blur the text even further in a continual "uncertainty" of endless deferrals: "In the course of time, the writing would become fainter and more illegible, until at last the paper itself would crumble away, and nothing would be left to him except the tears in his eyes" (*EO* 188). Time, for Cupcake, is his own illegible signature wavering in the text; it is his style.

IV

A Serious Trifling with History

And are not all things knotted together so firmly
that this moment draws after it *all* that is to come?
Therefore—itself too?
                                        —Nietzsche, *Zarathustra*

For Nietzsche, self, style, interpretation, and event are all finite perspectives, none of which can exhaust the richness of reality. History becomes, in this view, "a continuous sign-chain of ever new interpretations and adaptations whose causes do not even have to be related to one another" (*OGM* 77). A linear, sequential Time becomes an impossibility. For example, Nietzsche speculates on "whether some beings might be able to experience time backward, or alternately forward and backward" (*GS* 336). What Nietzsche uncovers, according to Foucault, is another base for history other than the continuity imposed by causality and memory, a base that is marked rather by disruption and differences, "a counter-memory—a transformation of history into a totally different form of time" (*LCM* 160). This form of time is "genealogical," the term Nietzsche uses to describe the eternal shifting of forces that are fluid, primordial; it is an always disruptive form, based upon an endless series of interpretive valuations and revaluations. Such a form of what we might call Critical Time is thus always deconstructing the central moments it nevertheless keeps positing for itself.

The primordial forces that Nietzsche describes find their metaphoric expression in historical structures. For Hollander, this occurs in his "Spectral Emanations." The "Spectral Emanations" are metaphorically suggested by the different colors of the spectrum that are at once continuous and discontinuous. The poem is on one level concerned with the fictive significations we might assign to the seven primary colors (which comprise the titles of the seven sections, each made up of a poetry and a prose segment), and to the boundaries between those sections. Taken as a sum, a final moment, the colors would combine, as we know from physics, to produce a white or invisible light. But, "*white* isn't the title of a section, only an un-reached sum, unavailable to sight, and timeless; the poem has to present the colors separately, sequentially, temporally" (*Acts* 200). What holds the poem together, then, its center *white*, is an absent sum, or rather, as it is diffused across the visible spectrum of history, an always displaced center. The result is a poem curiously in search of a subject to center itself on, and yet curiously undermining its own efforts to predicate a final subject, to predicate the history of its own presence.

This search is itself figured in the fictive plot, the "Recovery of the

88

Sacred Candlestick," that is the backdrop for the "Green" prose segment (which is reminiscent of *Reflections*) and indeed for the whole
poem. In the summer of 1972 Hollander stumbled across a section in
Hawthorne's *The Marble Faun* about the idea for a "mystic story or
parable" concerning the recovery of the Candlestick, really a seven-
branch candelabra, a story that would be written by seven American
poets. The origin of the poem, then, is itself a fiction within another
fiction, ultimately aiming back to what Derrida would call an
"erased" trace—that very erasure being the "text" of Hollander's
poem thus aptly subtitled, "A Poem in Seven Branches in Lieu of a
Lamp."

There is a radical doubleness to this erased text. While Hilda's call
is for an American poem in the Western tradition of an objective,
diachronic, spatialized time, Hollander also acknowledges Miriam as
muse, thereby invoking the more subjective, synchronic Time of the
Hebrew tradition. Parallel to this tension is a strife between a temporality of absence and a temporality of presence; each tradition
deconstructs the other at key points in "Spectral Emanations," no
matter how well the poem as a whole attempts to synthesize them.
Hollander's predicament here is much like that of Edmond Jabes in
The Book of Questions, who finds his Jewish origins a "hole," a "non-
place," an absence, a homeland of mere words and texts that under-
mine each other. At the same time, though, he strives, through those
very words that mark absence, to construct some provisional fiction
of presence. Thus his strategy—and it is Hollander's, too—requires
re-writings of history, redefinitions of time as a continual activity.
History becomes the matter of a future that is always already being
rewritten upon a present that is always already erased; it becomes
the matter of trace doubling upon trace. So, for example, Jabes says:
"The present is, for you, this passage too rapid to be seized. What is
left of the passage of the pen is the work, with its branches and leaves
green or already dead. The work hurled into the future in order to
translate it" (*BQ* 332). Such constant, discontinuous re-writing in a
poem as seemingly architecturally and spatially shaped as "Spectral
Emanations" is itself a sign of its deconstructive mode. The poem
ultimately reflects, as the "Green" prose segment suggests, "the inability of nature to signify beyond any one moment."

"Red," the first color section of the poem, plots the situation of a soldier in the Yom Kippur war of 1973 at the "red moment," which is his death. But the loss that is described is not simply a personal one, for the section is filled with references to Jewish history. When he dies, the "film of / The ages" disintegrates as it "runs in coils / Across his mind's eye." To supplement this radical loss of history, the text associates "redness" with the biblical richness of "Adam's kingdom"—also the Jewish state—with the red clay of Adam's name and with the other picture words for "Adam" ("Ax, door, water")—with, in short, the "wide realm of the red." The attempt here is to begin history once again by finding a "grounding sun" that will transform loss into birth, keeping the historical moment at one eternal threshold.

But this project is undermined at the end of the "Red" section when a "red singer," the narrator, looks back into the history he has sung, towards "the violet becoming black." That is, he glances towards, and moves backwards towards, the biblical moment of the origin of light, when all before was darkness. In terms of the architecture of the poem, it is a glance not to an origin, but an end—"Violet" is the last section of "Spectral Emanations." The singer's gesture, in other words, is to glance, Janus-like, both forward and backward from the delicate threshold of his own moment. However, the linear history of Western time that so dominates the early sections of the poem obliterates the desire for a synchronic time that would found a new age. The moment, and the section, fade into a radical, because so self-conscious, absence—"Blown dust makes a false threshold."

"Violet," on the other hand, is a more successful complement to "Red," though it opens with the false assurance that "at the song's beginning / Even as our voices / Rise we know the last words." But this teleology is immediately undercut when the last words themselves collapse and the narrator is left asking how to "shape / Our last stanza." No last words in the form of a "coda" emerge. Instead, we are faced with the emblematic image of a candle in a pitcher (according to Hollander, a Portuguese custom that unwittingly links Christian and Jewish traditions by a faded symbolism). The candle will "light up no path: / Neither will it go out," and it is set at a threshold, "at the easternmost / Edge of the sunset world." The question now becomes not the means to establishing a final text of white, but "what text will / The dallying night leave?" It is a question of re-beginning, of the flickerings of the mysterious candle and its lost traces of meaning—"the hidden candle, the locked clavichord of implications." The poem ends, then, with a dispersal, a promise of dissemination.

What path does "Spectral Emanations" take between "Red" and "Violet" that shifts the emphasis from "blown dust" to the poised play of presence and absence, text and trace, to time as the critical threshold? The most crucial text in this process is the middle section (another question of middles)—"Green." But before we examine that section we should examine the deconstruction of presences in "Yellow," which is a pre-text for "Green." The overt strategy of "Yellow's" verse is to establish presence as unchanging through echoings and doublings, an intensification of a pure "now" rather than "Red's" attempt to presence the past. It opens, for instance, with a description of a "whisper" of flowers reflected on the surface of a pond. And later, when a mythical "man of earth exhales a girl of air" in Stevensian fashion, the girl is seen as a pure presence, an "everlastingness." But the whisper of flowers is also an inscription on the water's surface, much like the inscription of traces on Freud's mystic writing pad of the unconscious, the absent: "It would remain an interpretation / Of the flimsy text, half unremembered, / Dimming evermore and diminishing." And the man of earth's girl occupies "the air within the circle of / His emptied arms." Now the hope of the "Yellow" verse section is that these two forces would synthesize by taking the form of a nineteenth-century dialectic. That form recognizes a war of contraries but attempts to reconcile them in a luminous moment: "to have eternized, for a moment, / The time when promise and fulfillment feed / Upon each other."

The prose section of "Yellow" dismantles this metaphysics, dispensing with the strategies of the verse in an opening citation: "All the eternal ornaments set down in dust will never live nor yet give birth. Pale, unenduring petals go to brown and therefore live in the soft mines of earth." A few paragraphs later, a celebratory group is described as chaotic when the revelers disperse in random directions. So chaotic is the scene that they fail to realize that the statue of Saturn they have gathered around, centered on as an emblem of cyclic, seasonal time, is really a statue of Mars, an image of Time's destructiveness—of the lost moment in "Red." It is this failure—indeed, the failure of the whole of "Spectral Emanations" up to "Yellow" to find a satisfactory theory of time—that leads to "Green."

In the absence left by these deconstructed moments of presence, and by the similar deconstructions we have seen occur in Hollander's work, there emerges a questioning of the very idea of Time. As Derrida says in his criticism of Husserl's attempt to bracket off moments of pure presence: "temporality has a nondisplaceable center, an eye or living core, the punctuality of the real now" (*SPH* 62). But as we have seen, and as Derrida sees in Husserl's texts, the pure present is compounded in fact by "nonpresences"—by traces, absences, loss. Thus, says Derrida, "what we are calling time must be given a different name" (68). Or, as Hollander's narrator remarks in "Green," what is needed is "a serious trifling with history." What they both eventually suggest is a "Time" Derrida calls a "divergence" (already suggested in the dispersals of "Violet" and "Yellow"), "deferral" and "spacing" (86). Even as this new Time emerges in the rhetoric, however, the text typically attempts, in its thematic assumptions, to establish a conventional Time based on presence. The play of the section, that is, is always dynamic and deconstructive—"perhaps I can determine a history as well, even as I plan to end it," reads the "Green" prose.

Thus the verse segment proclaims assuredly that "we / Desire nothing beyond this being green / Nor can we reach it," and attempts to interpret its color as the lushness of a noonday presence that would extend unchanged into night. This pastoral greenness "buzzes with what / Is, breathes with ever-presence, with its verity," as the closing lines of the verse section roundly conclude. But upon what, we must ask, is this pure Husserlian presence built? When we return to the opening stanza, upon which the others incrementally build, we find that green is seen as a "trace" that night will leave; it already marks its own absence. The birds in the scene chant, with a Stevensian doubleness, "of nothing that was to be." With similar duplicity, the second stanza enlarges the scene of presence as the green, localized in the first stanza, now encompasses a whole forest, but includes blue "far away" lakes. On the one hand, the green presence becomes more emphatic, but on the other hand it is only "a green hedge around blue wisdom. At the edge / Of things here and now." Presence becomes a matter of the periphery, already decentered. We are faced with a poetry that expands from an absent, displaced center. What the "Green" prose will subsequently work towards is a radical redefinition of the "now" in the light of this curious expansive yet emptying movement. The "now" becomes a moment so saturated with otherness that it must be written twice to suggest its own sliding away from itself:

> At the exact point of noon—at just noon—the sundial's vertical finger will be a knife edge, almost invisible. But even without the dial, we will know the moment from the grass: it will be at its greenest, remembering its early dimness when it awoke to light, invisibly dreaming its darkness to come. These are what saturate its hue, giving it depth and strength now, now.

In terms of the poem's strategy, the absence is the absence of the lamp which the text attempts to supplement. The lamp, then, is "an Object which is somehow like a Text." And the process of raising the lamp (a Cupcake-like cloak-and-dagger plot recorded anonymously) is a language problem: "Our nouns are chains and hydraulic lifts, the underwater gear our tropes." But what is an authentic text? The problem stems from the very beginning of the project, from the moment the plotters have found the lamp:

> the only representation we have all had to go on—is by its very nature uncanonical. It is as if one lived by a Scripture whose original tongue had been totally forgotten, all other texts in it lost or defaced, and that had only been preserved in a mocking and contemptuous translation, elegantly but insincerely done. And yet it would have had to have done for one's Text.

But even if this problem of the lost origin could be solved, "there is the problem of all the replicas." In fact, the author here, like Hollander, is most directly concerned only with a replica; his "sole charge is to remove [a] replica from future history, soundless unnoticed and without any consequences save for those that stem from the recovery of the lamp itself." And in order for the lamp to be free of its (false) representations, to be confined only to its own moment, "it has to be carried to its home in the unimaged region, bare of representations

93

save those of itself." Now this fictive activity that begins as a "lost or defaced" trace, that proceeds in a "soundless" way towards an "unimaged region" of further traces, is "an occasional vision, a wandering of the eye among accidents." This is not history, then, but romance—"Our romance is of a raising and bearing, the undoing of histories."

The recovery of the lamp, then, and the writing of the poem, are as suppositional as Cupcake's Final Cipher. It is a history with no time. The conspirators are both "too late" and "too soon," so that when the author can exclaim that he sees his "moment now," it is not a moment of "accomplishment—that instant is ever invisible." What he "sees" is rather a deferral, an openness—the invisible, a trace of a trace: "the fiction that the first text was itself a recension of whispers, a gathering of what had been half-heard among the trees" ("Violet") (*WD* 26, *SPH* 84–86). "Green," and indeed "Spectral Emanations," deconstruct the color symbolism, the representational grid, the history of their own progress. "Spectral Emanations" is "incomplete by virtue of its very closure: to finish is to leave undone the task of showing eternity, rushing out of the last event in a stream of consequences, mostly lost, like bubbles near a source" (*WD* 291).

The form that this history takes, finally, as an "opening," as a lost trace, is "not reconstruction, not restoration, but restitution." Written history becomes not a matter of attempting a duplication, or even the coveted recovery, but rather the futural task of anticipating a supplement, a restitution, which like all restitutions is inadequate, its tropes bubbling of something "mostly lost" even before it appears in any future history of itself. There is always, then, a reminder, and to see its traces we must interrogate the text still further. How, for instance, do we speak of the time or non-time of this history as restitution?—"The time of waiting is the time of the rock." And the time of the rock? The rock itself? A "canonical" replica, a "gleaming green stone, not standing for the thing itself, but speaking wordlessly of it." And how does it speak? By the "excited" play of light across its "facets" that seems to be reflected in the "smallest spill" or the "profoundest pool." That is, by the interplay of color traces as spectral emanations.

History, then, becomes a matter of historical illusion, the play of tropes, traces, anticipations—the play of always inadequate restitutions, of remainders. The remainder, in this context, is thus a surplus of signifiers; one could continue to make significant associations concerning the colors and their relationships in "Spectral Emanations" because their "meanings" are always left open—there is no bottom line, no center. The serious trifling with history that the poem accomplishes redefines it radically as a non-history of events whose "meanings" are always just emerging and just fading. Time becomes a symbol: colors, objects, events, and their rhetorical movements are its signs. Time becomes not a duration *in which* events take place; rather, the events themselves contain and determine themselves as "time." By this non-history, time is liberated as a style, as a symbolic style.

V

A Polyphonic Time

> Rather has the world become "infinite" for us all
> over again, inasmuch as we cannot reject the possi-
> bility that *it may include infinite interpretations.*
> —Nietzsche, *The Gay Science*

How are we to envision these events that determine themselves as Time? In the light of recent rereadings, we can say that for Nietzsche the openness of existence is affirmed in the Eternal Return, seen as a recurrence not of a particular thing or of being, but of recurrence itself as a principle of pluralism. That is, the Nihilism in Nietzsche's Eternal Return, like the "undoing" or "ending" of traditional history in "Green," has a positive thrust in that it is the basis of any change.

It affirms, as Zarathustra understood, our perspectivism. It is in this context that Time has presented itself in Hollander's work. Time, as a play of forces, becomes a time of endless reinterpretations, each interpretation marking a new beginning, but based upon the traces of previous beginnings and the anticipations, however provisional, of future traces. What recurs is the trace.

It is crucial to see that such a "structure" of Time is itself a symbol and, as a symbol, it imposes an order, however random, at least as much as it describes any play of forces. That is, the symbol of Time in Hollander's work is implicitly subject to further deconstructions, but at the same time it does propose a fictive order. This is felt, for example, in "Some of the Parts" (*BW* 8), where there is an "assurance" that the pieces of a scene that "flake apart" will be deployed under the rubric of an invisible structure. And when Hollander in *Blue Wine* questions "Lachesis," one of the Fates, about the random manner in which she cuts the fabric of our lives, he realizes that the fabric symbol itself is a playful figure, finally inadequate as a representation of Time:

> Asking what we are to do when our play,
> As with this very figure, fancying
> Up the old fiction for a moment, ends—
> Is this not all our late work?

We have not really drifted very far from our opening comments if we understand that this play of forces we have been describing as Time, as a play of infinite interpretations that interrupt one another, blurring in random tempo, uses the very terms of our description of style. It is the impulse to find meanings, for example, that motivates the endless play of Signifiers we have seen in all Hollander's work. Interpretation is a style of the poem. It is itself Time.

Interpretive Time, as a function of the play of language, is a polyphonic Time. A tempo of thought is interrupted by other tempos, brief moments that are fragments of other series, traces of otherwise interminable play. Each echo introduces another time and is itself interrupted. "Blue Wine," a poem of diverging perceptions, explores the intricacies of a polyphonic Time. The poem takes as its point of departure some wine bottles on which have been pasted mock labels and in which is a substance Hollander claims he could not identify—the poem is an attempt to "make sense out of what was apparently in them" (*Acts* 201). They are symbols, then, as well as objects. Each of the eleven sections provides a fragment of some fiction associated with the mysterious wine: some of these sections are set in an ongoing present, some in a religiously or historically colored past, some in a literary or mythic past, and the last segment in a suppositional future—there are no absolute referents for any of these. Around the non-existent wine, that is, a fictive history is suggested in a way that echoes the random allusiveness of "Green." Section four, for example, combines a reference to a non-existent Plutarch text on Blue Wines (there is something of Borges in Hollander's fictions); section eight is a mock-Homeric poem about the discovery of the wine; section seven alludes to some mysterious "master" who could exist at any time. What holds the poem together is its own textuality, the sense it projects of itself as an authentic document of interpretive history. The poem is, after all, a mock history, eager to deconstruct its own pretensions—"Perhaps this is all some kind of figure—the thing contained / For the container."

What Hollander has perhaps begun to discover with this poem, and indeed with all the poems in *Blue Wine* we have discussed, is the fact that not only is the trace invisible, but even our metaphors to supplement its loss always evade and fail us. The theory of poetry becomes the theory of Time. It is a theory that calls for a radical overturning of our traditional ways of thinking about Time. It is a theory that, ready to be overturned itself, incorporates the unexpected, the deferrals of meaning, the perspectivism we have been examining. Hollander's is a poetry that acknowledges, finally, the absence of the monotone presence, even of its own figures; it is a poetry whose metaphoric predications, always understood as impositions, invite interpretations beyond their own illusion of presence and within our own belated "epoch" as readers (*WD* 147).

> When some unexpected visitor
> Drops in and sees those bottles of blue wine, and does not ask
> At the time what they mean, he may take some drops home with him
> In the clear cups of his own eye, to see what he will see.

3

The Time of the Other

James Wright's Poetry of

Attachments

I

The Allegory of the Self

> Everything else is the language
> Of the silent woman who walks beside me.
> —Wright, "I Wish I May Never Hear of the
> United States Again"

Prefacing his translations from Theodore Storm, James Wright defines what he calls an essential quality of poetry, its *Stimmung*, as "a certain luminosity of descriptive language intended to express the author's emotional attachment to the objects and persons described" (*AWA* 576). Now this elusive definition touches on a number of complex issues. Not only are the terms "emotional attachment" and "certain luminosity" mysterious (for example, does "certain" mean "definite" or, more colloquially, "unnameable"?) but, as one begins to suspect in thinking about James Wright's own poetry, the mystery itself is perhaps part of any definition of these terms. And even if the individual terms themselves were more univocal, the relation between the "luminosity" and the "attachment" would still be problematic, though seemingly involving a Heideggerian presence. The issue in this case would rest upon the infinitive, "to express," which can mean simply a passive recording of some pre-linguistic experience, or a more active "squeezing" or "pressing out" of an attachment which is then simultaneous with, or perhaps even anterior to, language. If I seem to have wandered somewhat from the definition to illustrate its problems, it is with a sense that Wright's own poems, especially after the first two books, have tended to deconstruct the conventional notions of the simple presence of attachments the definition seems to propose.

We have entered already a "region," as Heidegger calls it, in which the language of Being and the Being of language begin to merge. Wright's explanation, in touching upon difficult and, according to Heidegger, nearly inexpressible aspects of poetic language, participates in that very inexpressibility the nearer it comes to capturing or "appropriating" it. This region, as we have seen in the discussion of Warren, is characterized, then, by a "withholding"—"There is some evidence that the essential nature of language flatly refuses to express itself in words—in the language, that is, in which we make statements about language. If language everywhere withholds its nature in this sense, then such withholding is the very nature of language" (*OWL* 81). If this withholding denies any easy solution to problems Wright's description raises, it also brings us "nearer" to a more "authentic" way of thinking about language and poetry. This experience, the "stimmung," of the approach along a "path" towards these attachments Wright aims for, and the underlying Heideggerian attachment to Being itself, is more important than calculative thought or meaning which for both writers is simply static and reductive; the approach, on the other hand, marks the Time of the self in the process of becoming itself. As a matter of fact, Heidegger himself uses the word *"Stimmung"* to describe "mood," which has an implicit connection to historicity and to the self's ongoing approach towards Being as Time (*HQ* 103–5). Now the "nearness" that is manifest in the approach is acted out, Heidegger says, in the notion of "Saying" as the Time of the "encounter" with the world (*OWL* 103–7). But in what context does this encounter occur? What does it lead to?

The short prose poem, "Time" (*TJ* 69), suggests the way this process of self-making can work.

Once, with a weak ankle, I tried to walk. All I could do was spin slowly a step or two, and then sit down. There has to be some balance of things that move on the earth. But this morning a small tern is flying full of his strength over the Ionian Sea. From where I stand, he seems to have only one wing. There is either something wrong with my eyes in the sunlight or something unknown to me about the shadow that hangs broken from his left shoulder. But the shadow is no good to me now. He has dropped it into the sea. There has to be some balance of things that move on the earth. But he is not moving on the earth. Both of my ankles are strong. My hair is gray.

The withholding here is manifest in the distance and separation of the narrator from the tern. Yet there is a certain parallel, emphasized by the verbal parallels ("wing" and "ankle," for instance) and repetitions. As we will see, more complex forms of attachment are increasingly built on modes of detachment. By focusing on the Other, the bird, the detached narrator gradually builds a relationship, only to discover in the end that he has also been building a self. The narrator gradually approaches himself, including his past self, through the Other. The discontinuity of time is made continuous. The poem, then, "balances" detachment and attachment, self and other, discontinuous and continuous, presence and absence. The sense of the self is invoked from the Other, from the "luminous" language that describes it. Similarly, at the end of "A Fishing Song" (*TJ* 60), he addresses the first fish he killed, which has become an emblem for all the ambivalent acts of his life. The fish, as an Other, also becomes the self—"Sweet plum, little shadow, he feeds my brother, / My own shadow."

It would be useful to refer to Jacques Lacan, who, echoing Heidegger and Wright, says that "the function of language is not to inform but to invoke. What I seek in speech is the response of the Other" (*ES* 86). What is encountered is this Other, as an object of desire whose identity progresses out of a narcissistic "mirror stage" as language develops, governs the "temporal dialectic that decisively projects the formation of the individual into history" (*E* 4). It is, in short, the object of attachment in Wright's poetry, that to which style is directed, the time-keeper of the poet. As Lacan says of Hamlet's predicament, the constant deferrals and withholding of action occur in the play because the young prince is so engaged with the figures of others that he is constantly "suspended" in the time of an Other—"Whatever Hamlet may do, he will do only at the hour of the Other" (*YFS* 55/56, 18). Thus, says Lacan, Hamlet "tries to find his sense of time in his object, and it is even in the object that he will learn to tell time" (17). Now obviously all poets do not suffer from Hamlet's neurotic condition, but something of this radical Otherness exerts some pressure on all poetic language. We need, then, to explore yet more fully the nature of the Other which interrupts the simple presence of the moment and, by its detachment, introduces the desire for attachment in Wright's poetry.

A little poem in the last section of *Collected Poems* provides us with a wedge to further open up Wright's definition. I refer to "Echo for the Promise of Georg Trakl's Life" (*CP* 179), which describes a "quiet voice" that seems to emerge from the "midst" of a battlefield's "blazing / Howitzers"—"Only the quiet voice / Speaks from the body of the deer / To the body of the woman." The mode of attachment in these lines is characterized as linguistic, though the nature of the "voice" that "speaks" in order to provide the "emotional attachment between two bodies remains problematic. The issue is made more complex when we realize that this voice is opposed to the sound of the battlefield, but that "Guns make no sound." So speaking and voice become defined by the attachment they produce. Speech, Lacan always explains in Heideggerian fashion, is also a *listening* to the Other. Speech is attachment. And who speaks this attachment for us? Who listens? Wright concludes the poem:

> My own body swims in a silent pool,
> And I make silence.
>
> They both hear me.
> Hear me,
> Father of my sound,
> My poor son.

The description of fact, the simple presence in silence, is interrupted and subverted by voice, both within the poem and by the existence of the poem itself, and in this deconstruction the call goes out to the other. The presence announced in the first two lines becomes predicated upon absence, and the seeming self-sufficiency of Wright's "I" is predicated upon the "listening" Others.

Voice is, paradoxically, both father and son of the attachment between the bodies in the poem, and between James Wright and those bodies—another version of time's balances. We are confronting here an infra-language, a silence that can be heard, which establishes the attachment that spoken language utters. This infra-language is something like the "determinative" pictures which Freud describes for the primitive Egyptian in "The Antithetical Sense of Primal Words"; these pictures, "placed against the alphabetical signs, are intended to give the sense of the latter and not to be spoken themselves" (*CP,* V 160). The difficulty is that these word-pictures can mean opposite things at once; a "reading" of them cannot take the form of a simple linear time. Rather, the words deconstruct each other, their relationships always fluctuating as they themselves attach meanings to each other; the Time of any such reading is always, in a sense, reversible, undercutting the progress of speech. The "path," as Heidegger often says, is an indirect and devious one—"silence," "sound," and "hearing" in Wright's poem have undecidable meanings, and the Time of the reading is endless. The notion of any Other as listener becomes, in the uncertain context I have described for this poem, highly problematic; it is, in fact, its evasiveness that underlies the undecidable language. The Other is the source of ambiguity.

The problem now becomes how provisionally to read these "determinative" signs, and it is this problem that we must address ourselves to in this chapter. But we have not even found our way out of the poem yet, and if we leap ahead to that strictly hypothetical point, where we are about to emerge from the poem, we find ourselves confronted with the title. The poem is an "echo"; and it is a silence, an attachment (but also, subtly, a detachment, as all echoes are an infra-language) that is echoed by the verbal utterance. Not only an echo of a past, but a future, too—a "promise." Or is the poem given rather as a substitute, an exchange for the promise of a life—that is, as another "body" to be figured in the structure of attachments? And if we extend this to the reader, what sort of attachment is he required to make? Once acknowledged or begun, where is this contexture of attachments to end? Is the end to be deferred indefinitely, suspended, as the "promise," the potential of anyone's life, of anyone's poem, his words, might be? Is that promise the source of the "luminosity" inherent in Wright's words for Trakl? Don't all these questions imply a rethinking of the whole problem of temporality? Is the end a detachment? *Is* there an end?

In order to situate Wright's strategies in a tradition of writing from which we can begin to confront some of these questions, I cite two texts. The first is a letter by Coleridge, in which he describes how he would work:

> to abstract and as it were unrealize whatever of more than common interest my eyes dwelt on; and then by a sort of transference and transmission of my consciousness to identify myself with the Object—and I have often thought, within the last five or six years, that if ever I should feel once again the genial warmth and stir of poetic impulse, and referred to my own experiences, I should venture on a yet stranger and wider Allegory than of yore—that I should *allegorize* myself, as a rock with its summit raised above the surface of some Bay or Strait [*CLC* 994].

The second text, also from the Romantic tradition, is a description from Kierkegaard's *Journals:*

> I felt so content in their midst, I rested in their embrace, and it was as though I were out of the body, wafted with them into the ether above—and the hoarse secret of the gulls reminded me that I stood alone, and everything vanished before my eyes, and I turned back with a heavy heart to mix in the busy world, yet without forgetting such blessed moments.

Both texts mark what Coleridge calls a "transference and transmission," what Wright calls an "attachment," that involves first an internalizing (an "unrealizing" or deconstruction of external reality), and then a projection of consciousness onto an external or detached object. Inherent in the description of these two "luminous moments," as the Romantics called such events, is a failure to reach a permanent identification, for there is always a difference that emerges in time. Kierkegaard turns away towards the "busy world" even in the midst of his observations; Coleridge writes from an autobiographical perspective, where the very possibility of poetry is questioned, and the whole last half of his rhetorically confident dithyramb is couched in subjunctive and conditional terms.

The process, then, has much in common with the process of transference, described by Freud and Lacan, which harbors a repression or resistance that must be faced and worked out according to an individual structure of Time (*LF* 77). Still, there is a triumph in each text; memory suggests that the self can be remade, or at least redefined, by its attachment to something "Other," and so the possibility of future renewal is carefully, if delicately, preserved. If the end of such a process is forever deferred, it exists at least as a "promise."

This deferral is achieved at no little cost; Kierkegaard and Coleridge, for instance, continually felt threatened by the loss of self in the philosophic and theological systems they simultaneously created and resisted. We might do well to consider Merleau-Ponty's notion that Time occurs only as a result of our relation to other things (*PP* 142). Time is not in a subject *per se*, for this would, for Ponty, provide simply a record of Time, nor is it only in other things, because this would ignore the role of the subject. Rather, Time is given in the "synthesis of transition" in which the present encounters or "meets" past and future; Time becomes, in this scheme, a "general flight out of the self" (*PP* 419), a progressive movement towards future attachments. There is a loss of the simple self as a center of Time. If, as the more radical stance taken by critics like Michel Foucault suggests, the contemporary linking of writing and death is to be understood as the author's self-effacement in his own text, we might suspect, in the context we have so far observed, that transference or attachment involves a sort of death (*LCM* 72). It is in fact a continuous association with death that effects the melancholy in Wright's work. "Names in Monterchi: To Rachel" (*TBPT* 53) describes a visit to a graveyard where names that are also the names of friends can be seen:

> In the little graveyard there,
> We are buried, Rachel, Annie, Leopoldo, Marshall,
> The spider, the dust, the brilliant, the wind.
> The tiny grapes
> Glazed themselves so softly in the soft tuft
> Of butterflies, it was hard to name
> Which vine, which insect, which wing,
> Which of you, which of me.

Here the metamorphosis of each thing into every other thing depends upon a double context of death: the literal graveyard of images the poet names, and a willingness to suspend the individuality of one's name to achieve identity with a class.

"I have left my body behind me," Wright says in another poem (*CP*). The attempt to produce metamorphosis thus involves an abandonment of the self. Here is "The Jewel" (*CP* 114):

> There is this cave
> In the air behind my body
> That nobody is going to touch:
> A cloister, a silence
> Closing around a blossom of fire.
> When I stand upright in the wind,
> My bones turn to dark emeralds.

The "cave," an emptiness, a silence, is what the self fears and what it hopes to supplement by its attachment to and identification with other things. Paradoxically, that emptiness itself, the luminous "blossom of fire," is what becomes "transformed"; the frailty of the flower, its link to mortality, is transformed into the impenetrable hardness of the precious stone whose facets and hues extend indefinitely.

One of the two introductory poems to the *Collected Poems*, "Sitting in a Small Screenhouse on a Summer Morning" (4), acts as a coda for the dynamics of this death process. The speaker has come to rest in Minnesota, ten miles short of South Dakota: "One more night of walking, and I could have become / A horse, a blue horse, dancing / Down a road, alone." Nested in his bower, he has seemingly negated time: "I have got this far. It is almost noon. But never mind time: / That is all over." Inauthentic time is replaced by the "nearness" of a more authentic Time, achieved by the negation of the self, an attachment of the self to the Other. This negation, finally, involves an ambiguous relation to death, for beyond the scene, "Among a few dead cornstalks, the starving shadow / Of a crow leaps to his death," and a "savage Hornet" strains at the screen. Even the "green" that provides a counter to the death images exists "at the edge of darkness," and it is a hue in which the speaker enters a death-like sleep. Finally, the poem ends: "I have come a long way, to surrender my shadow / To the shadow of a horse." Of course, the surrender of the shadow to another shadow, recalling the leap of the crow's shadow, is an image of death.

What Wright is working towards here is a movement from the physical world to the world of what Charles Deleuze calls the world of essences, the world of artistic as opposed to material signs, and it can be tracked in this poem by a movement into the world of shadows and hues. It is in this world that metamorphosis as incarnation and death occurs; it is in this movement that we must locate the source of Wright's "luminosity of language," its profound metaphoric quality, for "metaphor is essentially metamorphosis, and indicates how the two objects exchange their determinates, exchange even the names which designate them in the new medium which confers the common quality upon them" (*PS* 47).

II

A Wilderness of Voices

> I further had a suspicion that the discontinuous
> method . . . lies at the bottom of the origin of the
> concept of time.
> —Freud, "A Note on the Mystic Writing Pad"

The nature of Wright's attachment, if we can gauge by our inquiry thus far, ranges from an intense empathy whose strength can be measured by the kinds of wayward characters, places, and things that are its objects, to a form of Coleridgean identification, a spiritual metamorphosis of the poet himself into those objects. Whatever the mode of attachment, we find that it is most often motivated by a sense of a lost self, and a desire to attach whatever trace of the self remains to an object that provides a provisional substitute. This continuing poetic process itself provides a mode of self-definition, and so by its very nature suggests a re-definition of temporality that "promises" to transcend the losses Kierkegaard and Coleridge lament. We should remember Lacan's gloss on the temporality of such situations:

> I identify myself in language, but only by losing myself in it like an object. What is realized in my history is not the past definite of what was, since it is no more, or even the present perfect of what has been in what I am, but the future anterior of what I shall have been for what I am in the process of becoming [*E* 86].

Next to this let's place "Listening to the Mourners," a paradigmatic text for our purposes:

> Crounched down by a roadside windbreak
> At the edge of the prairie,
> I flinch under the baleful jangling of the wind
> Through the telephone wires, a wilderness of voices
> Blown for a thousand miles, for a hundred years.
> They all have the same name, and the name is lost.
> So: it is not me, it is not my love
> Alone lost.
> The grief that I hear is my life somewhere.
> Now I am speaking with the voice
> Of a scarecrow that stands up
> And suddenly turns into a bird.
> This field is the beginning of my native land,
> This place of skull where I hear myself weeping.
>
> [*CP* 153]

The speaker's self, his voice as it were, lost in "a wilderness of voices," is any and all of those lost "others" that extend miles and years in space and time, for in a sense all of these "have the same name." In a world where names are so arbitrary, the play of language becomes a means through which the voice attaches to various "others" and enters into a metamorphic process where Freud's "antithetical senses" are the rule. This, the scavenger voice of the speaker, becomes the antithetical "voice" of the scavenger, which yet becomes the voice of the scavenger bird it is meant to repulse. This "allegorizing" of the self, this process of antithetical identification could go on: the "field is the beginning," and the image of the bird suggests a movement beyond that field, and indefinitely beyond the verbal field of the poem. The self that is heard weeping as the speaker finishes is, paradoxically, more defined, more inclusive, and more anonymous, more voiceless; it becomes Lacan's "future anterior of what I shall have been for what I am in the process of becoming." Such a complex tense occurs throughout Wright's work, as, say, when he writes: "Nobody yet has walked across and sat down / at the edge under a pear tree" where he visited in the past ("With the Gift of a Fresh New Notebook," *TJ* 83).

As we have seen earlier, such an intertexture of voices itself constitutes the Other for writers such as Hollander and Lacan; moreover, this language of Otherness itself provides a link to the unconscious, for the unconscious, as Lacan repeatedly says, is structured like a language—"the unconscious is the discourse of the Other" (*E* 78–88). This helps explain the sort of random or "stream-of-consciousness" linkage of images here; images barely rise to the surface of consciousness when they are whisked away, erased, in favor of other images.

If we let this arbitrariness play itself a little further, we find that it resembles the Romantic "interpenetrability" that finds its most intense definition in Shelley's "The Sensitive Plant," where stars and flowers echo each other, where hues and odors, roots and boughs, winds and murmurings intermingle:

> And the beasts, and the birds, and the insects were drowned
> In an ocean of dreams without a sound,
> Whose waves never make, though they ever impress
> The light sand which paves it, consciousness.

> [*CW* 383]

The dynamics here are closely related to those described by Freud in "A Note on the 'Mystic Writing Pad' " which describes the workings of the unconscious. In the model, a waxed paper beneath the layer of celluloid receives stimuli from the preconscious system but forms no permanent traces, for when the two layers are lifted for a new perception, what has previously been written disappears. We seem to confront, at first, a simple temporal situation, a passage and loss. However, the situation is somewhat more complex for the trace remains as an invisible but, in Shelley's terms, impressed mark. Freud sees in the relation between the lifting and inscribing process, in a play of the differences between memory and perception (including the alternating back and forth of these two psychic "forces"), the basis for Time. Now it is important to note that Freud often distinguished the unconscious as timeless, the consciousness as timed. But we should do well to follow Derrida's advice: "We ought perhaps to read Freud the way Heidegger read Kant; like the *cogito*, the unconscious is no doubt timeless only from the standpoint of a certain vulgar conception of time" (*WD* 215). And so Lacan, too, in referring to consequences of his own work, writes: "the unconscious is the elusive—but we are to circumscribe it in a structure, a temporal structure, which, it can be said, has never been articulated as such" (*FFC* 32). Wright's poems continue this articulation.

Time is not linear but reversible, repeatable, correctable; one does not move towards an end as such, but keeps making provisional modifications. That is why Jacques Derrida sees these differences, or traces of impressions that do not leave a mark, as "moments of deferment." These traces are the invisible or voiceless "demonstrative" signs left by the unconscious: more specifically for Wright, they are prior attachments that are discarded on the way towards newer attachments, modulated repetitions—as in the poem above, the wind is abandoned for the telephone voices, for the voices of the scarecrow, for the unconscious, as the imagination works towards the "Other," as it constitutes Wright's luminosity of language. As Derrida notes: "Temporality as spacing will not only be the horizontal discontinuity of a chain of signs, but also will be writing as the interruption and restoration of contact between various depths of psychical levels: the remarkably heterogeneous temporal fabric of psychical work itself" (*WD* 225). Wright's is a language, as Hegel once wrote about his own luminous language of leaps in the *Phenomenology*, which "has the divine nature of directly turning the mere 'meaning' right about, making it into something else" (*PHM* 160). What the notion of the leap suggests, and what we have been working towards thus far, is a recognition of discontinuity, radical detachment, in what at first seemed a traditionally continuous structure of attachments.

Yet there is, curiously, a sort of continuity in the language of leaps—what Lacan calls a "logical time," a balancing, as we saw earlier, of past and future on the present inherent in language that must "reorder past contingencies by conferring on them a sense of necessities to come, such as they are constituted by the little freedom through which the subject makes them present" (*E* 48). It is logical Time which provides a structure of attachments.

"Rip" is typical of the large number of short, evocative poems in *Shall We Gather at the River*, and will serve to further explain this structure:

> It can't be the passing of time that casts
> That white shadow across the waters
> Just offshore.
> I shiver a little, with the evening.
> I turn down the steep path to find
> What's left of the river gold.
> I whistle a dog lazily, and lazily
> A bird whistles me.
> Close by a big river, I am alive in my own country,
> I am home again.
> Yes: I lived here, and here, and my name,
> That I carved young, with a girl's is healed over, now,
> And lies sleeping beneath the inward sky
> Of a tree's skin, close to the quick.
> It's best to keep still.
> But:
> There goes that bird that whistled me down here
> To the river a moment ago. Who is he? A little white barn
> Owl from Hudson's Bay,

Flown out of his range here, and lost?
Oh, let him be home here, and, if he wants to,
He can be the body that casts
That white shadow across the waters
Just offshore.

[*CP* 153]

The three points in the logical Time here mark an initial desire for attachment to a nostalgic past, a consequent understanding of the gap or detachment that opens between present and past, and finally a tentative attachment to a transfer object, the owl (*E* 48; *FFC* 32). What is achieved is a deferral of actual attachment and a repression of an actual desire. That is to say, the denial of time's passage, which opens the poem, expresses a hope that full identity with the past may be possible. Yet, despite the several continuities established between the speaker and his world (the "Whistle," for example), the return "home" is disturbed by the introduction of a difference from the past. By the middle of the poem, the past is the inaccessible trace of the girl's name that has been "healed over," though it remains close to an essence, a "quiet" that is absent. The owl, like the present "now," is lost, displaced, and the "promise" of the poem lies in its possible "attachment" to "white shadow," a trace of the detached past. Of course, this possibility is a deferred one, as marked by the conditional mood of the last lines, so that the linking of past and present is a futural event. This deferred attachment is thus marked by a difference, a gap, a lacuna, an absence, and the text itself becomes a supplement for this lack.

What is further curious about this poem is its refusal to name a referential base for Time. What is emphasized instead is a playful Otherness; the moment is defined by what is absent and invisible. Such a sense of Time is characterized, Derrida says, by "infinite depth in the implication of meaning, in the unlimited envelopment of the present, and, simultaneously, the peculiar essence of being, the absolute absence of any foundation" (*WD* 224). For example, in Wright's text the past, the inner or close space of a "home," dissolves into the temporal trace of a name that isn't named; the future, an outer space, dissolves into the indefinite region of the white shadow and of the owl vaguely beyond that. There is a sense of presence and resolution here, underscored by the subjunctive of the last few lines, and further suggested by the identity of the owl and shadow which echoes, supplements, the lost identity of the girl, the trace of her lost past and name. But it is a presence already subverted and redefined by the processes we have been examining, by the amorphous relation between the shadow and what casts it—Time, perhaps, the Time of the Other. Time becomes the logic of this playful movement in and out of the shadows, in and out of the unconscious, the Other.

Where a trace might be legible, as in "Living By the Red River" (*CP* 151), it is itself an enigma, leading to another time, a further time:

> Sometimes I have to sleep
> In dangerous places, on cliffs underground,
> Walls that still hold the whole prints
> Of ancient ferns.

Of course, this distance itself becomes the theme in some of the poems. In "Brush Fire" (*CP* 156), Wright comes across a dead bird, "Its throat bent back as if at the height of some joy too great / To bear to give." The possibility of any transference is lost and the evening itself seems detached from the speaker, separated by a gulf that is the reality of death which cannot be converted into an essence: "evening / Stands, in a gray frock, silent, at the far side / Of a raccoon's grave." In "Beginning" (*CP* 127), the speaker watches in a dream-like landscape where a woman seemingly "steps into the air, now she is gone / Wholly, into the air." But here, too, he remains detached in the midst of a metamorphic landscape: "The wheat leans back toward its own darkness, / And I lean toward mine."

"Redwings," the opening poem in *To a Blossoming Pear Tree* (3), modulates the play between differences and attachments that makes up the structure of the trace, and is one of Wright's most sophisticated poems. The speaker's empathy with the frailty and freedom of the "redwing" bird motivates an identification with the bird:

> It turns out
> You can kill them.
> It turns out
> You can make the earth absolutely clean.

My nephew has given my younger brother
A scientific report while they both flew
In my older brother's small airplane
Over the Kokosing River, that looks

Secret, it looks like the open
Scar turning gray on the small
Of your spine.

Can you hear me?

It was only in the evening I saw a few redwings
Come out and dip their brilliant yellow
Bills in their scarlet shoulders.
Ohio was already going to hell.
But sometimes they would sit down on the creosote
Soaked pasture fence posts.
They used to be few, they used to be willowy and thin.

One afternoon, along the Ohio, where the sewer
Poured out, I found a nest,
The way they build their nests in the reeds,
So beautiful,
Redwings and solitaries.
The skinny girl I fell in love with down home
In late autumn married
A strip miner in late autumn.
Her five children are still alive.
Floating near the river.

Somebody is on the wing, somebody
Is wondering right at this moment
How to get rid of us, while we sleep.

Together among the dead gorges
Of highway construction, we flare
Across highways and drive
Motorists crazy, we fly
Down home to the river.

There, one summer evening, a dirty man
Gave me a nickel and a potato
And fell asleep by a fire.

The structure of attachments here is quite complex. The speaker allegorizes himself as one of the birds that "flare / Across highways," and through that metamorphosis identifies with the others that comprise the "we," the characters from the past. But beneath that image is the image of the airplane that Wright's nephew and younger brother once flew over the river to observe the birds from earlier in the poem. In fact, we cannot be certain, I suppose, that the metamorphosis is not just a description of another (this time more playfully buzzing) plane ride, so powerfully does the trace of the first image operate. But the relation between them is unspoken, almost consciously forgotten; it operates on the level of the unconscious. It links the present with the past, but because the link is invisible, because it has the silence of the "determinative" picture we saw Freud describe earlier, it is accomplished in a timeless present which exists "at the moment" while "we flare," and which suggests an action continuing from the past—though, as an attachment of essences, it is also forever deferred.

Because of difference, then, the exchange of determinations that defines metaphor is never quite complete, and metaphor begins to reveal the inadequacies that are its motivation. We begin to feel differentiating links among river, sphere, coal shaft, and flight path; between the thin birds and the skinny girl; the scar and the nickel; the cleaning and the action of potato acid; nests and homes. The list begins to multiply. The nostalgia that was once the subject of the poem begins to be subverted by the *jouissance* (and I mean to conjure its meanings of sensual enjoyment, possession or attachment, use with a sense of interest gained; these meanings are implicit in the work of Derrida, Lacan, Foucault), yet maintained by this play of his proliferation of differences, this metamorphosis which does not occur. We suspect undiscovered laws of possibility—a movement not by linear connection, nor even by the concentric circles that structure Romantic poems, but by overlapping circles whose centers are all decentered from each other. The coal shaft weighs differently against the scar and the skinny girl, the scar differently against the speaker and the girl. The values of metaphors waver within the poem; the temporal systems that attachments and differences establish modify one another, become metaphors for one another. Can this system of entanglements end? Freud suggests the image of the navel, a dislocated center from which various strands radiate, a knot which can never be untied. Each metamorphosis becomes only a strand of the knot, or web of the whole poem, that vanishes in the tangle: "And still in my dreams I sway like one fainting strand / Of spiderweb, glittering and vanishing and frail / Above the river" (*TBPT* 35).

The image of the navel that Freud describes is a particularly happy one for us, as it suggests the severed attachment, the Other that is absent. Now Lacan and Derrida see movements similar to this play of image we have described as an endless series of signifiers. Says Lacan, "the subject is always a fading thing that runs under the chain of signifiers," and the "definition of this collection of signifiers is that they constitute what I call the Other" (*SC* 193–94). It is an identification of the subject and the Other—or the desire for attachment between them. How, then, does the absent Other, this unconscious, this severed attachment, operate in the poem? We need to locate the navel, the knot that will not come untied. "Can you hear me?" Wright asks in the poem we have been discussing, and he devotes a full paragraph to that utterance. Can *who* hear him? The rhetorical "you" of the first paragraph? the "you" whose spine's scar resembles the river? one of the others mentioned in the poem? one of the *we* who flares across the road? Is it a plural you? the reader? someone never mentioned, perhaps an alter ego? Wright's question slips out almost by accident; and the rest of the poem seemingly ignores this little knot that rests like the dark, impenetrable trace on a plank which shows where a branch attached itself.

Now, for Lacan, this Other is not to be identified with a specific person, but it does have a specific function. According to Lacan, "the first object of desire is to be recognized by the Other" (*E* 48). According to Leslie and Susan Brisman, this desire for recognition is the underlying motive for the lyric poet whose poems are always addressed to an implicit or explicit "you" (*LF* 29–66). We should add, too, that such recognition would provide a kind of authority for the poet, an authorization to write. The Brismans, furthermore, extend Lacan's understanding by identifying three sorts of auditors, and we in turn can extend the Brismans' sense to suit our purposes. In the first case, the poet addresses a mirror counterpart of the self who exists in a timeless space; in the second case, the poet addresses an "original" and "fully idealized Presence," God or some encompassing image like the sea—but in the temporalized setting of a particular exchange; in the third case, the poet addresses a mortal like himself in a conversational tone, in fully Time-oriented and structured encounter. Now the Brismans link these three cases, what we can call "modes of attachment," with, respectively, Lacan's three orders: the Imaginary, a pre-verbal realm of echoing and fluttering images; the Symbolic, the temporal structurings and linkages of language and conscious meaning; and the real, the Historical construct in which we live (*LF* 40–43). We could propose, for example, that Wright makes use of the third case or mode of attachment, but there is certainly an infringement by the other two which gives Wright's conversational voice its incantatory, reverential, and mysterious qualities. We might say that there is a movement, an approach towards this Historical dimension in his poems. "The Real lies ahead in the future," as Brisman says, explaining the psychological progress which results from a severing of misguided and overwhelming "attachments to the past" (*LF* 43) as a static entity. That is, the Real, as an Historical Construct, always remains unfulfilled, always is in the process of being re-attached by the speaker. The more Realistic the voice, the more inquisitive it becomes—and the less it simply submits to the authority of the Other.

In Wright's case, we can say that there is a small measure of control, a voice, as it were, over the shoulder, which exerts a silent pressure on the text. The Time of the Other modifies the pure voice of presence which has traditionally defined the lyric. We are reminded again of the demonstrative picture in Egyptian writing of the invisible trace on the writing pad. The poem's speech, in this context, is considered as one side of a conversation, however interior or exterior, that reveals a relation to truth not simply by what it says, but by its strategies of avoidance and deflection out of respect to the Other. In those spaces between paragraphs and after line breaks that Mallarmé became so intrigued with, the Other's demonstrative silences shift the tack of the poem towards new formulations. If we return to "Redwings," we can recognize the recurrent "themes" of Wright: isolation, the need for attachment, the attraction to socially wayward characters. However, it isn't these reductive themes, but the speaker's dialectically evolving disposition towards these concerns that forms the essence of the poem. He begins in a revelatory manner—"It turns out," the "scientific report," the open "Secret," and the insistent, "Can you hear me?" Hear what? we need to ask. What is said so silently?

What is revealed are secrets: the power to kill and, indirectly, a formerly hidden, now open scar. And the scar is not only to be associated with the speaker, but the whole land, the whole past—"Ohio was already going to hell"—the world of sewers and stripmines. Yet it is this very ugliness he feels attached to, as all "Redwings and solitaries are," even as it seems to reject him as the "skinny girl" once did: "somebody / Is wondering right at this moment / How to get rid of us." So the nest that he finds next to the sewer is his "home" too, as you are the "dead gorges." And the strategies he uses to deflect his attachment to what, in some senses, he hates or is repulsed by are like the flarings of the birds—erratic, testing. These flarings are a series of identifications with attitudes that become less troubled, as if he could gather strength from his own ability to talk: so that, at the end, his antipathies have been expelled and he confronts the past simply, purely, in an image that seems dissociated from the nest. Of course, it is not entirely dissociated; the nickel and the potato, for instance, complement the poverty implicit throughout. And the child's game of cleaning coins by inserting them in potatoes is probably not lost here—the image of value, momentarily slight but humanly rich, buried like the invisible trace at the center, and leaving only the hollow gap, the breach, on the surface.

"To the Silver Sword Shining on the Edge of the Crater" (*TJ*) addresses the Other more directly. The sword, he says, looks "like a lonesomeness / From somewhere else," the object characteristically attaching itself to the speaker's own emotions. What the narrator attempts to verify, as he does so often, is that he is "not a stranger here." Finally, he says, beginning to formulate a sequence of connections near the end of the poem,

> Whoever you are,
> Who may have made some kind gesture
> To me on my earth, you are welcome
> To me and mine.

The object becomes a sort of trace for the human history it symbolizes. "With the Shell of a Hermit Crab" (*TBPT* 19) also takes as its concern some of the notions we have been considering:

> This lively little life whose toes
> Touched the white sand from side to side,
> How delicately no one knows,
> Crept from his loneliness, and died.
>
> From deep waters long miles away
> He wondered, looked for his name,
> And all he found was you and me,
> A quick life and a candle flame.
>
> Today, you happen to be gone.
> I sit here in the raging hell,
> The city of the dead, alone,
> Holding a little empty shell.
>
> I peer into his tiny face.
> It looms too huge for me to bear.
> Two blocks away the sea gives place
> To river. Both are everywhere.
>
> I reach out and flick out the light.
> Darkly I touch his fragile scars,
> So far away, so delicate,
> Stars in a wilderness of stars.

What we are left with here are literally only traces: the tracks on some sea sand, too distant to see now, and too delicate to know, if one could be there, and of course the shell, a borrowed home in the first place. In the same way as in the previous poem, identifications merge: in place of his name, the crab finds the speaker and his lore. And the girl in particular, as a sort of other, is identified with the crab—both are gone. That is, in the line "You happen to be gone," the word "you" refers both to the girl as the "you" two lines above, and to the crab. But what face does he peer into? Not that of the physical body of the crab, for the face he sees is "too huge for me to bear." It is the face of its symbolic Other that is as encompassing as the sea: "Both are everywhere." And yet, it is a face, finally, which the speaker attaches himself to by a "touch" of sorts while the Other still remains forever elusive, forever absent: "Darkly I touch his fragile scars, / So far away."

The poem is not, finally, a pessimistic one of mere loss: the detachments and differences are seen as part of a complex structure of attachments. And this is the last, playful metamorphosis as "scars" echo into "stars," which suggests perhaps further metamorphoses as constellations of stars might form various patterns to the eye, as the play of language wanders, "looking for his name."

III

The Time of the Name

Mais Je t'écris Demain, Je le Dis toujours Au present.
—Derrida, *La Carte Postale*

This elusive process, occurring with the politically charged rhetoric of *Two Citizens*, produces an ambivalent poetics. *Two Citizens* is a book that struggles for detachment from an "ugly American" complex of images while unwillingly finding that its own language leads towards an uncovering of new bases for attachment. The "home" metaphor we have referred to several times becomes defined, as we might suspect, by this indefinable process, by being always already between attachment and detachment. The strategy of the book is to found a language that can hold in indefinite suspension the radical antinomies that a play of images leads Wright through. Here is the ending of "I Wish I May Never Hear of the United States Again" (20):

In Yugoslavia I am learning the words
For greeting and goodbye.
Everything else is the language
Of the silent woman who walks beside me.
I want the mountains to be builded golden,
And my love wants the cathedrals to be builded
By time's love back to their gray, as the gray
Woman grows old, the gray woman who gave us
Some cheese and whispered her affectionate sound
To my love and me wondering silent in the breeze
Of a strange language, at home with each other.
Saying nothing, listening

To a new word for mountain, to a new
Word for cathedral, to a new word for
Cheese, to a word beyond words for
Cathedrals and homes.

Beyond the two named words, "greeting" and "goodbye" that signify attachment and detachment, the language intimated here is one of silence and whispers (traces), the language of the Other who always walks beside the poet. It is a language that is always beginning, hence a "strange language" and one searching for the "new world" for something that will also transform the thing. The last few lines, especially in light of the lineation, are particularly ambiguous. Does the poet search for (1) "a word beyond the words for Cathedrals and homes," that is, the two dominating images of the particular book, *Two Citizens*, in an effort to surpass the concerns inherent in those images; (2) "a word beyond words," some meta-language of silences beyond conventional verbal patterns; (3) "a word beyond words for," that is, a word that does not need to "signify," as such, a particular "signified," but exists for itself? Probably, in a sense, all three, but the third is the most interesting, and the most problematic.

According to Derrida, while the "other originally collaborates with meaning," there is also "an essential lapse" which is inherent in the nature of language; and this lapse is a detachment that occurs within an ostensible structure of attachments (*WD* 71). The inability to name marks the ultimate failure to achieve full presence, complete attachment. Rather, the name names the undecipherable signature, the elusive Other, absence itself.

We must be careful not to construe this relation of supplementarity as a linear one. Of course, we must remember the continual reference to Horace throughout *Two Citizens* and the more frequent references to Horace, Virgil, Catullus, and the English Romantics in *To a Blossoming Pear Tree*, as well as earlier references not only to literary figures like Trakl but to other sorts of "fathers" throughout Wright's work. Poems increasingly become, as Derrida or Bloom would say, commentaries referring to prior texts, but in such a way as to effect a kind of exchange of positions. This is from "Prayer to the Good Poet" (10), addressed both to "Quintus Horatius Flaccus, my good servant," and Wright's own father:

> Every time I go back home to Ohio,
> He sits down and tells me he loves Italians.
> How can I tell you why he loves you,
> Quintus Horatius?
>
> I worked once in the factory that he worked in.
> Now I work in that factory that you live in.
> Some people think poetry is easy,
> But you two didn't.
>
> Easy, easy, I ask you, easy, easy.
> Early, evening, by Tiber, by Ohio,
> Give the gift to each lovely other.
> I would be happy.
>
> Now my son is another poet, fathers,
> I can go on living. I was afraid once

Four loving fathers meeting together
Would be a cold day in hell.

Quintus Horatius Flaccus, my good father,
You were just the beginning, you quick and lonely
Metrical crystals of February.
It is just snow.

Part of the poem's solution lies in the very luminosity of its language, in the ability of the language to produce the illusion that difficult problems can be metrically crystallized, and then transformed to something all embracing—the metaphoric snow of the last line. Thus, the repetitions that establish the links between Horace and the narrator's father, between the narrator and his own son, that transfer the word "secret" into the idea "father," can be understood as an exchange of gifts, a deconstruction of the linearity of time. The meeting of several generations in the moment of the poem suggests a process in which Wright's *particular* voice is self-effaced as it becomes a part of that very process of exchange and transformation.

This elusiveness at least partially explains the increasing tendency in Wright's work to undercut any "statements" the poems might make or infer. The first half of *To a Blossoming Pear Tree*, for example, is filled with self-effacing statements: "For all I know" runs like a refrain through "The Wheeling Gospel Tabernacle," which ends: "Little I know. I can pitch a pretty fair tune myself, for all I know." The disclaimers "I still do not know" and "I do not know" introduce crucial observations in "By the Ruins of a Gun Emplacement," and the second of these phrases echoes in a half-dozen other poems (and is the last line in one); events are attributed to "somebody" or "something," and there are numerous uses of the subjunctive, expressions such as "I hope so" and "maybe . . . ," along with numerous unanswerable questions. The point of all this is to defer meaning, any summing up, any bringing to pure presence, any ultimate attachment. When, later in the book, Wright explains, "Oh, I know," it is an ironic revelation of an enigmatic, "hopeless" world, a "sinking menace," and an expression of the doomed and endless desires of Romeos and Juliets: "Fumbling to touch hands in the dark, / Their hands fluttered into flares" (43). The attempt to reach sustaining certainties leads to utter pessimism. This tendency to subvert the self reaches an extreme in "October Ghosts" (*TC* 54), in which time seems such an oppressive external force that the poet must utterly diminish himself:

> Jenny, fat blossoming grandmother of the dead,
> We were both young, and I nearly found you, young.
>
> I could not find you. I prowled into my head,
> The cold ghost of October that is my skull.
> There is a god's plenty of lovers there,
> The dead, the dying, and the beautiful.
>
> But where are we,
> Jenny darkness, Jenny cold?
> Are we so old?
> We came so early, we thought to stay so long.
> But it is already midnight, and we are gone.
> I have nothing at all against that song,
> That minor bird I hear from the great frost,
> My robin's song, the ancient nothingness.
>
> Friends, I have stolen this line from Robinson,
> From Jenny and from springtime, and from bone,
> And from the quick nuthatch, the blooming of wing upon the sky.
>
> Now I know nothing, I can die alone.

And yet what saves the poet here is that the Nothingness is a Ghost, a "trace" in the language we have been developing, and a trace that is repeated, "stolen," as the lover's name "Jenny" is throughout the poem. The poem itself becomes, as we have seen earlier in other cases, an echo waiting to be echoed, avoiding the stasis of nothing while waiting for the author to re-emerge.

However, the writer, left with this self-effacing perspective that is a product of the absence and playfulness we have been describing, discovers an oblique attachment to countless "other lives," even in the midst of these forces for detachment, and based upon the metamorphic movement of his language. In the prose poem, "The Secret of Light" (*TBPT* 38), he describes a woman who seems like the secret black light at the center of a diamond (an image then of the vanished trace): "While I was trying to compose the preceding sentence, the woman rose from her park bench and walked away. I am afraid her secret might never come to light in my lifetime. But my lifetime is not the only one." The woman, the supposed subject, interrupts the time of writing and creates the chasm, the detachment, the poem strives to bridge. What the poem describes is a literalization of that moment when the subject wanders off towards others, only to be transformed as we have seen in several cases already. But if this writing cannot presence anything, it can at least project from its own emptiness a new beginning: "The very emptiness of the park bench just in front of mine is what makes me happy. Somewhere else in Verona at just this moment, a woman is sitting or walking or standing still upright. Surely two careful and accurate hands, total strangers to me, measure the invisible idea of the secret seen in her hair." No matter that all here is hypothesis, that the details may be one "or" another. The language has established a possibility born of a nearly random moment which keeps renewing its "secret." The present becomes the never realized possibility of the future. In fact, it is the writer who loses himself between these two tenses; "I feel like the light of the river Adige," he says, for he is always already skimming away, always already reflected towards something other.

If we have succeeded in describing a metamorphic play of traces, we have also evaded a direct confrontation with the nagging problem of whether this play is a product or creator of the "concerns" that a verbal text seems to establish. Or perhaps, more honestly, an answer has been assumed. And if we are to continue to talk about any such "concerns," we must also confront another problem: is there any bottom to this process whereby a text seems to continually fall away from itself? Let us look at another poem, "Lifting Illegal Nets by Flashlight" (*CP* 162):

> The carp are secrets
> Of the creation: I do not
> Know if they are lonely.

The poachers drift with an almost frightening
Care under the bridge.
Water is a luminous
Mirror of swallows' nests. The stars
Have gone down.
What does my anguish
Matter? Something
The color
Of a puma has plunged through this net, and is gone.
This is the firmest
Net I ever saw, and yet something
Is gone lonely
Into the headwaters of the Minnesota.

The poachers are perhaps so "frightening" because they combine the aimlessness ("drift") of the symbol, its play, with an intensity of single purpose that destroys the notion of the sport. But even these poachers, so intent upon gathering the fish, so methodical with their illegal nets, are unable to capture, to net, to circumscribe, everything. Probably the most "essential" image in the poem, that of the carp, remains "secret" throughout, and, in fact, becomes more and more a trace and less a substance as it (*is* it, though, the carp?) disappears in the form of a "something" losing its name, as it were, and identified only by its color (the *name* of the animal, by the way). The image of the "swallow's nests" that replaces the stars asserts all this, for the water-world itself now reflects a world defined by the dartings, the shadow traces of comings and goings that the swallows make.

Now what is curious in this poem is the position of the speaker's question, "What does my anguish / Matter?" Its context is not earned by direct statement elsewhere in the text, and it seems, like the question in "Redwings," to be dropped incidentally, perhaps an unconscious slip. Of course, the third line may tacitly imply a loneliness on the part of the speaker, or at least a melancholy, but it is a long way from loneliness to anguish. Yet the anguish is not structurally arrived at, but rather simply *assumed* in the question which questions only the significance of an individual's anguish in the light of the frightening event described, and not how it may have appeared, say, in relation to the event. That is, the anguish as such, though it may include anguish over the event, does not have a named and necessary attachment to it. The question of anguish achieves significance as it appears, seemingly incidentally, in the limiting context of the poem. In fact, so incidentally does the question appear that it seems as if the images momentarily have found this theme, this significance, to attach themselves to, rather than the writer's simply finding words to describe his emotion. The movement here is from what Lacan calls the Imaginary Order, a pre-verbal and visually oriented spatial grid of images lacking a phenomenological center of organization, into what he calls the Symbolic Order, into language itself, with its temporal structurings and grammatical sequences. Thus, the "concerns" of the poem emerge as the writer submits to this (unconscious) play of language: "there is involved a willingness on the part of the poet to trust the language a little more," Wright says in a recent interview (Heyen, 148).

Wright's question, then, marks what we might call, after Lacan, the *point de capiton* "by which the signifier brings the indefinite *glissiment* [transposition, sliding] of signification to a stop." It is a point from which we can read back into the rest of the poem various concerns of the poet. The production of the language of a text is much like the "sliding of signifiers" Lacan describes, and which we have seen in the transformations which defer signification in the poems of Warren, Hollander, and Wright. Now, for Lacan, this "point" (literally "upholstery stud") momentarily pauses this whirling motion: "The diachronic function of this anchoring point is to be found in the sentence, even if the sentence completes its signification only with its last term, each term being anticipated in the construction of the others, and, inversely, sealing their meaning by its retroactive effect" (*E* 303). Yet each sentence is followed by another; the point is a mark of punctuation that is effaced by the larger thrust of the paragraph, or stanza. Time refuses a complete structure. The "point" can also be understood as a "suture"—a time of arrest or moment of insight, a "conjunction of the imaginary and the symbolic, and it is taken up again in a dialectic, that sort of temporal progress that is called haste, thrust, forward movement" (*FFC* 118). The "suture" or "point," then, allows the Other to rise and speak, recognizing the subject, asserting its own silent voice as an ordering force upon the temporal movement of attachments and detachments.

Now for Lacan, as well as Derrida, the *point* is itself a trace. We might further suggest that the finished poem itself is a sort of *point de capiton*. Lacan says:

> The "pinning down" I speak of, or the *point de capiton*, is mythical, for no one has ever been able to pin a signification on a signifier; but on the other hand what *can* be done is to pin one signifier to another signifier and see what happens. But in this case something new is invariably produced . . . in other words, the surging forth of a new signification [*LS* 274].

The poem, then, as a melting place of various strands of signifiers, the poem as "knot." Its bottom, or "stopping" of the play of language, is mythical, but the mythical dimensions of the *point* are given by the conventions of literature, of poetry. In submitting to the play of language, the poet also submits to the myth of the *point*, and in inscribing his poem reveals his assent to and choice of a particularly "surging," evocative "point." *To a Blossoming Pear Tree*, for instance, "ends" with a reflection on this whole process:

> I know what we call it
> Most of the time.
> But I have my own song for it,
> And sometimes, even today
> I call it beauty.   [62]

The "it" refers to a remembered quality of light, and changing *its* name changes the thing. The book, then, ends tentatively, and with a casual naming, a sudden "point," and promises further alternative readings of "it." The book ends, literally, with a "certain luminosity," a provisional attachment to a past that is only a trace.

IV

The Reserve of Time

> When is it that it captures our attention and delights
> us? At the moment when, by a mere shift of our
> gaze, we are able to realize that the representation
> does not move with the gaze and that it is merely a
> *trompe-l'oeil.* For it appears at that moment as
> something other than it seemed, or rather it now
> seems to be that something else.
> —Lacan, "What Is a Picture?"

So far, this chapter has gradually uncovered, as we have seen specifically at several junctions, a psychological notion of time behind Wright's strategies. But how exactly does the *point de capiton* affect our thinking about time in Wright's work? The *point* is not a point as on a line or a linear duration, nor even the interval of a pure transcendent presence, for, as we have seen, it involves a complex alterity. The *points* occur where there is a radical break, a detachment, a turning away, as "when the moon / Is looking away" in "Late November in a Field" (*CP* 152), and the unseen tarantula "turns away" from Wright in "Discoveries in Arizona" (*TBPT* 26)—in short, whenever the writer, almost by accident, as we have seen, turns from the flow of the poem and interrupts himself. In this turning away a wholly different dimension of temporality emerges, suggested, for example, by the squirrels' paws that rifle for food in the momentary dark as the moon looks away, and by the strange darkness of the tarantula's private world—a temporality always defined as a trace, fading before it is even allowed to emerge.

This turning away is reminiscent of Lacan's notion of the "gaze" which can be explained by an analogy to the blind spot in the middle of the eye. What we look at we do not see, for there is always something repressed, veiled. "That they might not see what?" Lacan asks. "Precisely, that things are looking at them" (*FC* 109). Like the girl at the center of "Rip," the Other can possess a gaze that is too commanding. In most of Wright's poems, so carefully observed and focused, some "gap" or "chasm," as Lacan calls it—some "brissure," as Derrida calls it—uncannily opens up the text and introduces the Time of the Other. The prose poem, "The Turtle Overnight" (*TBPT* 7), for example, is an intensely focused, Steinbeck-like vignette set in an Italian ruins, but towards the end, just before the turtle disappears without leaving "a footprint in the empty grass," Wright makes an odd comparison: "The lines on his face suggest only a relaxation, a delicacy in the understanding of the grass, like the careful tenderness I saw once on the face of a hobo in Ohio as he waved greeting to an empty field from the flat car of a freight train." To what extent does the Time of the hobo incident—the structure of time since Wright saw him, the passing of the hobo himself on the train, the empty time of the empty field (but where is Wright in that scene), the structure of that fleeting moment itself—inform the present Time of the turtle incident? To what extent is this a poem about the hobo? About a larger sense of loss that informs Wright's Time? The poem is careful not to announce an answer but, rather, to suggest a kind of sliding of its signifiers along a field of possibilities.

Most of Wright's later poems, in fact, refer to or are set in historical places which provide multiple contexts that lead the self out of a focused and narcissistic world (Plumly, 151). The speaker's Time becomes not only the Time he operates in, but the trace of an historical past that is often just a fragment which enters the present to define it in terms of a future. Thus, in "A Lament for the Shadows in the Ditches" (*TBPT* 11), Wright's own past around "the beautiful river, the black ditch of horror," becomes associated with the melancholy noon in Rome, where the poem is set, and also the past, revealed in the "intricate and intelligent ditches" of the Colosseum.

"Greetings in New York City" (*TJ* 38) is a more dramatized account and reveals the depth of Wright's ambivalence about attachments. It begins: "A man walking alone, a stranger / In a strange forest," then introduces "One more stranger." Each lives separate for a while: "Two alone, two hours, they poise there, / Afraid, gazing across." What the gaze gradually accomplishes is a sense of separate but parallel activity as each becomes involved in similar labors. At the end of the poem their different histories remain attached/detached, but it is the narrator, it becomes apparent, who feels detached, the narrator who has, we remember, called both of the men "stranger" and who now pleas for an attachment, to be taken in to their histories:

> And then, when noon comes,
> Each stranger
> Has no room left in the light
> Except for only his hands.
> Here are mine. They are kind of skinny.
> May I have your lovely trees?

The gaze is often a suspended moment, too, as it is in "Jerome in Solitude" (*TJ* 72), which opens—"To see the lizard there, / I was amazed." What the narrator experiences is the type of religious experience Jerome would have had, for, as he watches, gazes, "I leaned close. / The deep place in the lizard's eye / Looked back into me." And if he "did not see Christ retching in pain, longing / to clutch his cold abdomen" as the meditation expands outward, he does conjure the image—attaches it in a detached way—to create an aura of reverence. The poem then ends in a sort of timeless, transcendent gaze: "He did not move. / Neither did I. / I did not dare to."

This sort of shift towards a transcendence, which occurs more and more as Wright's career progresses, is also apparent in "A Winter Daybreak Above Vence" (*TJ* 87), which dramatizes the poet's coming "face to face with the spring." As it turns out, the poem's time frames begin to include the mythic (Diana), the natural, the literary (the poets, Whitman and Ausonius), the autobiographical ("an American girl I know")—all combined in a Whitmanesque idyll. But the gaze is always broken—"Jerome" and this poem are both emphatically in the past tense, detached from the time they observe. Another poem, "Butterfly Fish," describes the trace of the fish in the moment after it leaves; as the poet gazes, he realizes the fish has gone to "His other world where I cannot see / His secret face." There is always interruption, absence, loss, detachment.

The "gaze" is itself the implicit topic in one of Wright's most accomplished poems, "By the Ruins of a Gun Emplacement: Saint-Benoît" (*TBPT* 12). The poem begins as two lovers walk the ruins:

> Behind us, the haystack rustles
> Into the summer dusk, and the limber girl's knees
> Alone are barely visible among the rust
> of grape leaves. We are one face
> Gazing into another, dim.

The "gaze," however, reveals not the narcissism of isolated love but other lovers who "scuffle" in the "dewfall behind us." Beyond that, the speaker can close his eyes and see where the moon, an image of traditional time's uncovering of our dark and protected places, reveals other lovers:

> There, no one at nightfall
> Pauses alone with his wine. There, no one
> At dewrise but only the moon
> Lifting deliberately, between the long slim
> Fingers, the startling faces
> Of night creatures. Who are they?

From these dream-like creatures, the poem moves to mention a snail observed in the past, what Max Jacobs is doing now, and swans Napoleon may have named over a century ago. Oddly, their names, "Dewfall," "Nightrise," and "Basilica," reveal not only the sense of seemingly arbitrary details that inform Wright's poems, but also a subtle texture of attachments as they actually refer back to the original setting of the poem. In terms of the gaze, "reality is marginal," as Lacan says; it is whatever the poem is about to include, the always-just-transformed Time that occupies the periphery of the gaze. The Time of lovers in this poem, for example, is defined by that of other lovers, other places at the same "now," the progress of the moon, the pastoral interlude of a fading Napoleon. The Time of the poem itself exists as a trace, a possibility somewhere amidst those various times and yet distinct from any one of them.

In "Two Moments in Rome" (*TBPT* 44), Wright says: "At noon on a horizon the Colosseum poises in mid-flight, a crumbling moon of gibbous gold. It catches an ancient light, and gives form to that light. Gazing at the Colosseum from a spot two miles away, I feel as though I had just caught a quick glimpse of a girl's face." At which point, with the form of light barely suggested, we are transported for several sentences towards the girl's world. Finally, the prose closes with a reflection on its own process: "Now, beyond the Colosseum, another moon, a day moon, appears in the sky. Even its little scars are ghosts." A poem by Wright can reveal such worlds for which we see only the trace of their pale day moons, or less. A poem becomes a "topography of traces, a map of frayings," a structure of attachments and detachments (*WD* 125).

A similar pattern suggests itself in "Dawn Near an Old Battlefield, in a Time of Peace" (*TJ* 59), where the narrator feels an immense distance from the historical events; he sees a young man—"How can he call to mind now, / And how can I, / His fathers, crawling / Blind into the grain?" And yet, though the past seems lost, perhaps the place, the river, "Upon washing his face in the water," will provide "Mercy," comfort, the attachment of home. Perhaps the strangers who so populate Wright's poems, dislocated and detached from human community, perhaps even Wright himself, deliberately detaching himself in Italy, in Europe, can re-enter time, perhaps can attach themselves through this sort of innocent baptism. At least that seems to be the hope in so many poems that wish to cultivate an historical sense by, paradoxically, beginning all over again, as in the intense bracketing off that the gaze affords.

The question of time, then, becomes—as it was with Hollander— one of timing; but also of the recurrence and repetition of points of incidental, perhaps arbitrary attachments within other structures of detachment. The poems comprise, Wright suggests, the "crude / rhythm of my time" (*TS* 17). As with Freud's mystic writing pad, time is an impossible synthesis of the linear and the simultaneous, the present and the absent: linear, in that one cannot write legibly until the paper is lifted and the previous marks erased; simultaneous, in that the ghosts of traces still remain. Time becomes, as Derrida would have it, a "spacing out of meaning" in which "concentrations are possible which no longer obey the linearity of logical time, the time of consciousness or preconsciousness, the time of 'verbal representation' " (*SPH* 60–87). Rather, poems become scenes from which a discovery about something other might be possible. So the poet in "To a Blossoming Pear Tree" addresses the tree that is "just beyond my reach" because, as it turns out, its "pure delicate body" is so distant from that of the aging homosexual who once confronted him. The man's wholly other life represents a structure of temporality alive to the narrator, a life that the narrator can conjecture only by hypothesis:

> He was willing to take
> Any love he could get,
> Even at the risk
> Of some mocking policeman
> Or some cute young wiseacre
> Smashing his dentures,
> Perhaps leading him on
> To a dark place and there
> Kicking him in his dead groin
> Just for the fun of it.

Paradoxically, it is precisely such a difference, such a divergence in the histories their lives have taken, that provides any hope for attachment. They are attached because of their detachment; or, more specifically, from the point where the difference is marked, "Both terrified / We slunk away, / Each in his own way dodging / The cruel darts of the cold." The whole poem is predicated upon chance. And we begin to suspect that poems by Wright could have been about almost anything, and perhaps to some extent still are. Especially in the last three books, they trace a radical difference, or detachment, a beginning burdened with infinite possibilities and relieved, as it were, by an incidental cast of the dice, the playful direction, the provisional attachment that is stumbled upon almost after the fact, and which provides a temporal dimension to what seems an infinite process.

In "Entering the Temple in Nîmes" (*TJ* 3), the sense of a reserve of time allows the poem, which opens Wright's last book, to project an incredible optimism. It begins by acknowledging Time's limitations:

"As long as this evening lasts, / I am going to walk all through and around / The Temple of Diana." But as he enters imaginatively into the story of the goddess, into her time, a time of fleeting glances, reverence, and the power of names to hold things, he can conclude:

> Allow me to walk between the tall pillars
> And find the beginning of one vine leaf there,
> Though I arrive too late for the last spring
> And the rain still mounts its guard.

Despite the progress of earthly time, there is another, part mythic, part transcendental time, a time of "the beginning" that may perhaps be made available.

It is in this context, this luminous *point*, that the temporality of Wright's poems emerges as a sort of reserve—not as something which simply passes, though certainly Wright's melancholy tone confronts this aspect, but more importantly as something which can be returned to. If things "other" are absent, they are also bound to emerge eventually at some point, and so, in a sense, are reserved. Thus in "Two Moments in Venice" (*TBPT* 47), Wright discovers, "All one needs to do is follow the sound of water." And as Wright follows that sound an old man emerges, in the first moment, from one of the canals, covered with slime. This prompts Wright to explain what hidden worlds might remain beneath Venice:

> How can I know what he was doing underwater? The very streets of the city are water; and what magnificent and unseemly things must sway underneath its roads; the perfect skeleton of a haughty cat, his bone tail curled around his ribs and crusted with salt three centuries ago; even a chimney, swept free, till this hour passes, of all the webs they weave so stoutly down there, the dark green spiders under the water who have more than all the time they need.

This sense of reserve allows him, in the second moment, to approach an evening from the perspective of Italian evenings enjoyed by "Byron on horseback," Ruskin "taking refuge," and other historical characters, who become part of the "present." And the evening itself, in this context, has always already been present, already discovered: "the old Venetians discovered the true shape of evening, and now it is almost evening." Wright's is a world of continual advances, or, to return to Coleridge's terminology, endless "approaches," that reveal infinite possibilities for attachment, infinite "Others" for the self's concern: "the Soul never *is*, because it either cannot or dare not be, any (one) Thing; but lives in *approaches*—touched by the outgoing pre-existent Ghosts of many feelings" (*NC* #3215). It is a world where "a dark moore bird has come down from the mountains / to test the season" ("A Dark Moore Bird" (*TJ* 13). The bird sings wildly, interrupting the narrator, who is, by his own attachment to what the bird represents, "hoping / He will never die."

This reserve of time is what sustains Wright to the very end, and beyond, in a sense, giving him more than all the time he needs. "The Journey" (*TJ* 30), one of his last poems, is a perfect example:

> Anghiari is medieval, a sleeve sloping down
> A steep hill, suddenly sweeping out
> To the edge of a cliff, and dwindling.
> But far up the mountain, behind the town,
> We too were swept out, out by the wind,
> Alone with the Tuscan grass.
>
> Wind had been blowing across the hills
> For days, and everything now was graying gold
> With dust, everything we saw, even
> Some small children scampering along a road,
> Twittering Italian to a small caged bird.
> We sat beside them to rest in some brushwood,
> And I leaned down to rinse the dust from my face.
>
> I found the spider web there, whose hinges
> reeled heavily and crazily with the dust,
> Whole mounds and cemeteries of it, sagging
> And scattering shadows among shells and wings.
> And then she stepped into the center of air
> Slender and fastidious, the golden hair
> Of daylight along her shoulders, she poised there,
> While ruins crumbled on every side of her.
> Free of the dust, as though a moment before
> She had stepped inside the earth, to bathe herself.
> I gazed, close to her, till at last she stepped
> Away in her own good time.

The Time of the Other

Many men
Have searched all over Tuscany and never found
What I found there, the heart of the light
Itself shelled and leaved, balancing
On filaments themselves falling. The secret
Of this journey is to let the wind
Blow its dust all over your body,
To let it go on blowing, to step lightly, lightly
All the way through your ruins, and not to lose
Any sleep over the dead, who surely
Will bury their own, don't worry.

The poem, obviously, attaches itself to an historical context, and suggests also a transcendental attachment. The wind, that is, not only blows the dust of history but the sense of mystery, a sense that the wind has been blowing endlessly. Here is the consummate poem, where everything else in the world is also at stake, a sense one gets of what Gaston Bachelord calls the intimate immensity of particular things, here the spider. The journey is the life and also the pacing, the timing of the poem itself and of the wind, as they strive to connect everything. There is a sense of abundance, of overflow, of more than enough time, and the source of this is the face-to-face encounter with the spider. What does the narrator find there? Listen again: "the heart of the light / Itself shelled and leaved, balancing / on filaments themselves falling." He finds the essence of light, the source of time, the pulsing between shadow and light which is at the very heart of time, yet threatened by time, so tenuous is this rest, and given in time, in wind, in an historical setting.

And, most dramatically, most moving, the poem reaches out finally to the periphery, to the reader, attaching itself to us yet keeping a certain detachment, a certain sense that the dead "bury their own, don't worry." It is, in fact, this gesture of detachment that makes the attachment so strong; it is this casting off of time that makes time such a powerful force; it is the timeless vision that gives meaning to this journey, this history. In the midst of dust, in the midst of ruins, everything begins again to attach itself, to temporalize.

Again, in the last poem of this last book, the narrator moves from a simple temporal setting towards a transcendental attachment, a sense of time's ease and surplus. It begins: "The night's drifts / Pile up below me and behind my back, / Slide down the hill, rise again." This undulating rhythm, along with a gradual expansion of consciousness to distant sounds, begins to blur dream and reality, consciousness and the unconscious. He sees reflections, sees his dream, a sort of pastoral, timeless, idyll, then—

> I turn, and somehow
> Impossibly hovering in the air over everything,
> The Mediterranean, nearer to the moon
> Than this mountain is,
> Shines.
>
> ["A Winter Daybreak above Vence" 87]

For a moment there is an illusion that the world is reversed—that the usual orders of time and space no longer hold. Then: "A voice clearly / Tells me to snap out of it." It is the voice of the Other, specifically here the voice of Galway Kinnell. And though he does "snap out of it," detach himself, something of the attachment to the transcendental realm remains, something of the reversal stays reversed, and just as the sea could seem to be above him, he can seem, with us, to be above the sunlight. Everything, finally, connects—all times, all Others—in the final lines of this final poem. There is, paradoxically, an increased awareness of his own mortality at the same time there is an increased awareness of things being out of season, out of time, transcended—

> Look, the sea has not fallen and broken
> Our heads. How can I feel so warm
> Here in the dead center of January? I can
> Scarcely believe it, and yet I have to, this is
> The only life I have. I get up from the stove.
> My body mumbles something unseemly
> And follows me. Now we are all sitting here strangely
> On top of the sunlight.

4

Nomadic Time

The Poetry of John Ashbery

I

The (W)hole Story

It is not the facts about time which we want to know.
All of the facts that concern us lie open before us.
But it is the use of the substantive "time" which
mystifies us.
                    —Wittgenstein, *The Blue Book*

"B ut, what is time anyway?" (*AWK* 17). That question
       marks the labyrinth that constitutes Ashbery's com-
       plex meditation on Time, a meditation that attempts,
as Derrida prescribes, to "emancipate" itself from the limits of a
traditional language whose symbols "determine things only by spa-
tializing them" (*WD* 16). If Ashbery must constantly, as he and Derrida often say, "violate" that language, it is because he realizes that
any emancipation must be in terms, as that word itself suggests,
which meet the conditions of any struggle for emancipation, that is,
which are not only conceptual but temporal—terms that put into
play endless deferrals of meaning, provisional pronouncements and
contradictions, metaphoric and metonymic sliding, transformations,
descriptions, detours (Shapiro, Chaps. 1 and 2). In fact, our original
question occurs in "Litany," a poem that is a dialogue between two
printed columns that test and subvert their own and each other's
predications about the moment, Time, history, and the self. For Ashbery, then, the poem about Time is necessarily volatile. As he writes
in "Clepsydra" (*DDS* 34), a poem whose title refers to a water clock,

142

> Each moment
> Of utterance is the true one; likewise none are true,
> Only is the bounding from air to air, a serpentine
> Gesture which hides the truth behind a congruent
> Message, the way air hides the sky, is, in fact,
> Tearing it limb from limb this very moment.

The "truth" of any utterance about Time becomes as undecidable as Time itself, as slippery as the syntax which defers a final or singular reading after the semi-colon in this passage. "There is so much in that moment! / So many attitudes toward that flame," he says in "Illustration" (*ST* 48). And so the poem about Time becomes a "fable," in the double sense of that word, as narration in time and as in life, one of the "Fables that time invents / To explain its passing" ("Years of Indiscretion") (*DDS* 46). We need to begin, then, by exploring the development of Ashbery's basic fables, metaphors for time.

Undecidable in this volatile sense, "time is an emulsion," Ashbery tentatively concludes in "Soonest Mended" (*DDS* 17), a poem that focuses many of the temporal contexts that occur in his first four books. What, then, can we make of this strange metaphor? As a suspension of small globules of one liquid in a second, an "emulsion" suggests not only the way Ashbery's moments are loosely suspended—that is, not solvent—but also the necessity of always agitating the suspension, to keep it in flux, "percolating," as he describes it recently in "The Prophet Bird" (*Sh Tr* 12). So, for example, Ashbery defines "The Skaters" (*RAM* 34) as a poem

> Which is in the form of falling snow:
> That is, the individual flakes are not essential to the
>   importance of the whole's becoming so much of a
>   truism
> That their importance is again called in question, to be
>   denied further out, and again and again like this.
> Hence, neither the importance of the individual flake,
> Nor the importance of the whole impression of the storm,
>   if it has any, is what it is.

However, to refer to a more technical definition (the preparation of silver halide grains in gelatin that is used in developing prints), an "emulsion" suggests not so much the flux of Time as the pictorial, discrete texture of Ashbery's poems, where fragments of different times are often pieced together, each retaining its own light point of identity, yet part of a more stable whole. Thus, for example, Ashbery says in "Years of Indiscretion," "each must live its own time." The word "emulsion," finally, comes from the Latin *emulgere*, "to drain, milk out," which is also the archaic English meaning of "emulsion," and which suggests the gradual passage of time, an emptying, an absence. The moment becomes, in this context, an "empty pair of parentheses" ("The Prophet Bird," *Sh Tr* 12). Now it is perhaps Nietzsche who is the primary antecedent for a vision of a Time that is always a suspension with various forces in agitation, always a dispersal of surfaces, of contradictions, of nothingness. And, too, the emulsive moment is, for Nietzsche as for Ashbery, "not a fact but a fable and approximation . . . ; it is 'influx,' as something in a state of becoming, as a falsehood always changing but never getting near the truth: for—there is no 'truth' " (*WP* No. 616). That is, the emulsion can never be, to use the chemical metaphor, a solution.

"Soonest Mended" itself deals with the problems of placing the self in Time somewhere between the "margin" of the opening lines, which refer to a past where the "we" of the poem has been lost in something like an Italian romance epic world, and the present, which is a more central Time, a "mooring." In that romance past, Time is blurred, as events happen too quickly and unrealistically to comprehend—"Only by that time we were in another chapter and confused." But the past must also be understood as something to escape from, "step free at last," though that recognition fades quickly, as it always does: "Alas, the summer's energy wanes quickly, / A moment and it is gone." But still, the hope of repetition, of deferral, of suspension, mutes that melancholy passage: "Night after night this message returns, repeated / In the flickering bulbs of the sky." The present itself is constituted by the "serpentine" movement we saw in "Clepsydra," a "flickering" that is present and absent, and, like this movement, given by language, by "loose meaning"—

> We are all talkers
> It is true, but underneath the talk lies
> The moving and not wanting to be moved, the loose
> Meaning, untidy and simple like a threshing floor.

The duplicity of each moment is underscored by the line break which suggests that all "talk lies"—what is underneath, any metaphysical stability, is literally also false, serpentine. And yet the poem also counterbalances this Nietzschean affirmation through negation by a nearly Heideggerian sense of a presence which resides perpetually at an origin, in "The being of our sentences, in the climate that fastened them."

What the poem as a whole marks, then, is Ashbery's particular brand of expanding threshold moment, "a kind of fence-sitting" that is "fantasy" and fable at the same time it is historical. The particular facts of "events" that are "solid with reality" do not change, but the fact that they are ordered by the fables of language, the fact that events must be "namable" to be remembered, gives that order, that vision, a certain tenuousness:

> These were moments, years,
> Solid with reality, faces, namable events, kisses, heroic acts,
> But like the friendly beginning of a geometrical progression
> Not too reassuring, as though meaning could be cast aside some day
> When it had been outgrown

But nothing is really "outgrown" in this poem, for all is suspended in the emulsion of Time: the past romance, associated with reading; the realistic accounts of the past, from critical autobiographical perspective; the present that is both dispersing and converging, and which implies a future in these motions; the sense that something of Time can be repeated, to at least counterpoint a sense of loss and passage; and finally the speaker's Time, the time of the "we" which also implicates the reader who has his own autobiographical and fabled times.

But Ashbery's emulsion, for all its gestures of dispersal, is not simply a shapeless play of temporal forces and perspectives; the linear movement of the poem, by giving emphasis first to one time and then another, gradually establishes a cyclic pattern. Eventually, the poem finds a tentative conclusion by returning to the lost origin in a passage that prefigures the Nietzschean sense of recurrence that will become a major force in the later poems:

> For this is action, this not being sure, this careless
> Preparing, sowing the seeds crooked in the furrow,
> Making ready to forget, and always coming back
> To the mooring of starting out, that day so long ago.

With its emphasis on a forgetting that is not a denial of the past, and on the paradoxical presence of all times, "Soonest Mended" seems, then, to echo Nietzsche's Zarathustra: "All things are entangled, ensnared, enamored; if ever you wanted one thing twice, if ever you said, 'You please me happiness! Abide, moment!' then you wanted all back" (*TSZ* 19). But "Soonest Mended" is not ready to take a larger, Nietzschean chance that would emphasize difference, isolation, and self-revaluation through recurrence, not ready to go beyond a simply cyclic view of history or to escape the comforts of the origin. In fact, the speaker here seems content to rest in a kind of nostalgic passiveness where he will "accept / The charity of hard moments" and where "probably thinking not to grow up / Is the brightest kind of maturity for us, right now at any rate." The situation, then, is like that described in *The Heroes:*

> Yea, a fine stifling mist springs up from the author's pure and moody mind. Confusion and hopelessness follow on the precise speech of spring. Just as, when the last line of this play is uttered, your memory will lift a torch to the dry twisted mass. Then it will not seem so much as if all this never happened, but as if parts continued to go on all the time in your head, rising up without warning whenever you start to do the simplest act [*TP* 502].

For Ashbery, then, the emulsion continues to go on, however confusedly, in what Derrida would call a process of fraying, diverging; the emulsion is not constituted by a central moment around which clusters other subordinate moments, but is rather a series of contiguous forces—the "repetitions, substitutions, transformations, and permutations" (*WD* 279) that characterize a "decentered" moment. There is, in this ferment, no hierarchy, no origin and telos, that structures a poem as a whole; the return to the origin, to the mooring, always fails because the mooring is itself characterized by a movement away from itself. Any language of presence, of an attempt to stabilize a simple now, as Michel Foucault explains, "always seems to be inhabited by the other, the elsewhere, the distant; it is hollowed by absence" (*AK* 111). So, Ashbery writes, the emulsive moment is never simply here, but

> more likely that such straining and puffing
> As commas produce, this ferment
> We take as suddenly our present
> Is our waltzing somewhere else, down toward the view
> But holding off.
>
> ["Young Man with Letter," *DDS* 41]

What is suggested by all this is a nomadic time, a time that is characterized by perpetual displacement, that abandons its own origins, an idea that is itself too mobile to be understood in any language but that of the emulsive poem (*PS* 146–47). What is required is something like a Keatsian negative capability, the ability to exist in doubt and uncertainty, to live otherwise, elsewhere. It is in this context, for example, that we can understand poems such as "The Picture of Little J. A. in a Prospect of Flowers" (*ST* 27), where the speaker "cannot escape" the past represented by the picture yet cannot avoid anticipating a future that will repeat that elusive non-present, "As though the rolled-up future might stink / As loud as stood the sick moment / The shutter clicked."

The continual ferment and repetition that characterizes the emulsion is not an expression of pure subjectivity, for there is no simple present or presence to base a subject in. Yet, an Ashbery poem seems to mark a self-referential progress, always coming back to the mooring, the non-origin. For Ashbery, though, this self-referentiality is a complex process:

It seems to be that poetry has to be self-referential in order to refer to something else. I think many people feel a poet should take a subject as an essayist would, and then write about it in order to come up with some conclusions and the whole matter would then be solved to everyone's satisfaction. But poetry, as has often been said, is made out of words; it is an affair of language. The situation is parallel with painting, for a painting does not make a "meaningful statement." I think that this is why the Impressionists were harshly criticized at first, yet their work is actually a kind of realism superior to what had been done when they began to work. The interests of realism in poetry are actually enhanced in the long run by a close involvement with language; thought created by language and creating it are the nucleus of the poem. Self-referentiality is not a sign of narcissism, but actually is a further stage of objectivity [*Acts* 69–76].

But neither is this "objectivity" a form of transcendence, as John Koethe suggests (*BA*). In the emulsion, the now-points do not interpenetrate, as they would in a "solution," for these now-points are always exterior to one another. There is no single consciousness that attempts a resolution, only a plurality of voices and perspectives that deny the closure of a metaphysical or Cartesian subject, only the intricate evasions of language, the validity of "Each moment / Of utterance." As Derrida notes, "The absolute alterity of each instant, without which there would be no time, cannot be produced—constituted—within the identity of the subject or the existent" (*WD* 91).

Now this alterity of the time and the self is expressed, for Ashbery, in a poem like "Rain" (*TCO* 28), which concerns "the time / We do not live in but on." That the speaker would be always an outsider, even to the temporal processes that define him, poses a series of difficult problems. For example, in "A Last World" the speaker recalls: "These wonderful things / Were planted on the surface of a round mind that was to become our present time." The use of the past tense here reveals that the "present" has not, in fact, occurred, and the speaker senses from the vast emulsion of history that time has reached a state of entropy. Without the possibility of a transcendental synthesis, faced with a continual dispersal that seems to lead only to endless repetitions, the speaker waffles. He observes—"Once a happy old man / One can never change the core of things," and yet "the passions are divided into tiniest units / And of these many are lost, and those that remain are given at nightfall to the uneasy old man / The old man who goes skipping along the roadbed." In this last world, one wishes "to go far away from himself." From such an outsider's position, duration is replaced by apocalypse as "a last world moves on the figures" of the poem. Here, it seems, "Everything is being blown away; / A little horse trots up with a letter in its mouth, which is read with eagerness / As we gallop into the flame."

The problem becomes, then, how an outsider can read the secret letters, the utterances that constitute time—how he can experience the emulsion as a duration rather than an entropy. Duration thus becomes crucial, for it always seems to the outsider that "duration / Only conjugates the last happening / Is seen as adequate only after the passing of much else varied stuff" ("Litany," *AWK* 3). We can return to "Clepsydra" (*RAM*) for a more elaborate exploration of the problem. The poem opens with an implicit comparison between the passage of time and the changes of color, brightness and cloud, that the sky registers. But the notion of simple change becomes quickly modified with the recognition that any moment is "scarcely called into being / Before it swells, the way a waterfall / Drums at different levels," and yet is also part of the "recurring whiteness." Elongation and recurrence, progress and repetition—the hope of the poem is to modulate these constitutive elements of duration. The poem, then, is interested in

> Those mysterious and near regions that are
> Precisely the time of its [dialogue's] being furthered.
> Seeing it, as it was, dividing that time,
> Casting colored paddles against the welter
> Of a future disunion just to abolish confusion
> And permit level walks into the gaze of its standing
> Around admiringly, it was then, that it was these
> Moments that were the truth, although each tapered
> Into the distant surrounding night.

This "tapering" or "lingering" and "dividing" is accomplished here by a play of tenses. What seems at first to be a simple past is subverted by the fact that it is apparently a still incomplete past, a past in which a certain "spacing," as Derrida calls it, occurred in order to allow one to walk around in a time whose "confusion" has been deferred to the "distant surrounding night." But that past time, so effectively deferred, is called into question when the speaker realizes that no one "would ever see his way clear again." In addition, the "distant surrounding night" begins to sound, in the context of the poem's movement in traditional time through the course of a day, like the approaching present evening, but distinctly a present whose only identity is as the future of something else, a present where "expossibilities become present fact." In this way, temporal duration is allowed to assert itself as "Each moment seemed to bore back into the centuries."

The present, then, is both a presence and an absence, "comparable to exclusion from the light of stars / That drenched every instant of that being." It is, the narrator writes, a "round time," which suggests not only the possibility of repetition but, simultaneously, the enclosure and detachment that is the "look of the horizon." What the poem hopes to enclose is "A moment that gave not only itself, but / Also the means of keeping it," though detached, in a "distant" time. To achieve this complex situation, time must become "elastic":

> But the condition
> Of those moments of timeless elasticity and blindness
> Was being joined secretly so
> That their paths would cross again and be separated
> Only to join again in a final assumption rising like a shout
> And be endless in the discovery of the declamatory
> Nature of the distance traveled.

The moment here is not a simple repetition, for there is a teleology—even if it is only an "assumption" to be later corrected, even if "An invisible fountain continually destroys and refreshes the previsions." The notion of the lost origin, the mooring that cannot be held, gives way to a genealogical vision that forgets origins, as Foucault would have it, or that concentrates on the play of supplements, in Derrida's terms: "there was no statement / At the beginning. There was only a breathless waste, / A dumb cry shaping everything in projected / After-effects." The past, then, becomes something "to make absurd elaborations with / And in this way prolong your dance of non-discovery." This structure of "Prolongations of our reluctance to approach" finality is precisely what constitutes duration in "Clepsydra," where the danger becomes not the entropy of repetition but a dissolving, a loss of the emulsive quality of time, a loss of impetus—

> . . . it could only happen here, on this page held
> Too close to be legible, sprouting erasures, except that they
> Ended everything in the transparent sphere of what was
> Intended only a moment ago, spiraling farther out, its
> Gesture finally dissolving in the weather.

"Sprouting erasures"—that phrase, which is uncanny in its recollection of Derrida's "erasures" or "traces" transforms the very notion of traditional time. Ashbery says, late in the poem: "the windows no longer speak / Of time but are themselves transparent guardians you / Invented for what there was to hide." Metaphysical or traditional time gives way to a play of transparencies, traces, erased "previsions," to the elongation and repetition of "after-effects." The trace is like the child's invisible writing held over a flame to decipher it in "The Skaters." The trace that structures duration becomes "both mirage and the little / That was present, the miserable totality / Mustered at any given moment." That is, it marks what Derrida coins a *differance*—the "difference" between the mirage and what is present, a difference that marks the generating conflict of "Clepsydra," and a "deferral," a mustering that is always provisional (see Derrida, *SP* 136). The traditional categories for thinking duration must be reformulated; as Derrida notes, "concepts of *present, past* and *future*, everything in the concept of time and history which implies evidence of them—the metaphysical concept of time in general—cannot adequately describe the structure of the trace" (*OG* 67). Duration, then, becomes a matter of what Derrida calls "spacing," the progress of utterances that are always inadequate, what Ashbery calls "spaced-out times of arrival," a paradoxical sense of things always ending yet always needing to be supplemented.

The difficulty with this trace structure for duration is that it supposes, even in its "dance of non-discovery," a certain totality, however transformed it is by the radical temporality of the poem: "we must progress toward the whole thing / About an hour ago." In fact, words such as "whole," "total," and "horizon," and metaphors of roundness, closure, characterize the vocabulary of "Clepsydra" as much as any deconstructive vocabulary. Thus Ashbery refers to a "round time" and to the fact that "the words / 'After all' are important for understanding." The difficulty for such paradoxical thought, as Nietzsche explains it, is that becoming cannot be thought with respect to wholeness or totality which would deny becoming altogether: "If the motion of the world aimed at a final state, that state would have been reached" (*WP* 708).

How, then, does the notion of duration, with its sense of teleology, affect the process that is the "delta of living into everything," as Ashbery calls it in "The Skaters" (IV) (*RAM* 34ff), which follows "Clepsydra"? If we return to that poem "in the form of falling snow" in the light of the problematic of duration and closure, we discover that its vision of time seems to be continually failing: "The sands are frantic / In the hourglass." The reason is that the poem often relies too much upon a simple dualism between presence and absence, the "positive" and the "abstract," the real and imagined settings of the adventure, say, in section III: "the carnivorous / Way of these lines is to devour their own nature, leaving / Nothing but a bitter impression of absence, which as we know involves presence" (I). The result is a poem that, despite its virtuoso performance as a poem of faith in the manner of Eliot's *Four Quartets*, is essentially passive in its stance towards time: "I am, then, continuing, but ever beginning / My perennial voyage, into new memories, new hope and flowers / The way the coasts glide past you."

But there is a difference between time in "The Skaters" and in the other poems we've discussed, a difference in that "perennial" events are not simple repetitions, or even attempts to enclose the trace, but rather a difference marked by "new" memories, "new" hopes—a new past and future. The image of linear or circular time is replaced by "lengthening arches," the movement of the skaters in and out of the emulsive "mass" at a varying "distance, like fishing boats developing from the land different parabolas" (1). With the image of the parabola, the always incomplete figure nevertheless fully inscribed on a cone, the figure always incompletely drawn, trailing off, the poem finds a figure for its "dance of non-discovery." Like the parabola, the poem is always provisionally complete but without a static or Platonic "pre-vision," always figuring a "round time" on a circular shape that will not close, a duration that can be teleologically structured and yet left "postponed" (IV). Thus in the last part of the poem the mentions of temporal passage, seasons, "climax," defeat, "completing the puzzle," a matrix of anticipatory resolutions, finds completion in the "perfect order" of rising constellations at the close of the day that helps structure the poem's progress, in the distant fullness that only an outsider can experience. Completion belongs, here, in the realm of the astrologic, the mythic, the supreme fictions, as Stevens called them.

To move from "The Skaters" to "Fragment," the culminating poem in *The Double Dream of Spring*, is to mark a development from a parabolic figure of time to more complex "signs of the oblong day" (st. 1). The oblong, which can tend both towards the rectangle or the ellipse, is a problematic figure whose center seems often decentered, whose shape seems often a distortion carrying the trace of another shape. It is not surprising, then, that a poem titled "Fragment," a poem whose rhetorical surface describes a relationship to a former lover and indeed proceeds in the dialectic style of a Platonic dialogue, begins by questioning its own center or origin in that lover. That origin quickly becomes recognized as only a "version" (4), a "wish," a sequence of "passages of being" (2). There is always a hope, though, that the endless process of fictionalizing and supplementing origins may be framed by something larger: "The stance to you / Is a fiction, to me a whole" (2). What the narrator is momentarily teased with here is the possibility of a history that forgets its own perspectivism, a Bergsonian duration unconcerned with the status of the other. In this case, the poem of the self, a "flame . . . / Without meaning," would attempt only to establish "that flame's idealized shape and duration" (10). But this temporary musing arises from a crucial synthesis for the poet who has been an outsider: "You can look at it all / Inside out" (3). That is, more specifically, "your only world is an inside one / Ironically fashioned out of external phenomena / Having no rhyme or reason" (10). Here Ashbery uncovers the principle that will be crucial for all his later work. As Derrida notes, the outside *is* the inside, for in a process of continual supplementarity, of moving away from the mooring, the horizon will always shift. This produces its own difficulties concerning the narrator's point of view, for he finds himself "More outside than before, but what is worse, outside / Within the periphery" (16) as the dialectic of the poem intensifies. But this will force him to make an active choice, to define his time rather than passively ride it. The poem becomes not a distant symbol or representation, but the thing itself; he finds himself always already within its linguistic structure of supplements. The "whole story" is always "interrupted," fragmented in an "endless process of invagination," as Derrida calls it, a process underscored in "Fragment" by the grottoes, caves, and husks that permeate the poem (*OG* 44ff and *D* 98ff).

The narrator, then, is both an insider and an outsider, moving not simply upon the linear edge that marks the horizon of a decentered geometric figure. Rather, he moves over and within the figure of an oblong time, that is, of an *opening*, a cave of time turned inside out, an abyss within the self and in which the self progresses, the whole of a fictional duration that is also, the narrator puns later in the poem, "The hole, towering secret" (37) of time, the (w)hole that is the "hollow center," the "cave of winds," of breath, of the fragmented story. The notion of closure as a (w)hole thus radically restructures the problems we have been examining when the linearity of time is replaced by a hollow, an absence that must be filled: "The sense of that day toward its center / Is perforated and crisscrossed" (14).

It is useful to consider this radical opening, in Nietzschean terms, as a drift from horizontal to vertical time. In the fourth part of *Zarathustra*, Nietzsche's character, lulled by a false sense of fullness, completed duration, a "world become perfect just now," suddenly realizes the emptiness he faces: "What happened to me? Listen! Did time perhaps fly away? Do I not fall? Did I not fall—listen—into the well of eternity?" (*TSZ* 389). As the bottom literally falls out of the moment, the question of time must be re-thought criss-crossed over the abyss. In this vertiginous situation, the (w)hole becomes "not withdrawn / And never yet imagined: a moment's commandment" (1). Time as perforation then, as the opening within and without us.

In (out)side that Nietzschean well, that (w)hole, time becomes a series of pictures "told in an infinity of tiny ways // Stories of the past: separate incidents / Recounted in touching detail, or vast histories / Murmured confusedly" (17–18). What "Fragment" asserts is that "There was lots of time left / And we could always come back to it" (31). That is, time is the (w)hole of our words, our fables about it. So, for Ashbery, the language of phenomenology, clock time, myth ("Autumn was a giant," he says), biography, novels—any number of competing languages—are interwoven across the (w)hole. To assert the validity of any one theory is to tumble into the well as some "ancestor" does when he presents an Aristotelian view of time as a "future" that is "invaded by a present" (38). All such interpretations must be recognized as "allegorical" (43), as "slogans" (48), as "dwarf speculations / About the insane, invigorating whole they don't represent" (46). The (w)hole is the emulsion, the oblong that contains all versions yet contains none. The movement of the poem, then, marks its own time, its own tenuous, fragmentary duration, as an "after-all" after all:

> It is that the moment of sinking in
> Is always past, yet always in question, on the surface
> Of the goggles of memory. Nothing is stationary
> Nor yet uncertain; a rhythm of standing still
> Keeps us in continual equilibrium, like an arch
> That frames swiftly receding clouds

The equilibrium here is not a stasis, an entropy, but rather a more Nietzschean force; the (w)hole is originless, non-teleological, a "round time" that tends to turn parabolic or oblong, an abyss that is yet always full—

> Without beginning, without end; a firm, iron magnitude of force that does not grow bigger or smaller, that does not expend itself but only transforms itself; as a whole, of unalterable size, a household without expenses or losses, but likewise without increase or income; enclosed by "nothingness" as by a boundary; not something blurry or wasted, not something endlessly extended, but set in a definite space as a definite force, and not a space that might be "empty" here or there, but rather as a force throughout, as a play of forces and waves of forces, at the same time one and many [*WP* 1067].

The (w)hole, then, serves as a sort of container for the emulsion of time, a receptacle of past traces, yet also a catalyst for further transformations within a rather chemical equilibrium. It suggests both "sleeves / In the weather time after the doubtful present saluted" (44) and, in the closing lines of "Fragment," "words like disjointed beaches / Brown under the advancing signs of the air."

II

Recurring Waves of Arrival

> Thus it can come about that we aren't able to rid
> ourselves of the implications of our symbolism,
> which seems to admit of a question like "Where
> does the flame of a candle go when it's blown out?"
> "Where does the past go to?" We have become ob-
> sessed with our symbolism.—We may say that we
> are led into puzzlement by an analogy which irre-
> sistibly drags us on.
> —Wittgenstein, *The Brown Book*

We have raised, then, the question of the textuality of Time, of Time as the history of writing and the writing of history, a question that is the major inscription in *Three Poems, Self-Portrait in a Convex Mirror,* and *Houseboat Days.* Any discourse, writes Michel Foucault, is "from beginning to end, historical—a fragment of history, a unity and discontinuity in history itself, posing the problem of its own limits, its divisions, its transformations, the specific modes of its temporalities rather than its sudden irruption in the midst of the complicities of time" (*AK* 117). If *Three Poems* seems a "segment, more, of reality" (6), a surplus that seems to emerge from an unnamed discourse which can never be pinned down, that is, if the text seems more self-referential than earlier texts, it is because it refers implicitly to its own history, to the "transformations" and "divisions" in earlier Ashbery texts which brought it about and which continue to produce that history in *Three Poems* itself; the referent is thus always a "fragment," always being transformed and divided, yet always recurring.

While the narrator begins by simply questioning his own earlier vacillation between inclusive and exclusive styles, styles where he would "put it all down" or "leave it all out" (3), the very process of questioning leads to what Derrida calls the "crypt," a figurative "tomb" or "monument" that commemorates not a past but what is hidden by a past—a figure, then, that is also a "cleft." For Derrida, the crypt marks a secret word or name that governs a text (*GR* 65–72 and *YFS* 133). Thus the narrator writes: "We have broken through into the meaning of the tomb. But the act is still proposed, before us." Then he fractures the paragraph itself in mid-sentence, to resume, "it needs pronouncing. To formulate oneself around this hollow empty sphere . . ." (5). What needs pronouncing is, as Ashbery later explains, "the word that everything hinged on [and] is buried there," a word "unexamined" originally "when it was pronounced," yet which "is doing the organizing" (95). Putting the crypt, the unnamed word, into play across the silence of the fractured (w)hole of the text is thus to motivate a history, the textuality of Time: "there is now interleaving the pages of suffering and indifference to suffering a prismatic space that cannot be seen, merely felt as the result of an angularity [Derrida's term, too, in describing the workings of the crypt] that must have existed from earliest times and is only now succeeding in making its presence felt through the mists of helpless acceptance of everything else projected on our miserable, dark span of days. One is aware of it as an open field of narrative possibilities" (41). It is helpful to note that Foucault, describing the history of texts, describes the fracture or crypt as "that rent, devoid of chronology and history, from which time issued," as a gap where the idea of the origin, the hidden words of Derrida and Ashbery, are "forever promised in an imminence always nearer yet never accomplished" (*OT* 332). And so, for Ashbery, the crypt or "tomb" is where everything, including its own history, "is still postponed," and yet where "whole eras of history have sprung up in the gaps left by these pauses, dynasties, barbarian invasions and so on until the grass and shards stage, and still the answer is temporarily delayed" (98).

But putting the crypt into play is not to possess the "hollow sphere," the hidden word, within oneself, for *Three Poems* continually regenerates the crypt through the process of invagination we saw at work in "Fragment"—"We see this moment from outside as within" (5). That is, one is held within the very words and their history one hopes to contain; in fact, in this context, the "self has dwindled and is now at last vanished in the diamond light of pure speculation" (41). That invagination also involves the two elements separated by the fracture: the tomb and its lost pronunciation; writing and speaking; the playful typographical lacunae, ellipses, shifts between prose and poetry which are meant to defer progress, and the unwavering linearity of speech with its hope for pure presence; each is constantly sheathed by the other. *Three Poems*, then, is marked by the double inscription of Time, by detour and by progress: "The whole thing is calibrated according to time's way of walking sideways out of the event, at the same time proceeding in a straight line toward an actual vanishing point" (23). The double inscription thus aims not simply at repeating by deciphering a vanishing past, but at the surplus—the digressive interruptions, the sideways movement, the supplement, the addition, the "new" that is not simply the introduction of a variant as promised in "The Skaters"; it is "the new merging, like ancestral smiles, common memories, remembering just how the light stood on the water that time. But it is also something new" (5).

And yet the "new," the "narrative possibilities" that might emerge from any questioning of the crypt are curiously thwarted by both the conclusion and the structure of "The New Spirit," the first of the *Three Poems*. In its last pages (50–51), the "tomb" has become the "horrible vision of the completed Tower of Babel," a "metaphor" that seemed about to erase them [constellations; i.e. "reality"] from the sky. But just as the metaphor could itself be erased when "it was not looked at," the constellations themselves are only figures, mythic arrangements that seem to pronounce a history. Thus the "Archer" can always aim "still higher," a gesture that may seem "no longer a figure of speech but an act," but his "history" is always another metaphor, the hidden words of the tower, the poem. If this conclusion, then, only enlarges the crypt, only repeats it on a grander scale, does that not suggest that the history of this writing is always a recurrence of itself? "The New Spirit" returns, despite its thesis of progression of beginning anew, to its own beginnings. It is a poem that ends by re-pronouncing its own earlier key words—"propose," "formulate," "question" ("We must remember to keep asking the same question / Until the repeated question and the same silence become the answer," p. 6):

> . . . just their presence, mild and unquestioning, is proof that you have got to begin in the way of choosing some one of the forms of answering that question, since if they were not there the question would not exist to be answered, but only as a rhetorical question in the impassive grammar of cosmic unravelings of all kinds, to be proposed but never formulated.

The return is, as Nietzsche says, a question of textuality, an "illusion" or fiction (*WP* 552 and *GM* 2.12, 2.13), an interpretation or re-inscription; it is a metaphor for what cannot be spoken, the crypt/tower, "having no live projection / Beyond the fact of the words in which it was written down" (40). It is, as he explains, a thought, a "what if."

Unspoken perhaps, but certainly imaged as the "horrible vision" glimpsed briefly near the end of "the New Spirit,"a vision that echoes Zarathustra's initial "Nausea" at the idea that individuals, as we have seen Ashbery say, "dwindle," that events are no longer unique (*TSZ* 370). In *Will to Power* Nietzsche writes: "Continual transition forbids us to speak of 'individuals,' etc; the number of beings is itself in flux" (*WP* 520). In "The System," the second of the *Three Poems*, Ashbery once again confronts the problem of the (w)hole, but here through the problematic of "uniqueness," through the confrontation between individual moment and historical system. Thus Ashbery writes: "You see that you cannot do without it, that singular isolated moment that has now already slipped so far into the past that it seems a mere spark. You cannot do without it and you cannot have it" (34). It cannot be had, that is, because the moment is not a simple entity, not a simple whole, a simple duration; each moment is linked to others in such a way as to *become*, as Nietzsche says, those others. The moment cannot be had because it is had again and again through the multiple perspectives, the repetitions of the same problem in different contexts throughout *Three Poems*. The question then turns on itself in Ashbery's usual dialectic fashion: "What if it were true that 'once is enough'?" (76). Could all "resonances," Ashbery asks, be cut off, "even if the uniqueness were meant to last only the duration of its unique instant," before qualifying his qualification ironically—"which I don't for a moment believe"? (77). "For a moment"—that is precisely what is at stake here, the phrase, the issue, complicating the very inquiry that hopes to resolve it. Just as nothing could be "after all," can anything be "for a moment"? Ashbery provisionally answers with the notion of an "aura" that is "meant to linger." But then, what is the ontological relation between event or word and aura? In Nietzsche, the aura is the "phantasm," the "demon" that hypothetically announces the eternal return in the *Gay Science*; it stands for the Dionysian fervor where everything dissolves and forms again, where what recurs is recurrence itself, the phantasm of itself, the thought, the metaphor of the return (34). And as Foucault explains the phantasm, it involves the relation between events, the invagination of inside (spirit) and outside (sign), the multiplicity of perspectives, the polysemic nature of words, the repetition of what is hidden or missing, oscillations in time, a surplus or "excess"—in short, the structure of recurrence as we have seen it gradually develop in Ashbery's poems is suggested by the metaphor of the "aura" (*LCM* 169–77).

Most of the earlier parts of the poem deal with possible systems of Time and history: whether history ought to simply record central events or rather the internal pacing and seemingly random movement of everything as in Nietzsche's "genealogy" (54–55); whether it ought to focus on a consciousness of individual loss or larger "rituals" (69–70); whether it ought to find hope in sudden events or latent eventualities (70 ff); whether, as historians, we are ourselves in or out of time (89). These concerns build gradually, until Ashbery stumbles across the inevitable truth of his own version of recurrence. He describes a fork in a path, parodying Frost's notion that choosing one or the other makes "all the difference," where a "you" has taken first the worn path, rather than the "more tangled way," only to make an uncanny discovery:

> In doing so you began to realize that the two branches were joined together again, farther ahead; that his place of joining was indeed the end, and that it was the very place you set out from, whose intolerable mixture of reality and fantasy had started you on the road which has now come full circle. . . . Nothing remains but to begin living with the discovery, that is, without the hope mentioned above [90].

For Nietzsche, the idea of the eternal recurrence is extremely complex and ambivalent. Zarathustra's versions of the return are never fully, finally stated, and even in *The Will to Power* this "horrible vision" must remain fragmentary because it is so overwhelming. When, for example, the animals describe their version of the return to Zarathustra as a coming "back eternally to this same, selfsame life, in what is greatest as in what is smallest," Zarathustra falls asleep, bored (*TSZ* 370). There is a buried word in Nietzsche's idea, and that is "difference," or better Derrida's *differance* as both a difference and a deferral. Earlier in Nietzsche's text, when Zarathustra explains the idea to the dwarf, who thinks of the eternal recurrence as simple repetition in time, Zarathustra describes two similar events in which a dog first "howled" and then "cried"—the difference being one of quality and also an accounting of a movement *in time* (365). As a metaphor, an inscription on the "tomb," the eternal recurrence is the "system" as a (w)hole. It does not preclude Time as a dispersal of moments, but rather hovers over Time like the constellations in "The New Spirit," constituting a *Stimmung*, a tone for time. Thus Ashbery says a few lines after making his own discovery:

> One must move very fast in order to stay in the same place, as the Red Queen said, the reason being that once you have decided there is no alternative to remaining motionless you must still learn to cope with the onrushing tide of time and all the confusing phenomena it bears in its wake, some of which perfectly resemble the unfinished but seemingly salvageable states of reality at cross-purposes with itself that first caused you to grow restless [*TP* 90–91].

What is required, now, is to make choices about those "salvageable states," to become, as Nietzsche says, more selective, to continue, as Ashbery says, to question. That questioning, with its implicit perspectivism, is not so much a movement in Time as a deconstruction, that is, re-creation of it. Time becomes surprise, a uniqueness, a structure in which dimensions and movements are absolutely relative:

> No, one must treasure each moment of the past, get the same thrill from it that one gets from watching each moment of an old movie. These windows on the past enable us to see enough to stay on an even keel in the razor's-edge present which is really a no-time, continually straying over the border into the positive past and the negative future whose movements alone define it. Unfortunately we have to live in it. We are appalled at this. Because its no-time, no-space dimensions offer us no signposts, nothing to be guided by. In this dimensionless area a single step can be leagues or inches; the flame of a match can seem like an explosion on the sun or it can make no dent in the matte-grey, uniform night. The jolting and loss of gravity produce a permanent condition of nausea, always buzzing faintly at the blurred edge where life is hinged to the future and the past [*TP* 102–3].

And yet, "The Recital," a coda of sorts to *Three Poems*, poses still another reversal. It begins: "all right / The problem is that there is no new problem" (107), and continues with such proclamations as "our apathy can always renew itself" (110) and "We are stuck here for eternity and we are not even aware that we are stuck" (115). And there is a curious narrowing, perhaps stagnating, that is named by the successive titles with their successively shorter texts—a new spirit is first systematized and then recited. Recital, then, is not only performance, the old film re-shown before an audience whose applause echoes in the empty hall at the end of *Three Poems*, but a re-play of something previously rehearsed, and a re-telling, a history. In fact, it is this lack of a problem that is the central issue of Ashbery's following book, *Self-Portrait in a Convex Mirror*, where perspectives tend to exist lethargically on "the great relaxed curve to time" ("Ode to Bill"), and where the double inscription often seems to have been erased. And yet. And yet. Perhaps within the crypt of "The Recital" another word is hidden, the cognate *recit*, a story, a saving fiction, a faint "glimmer" even if of a "false dawn" (117), a hope that a "conjugating" and "transforming" (repeating with a difference) of the "anonymous matrix without surface or depth "may yet be acted out" (118) in later texts (*WD* 162ff).

As the problem is re-cited in "Grand Galop" (*SP* 14), it emerges from the very structures of recurrence and dissemination that had been established to overcome it. For example, the poem begins: "All things seem mention of themselves / And the names which stem from them branch out to other referents." And later the narrator writes: "The words had a sort of bloom on them / But were weightless, carrying past what was being said." The difficulty emerges with a consciousness of the space between the words and what is being said, between the signifier and the signified; the narrator, finding himself within a system of recurrences which seems to anticipate its own future ("the same as having reached the end"), always seems to be ahead of himself, is always tempted to "wait" for time and meaning to catch up, and thus tends to impose a closure that will limit or halt dissemination. The poem, like many others in *Self-Portrait*, begins to anticipate its own directions, a gesture that Derrida analyzes in "Genesis and Structure" as a desire to establish "the unification of the temporal flux of consciousness just as it [the infinite] unifies the object and the world by anticipation, and despite an irreducible incompleteness" (*WD* 162). This is not, then, a question simply of totality, of the "after all," or the problematics of felt duration. The poem would take the parentheses out of the (w)hole and substitute the order of a "horizon . . . of recognition," however provisional—the "imperfect knowledge of the featureless whole." And the result would be an "inertia that once / Acknowledged saps all activity" ("Self-Portrait"). This seeming to be ahead of oneself, this anticipation which is not the dynamically expanding horizon one finds in Heidegger or in such poets as Robert Penn Warren and John Hollander, but rather a sense of already having arrived, is manifest in the increased attention paid to consequences and eventualities in this volume, and to the relaxed tone of such key words as "benevolence," "polite," and "tame." The result is that the marking of the horizon becomes "A protracted wait that is also night" ("Farm"). Near the opening of

"Grand Galop," the narrator situates this waiting within the structure of recurrences:

> And now it is time to wait again.
> Only waiting, the waiting: What fills up the time between?
> It is another kind of wait, waiting for the wait to be ended.
> Nothing takes up its fair share of time,
> The wait is built into the things just coming into their own.
> Nothing is partially incomplete, but the wait
> Invests everything like a climate.
> What time of day is it?
> Does anything matter?

From this retrospective position the question of the "fair share" emerges, that is, the economy of various temporalities in an historical system; it becomes, then, a question of the tropes one has used, a question of the *recit*. Thus the moment of waiting already begins to disrupt its own unity because of the relativity and historicity of its own terms—it deconstructs itself, Ashbery says later in the poem, as a "moment of indecision." Even the undecidable meaning of the line "Nothing is partially incomplete, but the wait," enforces this.

Now this very indecisiveness, this waiting, constitutes what the narrator calls "pauses," a term which recalls the "gap" or "fracture" we saw near the beginning of *Three Poems*. But it is important to distinguish the pause in "Grand Galop" from the "hollow empty sphere" that is the hidden singular word in *Three Poems*. In "Grand Galop" the pauses are the result of a surplus of tropes; they measure not the absence of a past that must be supplemented, but a past so supplemented it has overtaken its own future, a past which pronounces itself everywhere. And more, these pauses are spoken as Times bounded by shifting, indecisive horizons—they are fractures with "sides," and they are plural—

> And their steep, slippery sides defy
> Any notion of continuity. It is this
> That takes us back into what really is, it seems, history—
> The lackluster, disorganized kind without dates
> That speaks out of the hollow trunk of a tree
> To warn away the merely polite . . .

The pauses thus rediscover history in the phenomenological *hyle*—the discontinuous, the incidental, the formless and the accidental, what is not yet subjected to any chronology, what Derrida calls the "very possibility of genesis itself" (*WD* 163). And so the horizon itself is absorbed into the system of recurrences where it begins to mark this double movement of an invitation and a warning, a return and a difference. The horizon and its pause thus need not mark an inertia but rather a profound discontinuity, "rumours - Of things being done on the other side of the mountain" which provide by their very fictiveness, their marginal status, a surplus of tropes that still "remains, a still perfect possibility," a future.

What has occurred here is the invagination of the horizon and the crypt, the pause and the fracture. It is because of this arche-writing, as Derrida calls it, a writing that would rupture the "impossible" horizon that seems to close "Grand Galop," that "Self-Portrait in a Convex Mirror" can be written (see *OG* 60–65). That poem is literally a marginal text, not a mimetic "codification" but a supplement to an already distorted, vanished origin, the crypt—the artist named Parmigianino, whose image, reflected in a convex mirror, has been painted, and now written into the name, Ashbery—"until no part / Remains that is surely you."

The situation recalls the textual mirroring in "Scheherazade" (*SP* 9ff), appropriately titled to suggest the endless invagination of stories and narrative contexts in *The Arabian Nights*, a mirroring that opens up an infinite space of reverberations, of language listening to and echoing itself (see *GS* 310). In that poem, the stories exactly inscribe a world: "nothing in the complex story grew outside." The difficulty that the poem describes, though, occurs as a result of this enclosure:

> Some stories survived the dynasty of the builders
> But their echo was itself locked in, became
> Anticipation that was only memory after all,
> For the possibilities are limited.

Thus, though "the moment of telling stayed unresolved," it cannot progress or change in its repetitions, "its growth a static lament." The mirroring in "Scheherazade" becomes simple repetition.

But during the course of its six related meditations, "Self-Portrait's" margins and horizons are thoroughly ruptured: "Today has no margins, the event arrives / Flush with its edges, is of the same substance, / Indistinguishable." The poem thus becomes a "recurring wave / Of arrival" from the past to where the narrator now waits. The structure recalls Nietzsche's ever approaching wave that "crawls with terrifying haste into the inmost nooks of this labyrinthine cliff. It seems that it is trying to anticipate someone; it seems that something of value, high value must be hidden there . . . Has it found what it looked for? . . . But already another wave is approaching . . ." (*LCM* 66–67). In this recurring process, "All time / Reduces to no special time." The time of writing and the time of painting are thus reversible in the sense that the mirror holds a reverse image, that the poem is always a re-versification of both the hidden words of the crypt and the surplus of the margin, that these binary poles are always reversed, that is to say, turned inside out, invaginated. And there is a disruption of the usual relation between critical and creative texts, events and their histories, for the painting is not doubled, as Derrida would say, by its poetic "analysis," but rather a new set of signifiers, an endless set of implications, is catalyzed by the poem. The poem creates more "nooks" than it ostensibly proposes to probe, for it cannot help mirroring its own concerns, generating discrete "parts" that will imply the "whole" as (w)hole—"Here and there, in cold pockets / Of remembrance, whispers out of time," beyond the time of the poem, deferred. The poem itself remains

> a gauge of the weather, which in French is
> *Le Temps*, the word for time, and which
> Follows a course wherein changes are
> Features of the whole. The whole is stable within
> Instability, a globe like ours, resting
> On a pedestal of vacuum, a ping pong ball
> Secure on its jet of water.
> And just as there are no words for the surface, that is,
> No words to say what it really is, that it is not
> Superficial but a visible core . . .

Change within the (w)hole within an instability; words that cannot name the surface-core, the horizon-crypt, the wave-nook—these strategies are now familiar to us. But what is the nature of that unspoken surplus and/or crypt which motivates these lines, which provides this poem with its "course"? What is that unstable system of mirrorings which allows "words" and surface or core to differ, defer, and trace each other's Times in a random, fragmentary fashion?

A recurring system of endless dispersals and ruptures, of transformed horizons, decentered fragments, self-referential fictions—does this not describe Foucault's archive? Borges' library? Nietzsche's world as infinite textuality, as chance? Conventional history only reflects a static past:

> The past in each of us, until so much memory becomes an institution
> Through sheer weight, the persistence of it, no,
> Not the persistence, that makes it seem a deliberate act
> Of duration, much too deliberate for this ingenious being
> Like an era that refuses to come to an end or be born again.
> ["Train Rising Out of the Sea," *AWK* 87]

This history is something, Ashbery goes on to say, that needs to be taken from us, "To be deposited elsewhere." But where? What is the "site," in the Heideggerian sense of that word, of the library? In *Three Poems* Ashbery writes: "we are rescued by what we cannot imagine: it is what finally takes up and shuts our story, replacing it among the millions of similar volumes that by no means menace its uniqueness but on the contrary situate it in the proper depth and perspective" (104–5). This library, for Foucault, is the place where "even the infinity of language multiplies itself to infinity," a place where language "postpones death indefinitely by ceaselessly opening a space where it is always an analogue of itself" (*LCM* 66). Here the traditional idea of the book is antiquated, "the gilded species of these tomes blaze too bright" ("Drame Bourgeois," *HBD* 44), for, as Foucault says, "it is a site that is nowhere since it gathers all the books of the past in this impossible 'volume' whose murmuring will be shelved among so many others" (*LCM* 66). Uniqueness and infinite play, infinite recurrence, are part of a paradoxical system whose (w)hole can never be experienced in any one moment, but only implied by a series of chance encounters. As Ashbery describes this, the archive is a process:

Into the house within, its many chambers,
Its memories and associations, upon its inscribed
And pictured walls, argues enough that life is various.
Life is beautiful. He who reads that
As in the window of some distant, speeding train
Knows what he wants, and what will befall.

["Houseboat Days" 39]

Constructing the system that shows "what will befall" is an endless task of reading oneself onto those walls, the task of *Houseboat Days,* really, for with each glance from the train, each "perspective" on the library and its impossible texts, "the old poems / In the book have changed value once again" ("Collective Dawns"). As Foucault describes his archive, its "dispersion itself—with its gaps, its discontinuities, its entanglements, its incompatibilities, its replacements, and its substitutions—can be described in its uniqueness" (*AK* 72) by uncovering the anterior discourse, the hidden language of the crypt, that allows it to be written.

Ashbery's archive demands a fluid language, that is, a language with no subject other than itself, its own infinite play of mirrors, a language that transgresses the limits of language in order to pronounce what cannot be pronounced. It is a language of false causalities, incomplete references, dead-end allusions, periphrases, hyperbations, etc. Thus, in "Drame Bourgeois," writing takes place at the ruptured horizon where the "moment of outline recedes / . . . always darker as the vanishing point / Is turned and turns itself / Into an old army blanket, or something flat and material," that is, into the random, the unexpected signifier. As the editor of the *Yale French Studies* issue on "Graphesis," where this poem first appeared, points out, the poem talks about the non-referentiality of the imaginary process: objects are turned into ideas and can be grasped only at the limit of some " 'non-real' border line or 'vanishing point' " (*YFS* 52). The experience of poetry at Ashbery's "vanishing point" is what Foucault calls an act of transgression:

The moment when language, arriving at the confines, overleaps itself, explodes and radically challenges itself . . . and where it remains fixed in this way at the limit of its void, speaking of itself in a second language in which the absence of a sovereign subject outlines its essential emptiness and incessantly fractures the unit of its discourse [*LCM* 48].

At this point, "All of our lives is a rebus," a puzzle that is constituted by a violated language, Ashbery writes in "The Wrong Kind of Insurance." The crypt itself, that unsolvable rebus, that (w)hole, that emulsion, or whatever metaphor we invent for its varying functions, is also the archive, the always already transgressed text for which we have a "divine recollection." In "Blue Sonata" (*HBD* 66), for example, a poem concerned with the past as archive, and that situates itself on the way toward a previously imagined horizon, Ashbery writes:

> It would be tragic to fit
> Into the space created by our not having arrived yet,
> To utter the speech that belongs there,
> For progress occurs through re-inventing
> These words from a dim recollection of them,
> In violating that space in such a way as
> To leave it intact.
>
> [*HBD* 67]

"Progress," temporality, can only be structured through "re-invention," recurrence with a difference, not a mimetic or anticipatory utterance. Re-invention is always a violation that does not fully violate, a deconstruction that restructures, a "destiny," as Ashbery says earlier in the poem, that is also a "new way." And so he begins "And UT PICTURA POESIS Is Her Name," a poem that constitutes an *ars poetica*, with the line: "You can't say it that way any more." The poem goes on to construct a poetics of the random, the anti-poetic, a shopping list of unlikely ingredients, "so that understanding / May begin, and in doing so be undone." Undone, that is, not only in the sense of being unfinished, but also unmade or not attempted, untied or unravelled, subverted or done in—a concept of progress that must always dismantle its own definition. As he says later in "Flowering Death" (*AWK* 79): "We must first trick the idea / Into being, then dismantle it, / Scattering the pieces on the wind."

Is any history possible for this poetry of undoings? Ashbery's "Pyrography" (*HBD* 8) reconsiders the ideological and cultural history of nineteenth-century America's westward movement and its present eventualities. The aim is to deconstruct our myth of completion, our sense of having constructed an edifice of authoritative history in which to center ourselves. Ashbery attempts to uncover a different structure:

> How are we to inhabit
> This space from which the fourth wall is invaribly missing,
> As in a stage set or dollhouse, except by staying as we are,
> In lost profile, facing the stars, with dozens of as yet
> Unrealized projects, and a strict sense
> Of time running out, of evening presenting
> The tactfully folded over bill?
>
> [HBD 8]

The "answer" is provided by a Nietzschean genealogy concerned with a provisional rather than a final structure of events (*GS* 7; *GM* I, 2). As Foucault defines it, genealogy "must record the singularity of events outside of any monotonous finality, it must seek them in the most unpromising places, in what we tend to feel is without history— in sentiments, love, conscience, instincts; it must be sensitive to their recurrence, not in order to trace the gradual curve of their evolution, but to isolate, the different scenes where they are engaged in different roles. Finally, genealogy must define those instances where they are absent, the moment when they remain unrealized" (*LCM* 252). This refusal to focus on major events that can be arranged to suggest a continuous, stable pattern, this patient attention to singular details no matter how disruptive or discontinuous, establishes a "counter-memory—a transformation of history into a totally different form of time" (*LCM* 160). Ashbery's version is to reveal the "prismatic / Features of this instant"—

> If we were going
> To be able to write the history of our time, starting with today,
> It would be necessary to model all these unimportant details. . . .
> And not just the major events but the whole incredible
> Mass of everything happening simultaneously and pairing off,
> Channeling itself into history.
>
> [HBD 9]

This genealogical approach explains Ashbery's radical shifts in diction, from the philosophical style of *Three Poems* to the mannerist technique of *Self-Portrait* to the low, cliché-filled diction that occupies such an important place in all his work; each style brings forth metaphoric possibilities based on its histories. The poet becomes, in Foucault's words, an analyst of "discursive formations," a genealogist. That is, he writes what Nietzsche calls an "effective history," as opposed to a "monumental" or "antiquarian" history; he writes a history that parodies convention, as in "Daffy Duck in Hollywood" (*HBD* 31), that dissociates itself from the unity of simple memory, and that subverts the notion of history as metaphysical truth. Thus, Foucault writes, "A discursive formation does not play the role of a figure that arrests time and freezes it for decades or centuries" (*LCM* 160–64), but rather becomes the basis for a radically temporal history.

The genealogist, then, is both an explorer and creator of archives. But what becomes of the post-genealogist in such a complex history? As Ashbery says in the penultimate poem of *Houseboat Days,* "Syringa," which powerfully reflects Foucault's main theories, the poet must "forget" the Orphic desire to dwell upon repetitions, upon the lost presence of his Eurydice. He must realize that it is "the nature of things to be seen only once" in their uniqueness, that he cannot "treasure / That stalled moment. It is too flowing, fleeting." He must realize that his "subject" is soon "no longer / Material for a poem" (71), for any subject, as such, is too intent upon revealing a stable meaning:

> While the poem streaked by, its tail afire, a bad
> Comet screaming hate and disaster, but so turned inward
> That the meaning, good or other, can never
> Become known.

In one interview, in fact, Ashbery notes that he takes pains to avoid the context of a subject (*CP* 117–18). But this is not a sophisticated solipsism. The poet must realize that he, too, must cut himself off from the poem, that he, like it, must disappear at the "vanishing point" as both become part of the "archive," to be subject to later archeologies, genealogies. The author, man ultimately, "disappears" in the sense that he is no longer the central issue. He becomes literally the text's *rebus*, the "hidden syllables" of the crypt.

This is not simply the gradual loss of identity we saw in *Three Poems*, the "clear, compact shape of the plot of a novel," for the notion of narrative itself as a "gradual curve" or "evolution" disappears. I quote from the closing lines of "Syringa"—

> The singer thinks
> Constructively, builds up his chant in the progressive states
> Like a skyscraper, but at the last minute turns away.
> The song is engulfed in an instant in blackness
> Which must in turn flood the whole continent
> With blackness, for it cannot see. The singer
> Must then pass out of sight, not even relieved
> Of the evil burthen of the words. Stellification
> Is for the few, and comes about much later
> When all record of these people and their lives
> Has disappeared into libraries, onto microfilm.
> A few are still interested in them. "But what about
> So-and so?" is still asked on occasion. But they lie
> Frozen and out of touch until an arbitrary chorus
> Speaks of a totally different incident with a similar name
> In whose tale are hidden syllables
> Of what happened so long before that
> In some small town, one indifferent summer.

[71]

The world, as Nietzsche says, is an "infinite" series of ever more powerful, more willful interpretations, the promise of the text as it breaks its own horizons (*GS* 374). The history that evaded the narrator at the beginning of *Three Poems* emerges here as a function of chance, the only rule of the archive. Nietzsche neatly summarizes this history in the *Genealogy of Morals:*

> The entire history of a "thing," an organ, a custom can in this way be a continuous sign-chain of ever new interpretations and adaptations whose causes do not even have to be related to one another but, on the contrary, in some cases succeed and alternate with one another in a purely chance fashion. The "evolution" of a thing, a custom, an organ is thus by no means its *progressus* toward a goal, even less a logical *progressus* by the shortest route and with the smallest expenditure of force—

but a succession of more or less profound, more or less mutually independent processes of subduing, plus the resistances they encounter, the attempts at transformation for the purpose of defense and reaction and the results of successful counteractions. The form is fluid, but the "meaning" is even more so [*GM* II, 12].

Ashbery's archive, then, promises a new freedom for readers; it is our "arbitrary chorus," as critics and as poets, which retrieves texts from the archive, though it may be by a chorus that "Speaks of a totally different incident with a similar name." Not only does the Ashbery poem attempt to mirror or supplement the hidden words of the crypt within it, but it becomes itself a crypt, an essential emptiness and openness that is always transgressed by reading; this play of mirrors is the archive, the crypt as it functions beyond the individual text. This, for example, is the thrust of "Paradoxes and Oxymorons" (*Sh Tr* 3), which begins:

> This poem is concerned with language on a very plain level.
> Look at it talking to you. You look out a window
> Or pretend to fidget. You have it but you don't have it.
> You miss it, it misses you. You miss each other.

While the direction underscored here is away from the (traditional) poem as a center of concern and towards the glance and private activity of the reader, the text does in fact act by "Bringing a system" of reader responses "into play" in a "dreamed role-pattern" that is always "Open ended." It is by this indirection, the way the poem and reader miss each other's phenomenological intentions, that a more intimate relation is paradoxically established, one that blends author, text, and reader in an indistinguishable emulsion. Thus the poem ends by appropriating the wandering reader: "You aren't there / Or have adopted a different attitude. And the poem / Has set me softly down beside you. The poem is you." So if the author has been lost in the random eventualities of a text like "Syringa," he can inscribe himself as the reader who finds, in a sense, his own name echoed in the crypt. In this way, the narrator-reader produces his most radical de-centering, a production that is Time itself, a style that is matter-of-fact enough to include all facts, all times. Thus Shelley, certainly

one of the hidden names in Ashbery's crypt, one of the greatest dis-
mantlers: "All high poetry is infinite, it is as the first acorn which
contained all oaks potentially. Veil after veil may be undrawn . . . ,
and after one person of one age has exhausted all its diverse effluence
which their peculiar relations enable them to share, another and yet
another succeeds, and new relations are ever developed" (*CW, 609).*

III

The Parallelograph of Time

> The two senses stand side-by-side; the sense for
> the real is the means of acquiring the power to shape
> things according to our wish. The joy in shaping
> and reshaping—a primeval joy! We can comprehend
> only a world we ourselves have made.
> —Nietzsche, *Will to Power*

The question of Time now becomes the question of form: how best
to release an extra-textual world of random eventualities within the
printed text itself; how to write a text that will re-invent itself in a
discontinuous way; how, that is, to "save the text," as Hartman
phrases the problem with respect to a general deconstructive project.
The history of this question is implicitly described in "The Sun," the
penultimate poem in *As We Know* (the title suggests, in a way we
saw earlier, a volume of endless self-referentiality). The poem puts
into play the metaphor of a family history; though it begins with the
notion that all history is spoken from the trace or "watermark" in a
text, from the crypt, it seems for a while that the poem will not escape
the burden of an "invariable law," a monumental history of "millenial

growth," the "idiot" cycles of the sun, as Ashbery phrases it in "Collective Dawns" (*HBD* 5). As an initial solution, the poem calls upon the problematics of recurrence as we have described it; events in this history occur "decade after decade, and it never stops / Being refreshing," the tension between the endlessness of identity and the refreshening of difference emphasized here by the line break. In its last lines, the poem suggests that any event will be "transfixed" by the archive, that is, both impaled or deconstructed and held fast or reconstructed, as that word's double nature suggests. Thus an event, like the hidden words of the crypt, will

> pass unnoticed, until the deeply shelving
> Darker pastures project their own reflection
> And are caught in history,
>
> Transfixed, like caves against the sky
> or rotting spars sketched in phosphorus, for what we did.

[5]

The fluid meaning of these lines borders on chaos, is almost undone by itself. To be transfixed in history is not to be rendered motionless, after all, but to be thrust into a temporal structure, transformed. But it is a structure that is invisible, the empty space of a cave upon the vast emptiness of the sky. And it is a structure whose terms disseminate wildly; doesn't, for example, "spars" echo "stars" ("Caves against the sky") and "spears" (instruments of impalement), by what Riffaterre calls an ungrammatical relationship? (*SP*). What this little passage reveals is a hidden form in Ashbery's poems: "We know we can never be anything but parallel / And proximate in our relations, but we are linked up," he writes earlier in this poem. This parallelism is what holds a poem of seemingly endless proliferations together: "variety implies parallelism" when one approaches the infinite, he had written in *Three Poems* (101). Time exists as a form of "parallel thought," he writes in "Fragment" (33). So, in this poem, several alternative forms of the family history exist side by side—an emulsion never fully separated, a (w)hole never fully conceived, a crypt never fully deciphered. On various readings, a more conventional or more

175

radical history may dominate; time may seem deconstructed, reconstructed, or both; the events may seem to pass or they may be reflected. Time becomes not only a discontinuous form, predicated by one or several schemes, but is also produced by the parallelism of the relations themselves, a relational Time.

Ashbery's "Litany" (*AWK* 3) is literally such a parallel text, not only in its subtle parodies of other texts, including some of Ashbery's own, not only in its deliberate returns to recast more of the problems we've already described, but in its very graphic form, its two columns erected over sixty-five pages. It's a text like Derrida's columned *Glas* or many of Ammons' *Snow Poems*, in that it enciphers within itself a radical otherness; it is a text that, from the very beginning, faces two different directions, two tempos, a vertigo of text in and about Time, whose only center is the white margin, the blank crypt between columns. The poem of ultimate decentering. Or perhaps not columns—perhaps two towers of Babel, an uncanny doubling of the end of *Three Poems*, the radical otherness of a discourse, an archive, fractured into its own false echoes. Graphically, the poem presents two independent structures, two towers with their own patterns of questioning, their own pacing, their own Times. But they are also two dependent structures; narrator A mentions topic X before or after B does, or perhaps B never mentions it at all. Then, of course, the questions arise—why not? or why *this* juxtaposition? does B supplement or subvert A on this or that particular point? And the tower-columns themselves are broken into three sections, and then broken into paragraphs, even larger white spaces. Why has A chosen to make a paragraph at this point, leaving a white space parallel to a line of B? Why let B have the stage all to himself? What role does chance play in these relations and fracturings? Then another series of questions: must the text of "Litany" be listened to, taken in simultaneously, that is to say, incompletely, as a series of fragments whose sequence and composition change with each hearing? As a written text, can one assimilate a page, then balance it after-the-fact like a verbal see-saw? What is the difference between the oral and written effects? And finally, a disturbing effect: someone is always talking—words, relations, Time cannot be eluded. Too much is always happening in this poem of ultimate surpluses. As A states at the beginning of section

III: "these things are part of time, / Or are rather a kind of parallel tide, / A related activity" (58, A).

The form of the poem is perhaps what Julia Kristeva, following Bakhtin, would call "dialogic." The discourse of one column refers us always to the discourse of the other, where language is revealed as essentially ambivalent (*DL* 67ff). The parallelism often tends to disrupt the linear logic of sentences in favor of a linguistic relationship of signifiers. For example, when column A is describing a "plunge" into meditation, B describes a stream; but since A thinks of the plunge as a pause from Time, B's stream then suggests the conventional image of a stream of Time. Since B's description is of a slow-flowing stream, it supplements A's desire to escape the "rat race," but subverts his desire for an absolute pause. These complex relations must then be read back into the continually disrupted flow of the larger passages they are a part of (38). In fact, such connections (corrections), such "readings back," are endless. Sometimes the relationships are parodic; when A discusses the way experiences can be savored ("the knowledge / Will always remain with me that there is one"), B sarcastically comments in the exactly parallel lines: "you enjoy / The mellow fecund death of that past." While this "you" is not necessarily A (though both A and B are discussing failed affairs throughout), the parallelism certainly leaves such a possibility open (48). A dialogic relationship, as Bakhtin describes it, is carnivalistic; language relativizes itself—it is both representational (the affairs behind the discourses and the ostensible topics) and non-representational (each column is centrally interested in a proliferation of metaphors and dialects that reflect against the other column and back on itself). It is a deconstructive language of non-exclusive oppositions and often what seem to be inconsequential statements. At the end of section II, for example, A discusses the otherness of Time, B the persistence of memory; suddenly B shifts to mention the popularity of the Yellow River, a dramatic break in discourse. The connection is never fully severed, however, for B uses the stream image to discover how we always "enter / A new chapter" and A describes love as "perennial as time"—the two columns together mark the notion of repetition with difference. We might note, too, that there is a tenuous connection here between A's discussion of the way time

> takes from the idea of itself
> Each of us has, and knows not, except
> To recognize, and feel secure again about its growing:
> I mean that it is a replica
> Of itself, which is itself the replica,
> Counterfeited from itself,

and B's emphasis that he speaks of the Yellow River itself and not the novel; they seem to deconstruct each other. In fact, B seems to deconstruct A's deconstructions of phenomenological time, his insistence upon Time's textuality. Yet B, in furthering his argument, does construct a hypothetical narrative that we suspect has some basis in the novel itself, and so undercuts his own anti-textual position (56–57). This sort of labyrinthian relationship, where language, like Time, is involved in a system of endless becoming and mirroring, is precisely the dialogic method. The text is, in DeMan's sense, unreadable, infinite.

Parallel to this dialogic system, where almost any random word, phrase, sentence, or line seems to play endlessly against its counterpart in the other column and against itself, ensuring a kind of infinite structure, there is a certain sense of flow, of development in the general argument about Time. It is in the play between these two structures that a general theory of Time is re-inscribed. In the first section, column A begins with a meditation on presence, on time as recurring as a continual presence (12), then begins to perceive the trace structure of the moment and, finally, acknowledges an essential otherness to the moment. B, on the other hand, begins with a more complex sense of Time as always Other, for "nothing directs / To the present" (3); yet precisely because there are "Too many coils / Of remembrance," B ends the section on a nostalgic, almost defeated tone. At one crucial point (12), A describes the moment as

> the fixed wall of water
> That indicates where the present leaves off
> And the past begins, whose transparencies
> Admit impressions of traceries of leaves
> And shallow birds among memories.

The moment, so filled with a Heideggerian language of betweenness, of phenomenological presence, is undercut by the corresponding section of B, which is constituted by a language of "Refrains," of "conjugation," of "being turned inside out"—in short, the language of recurrence, deconstruction, and invagination. In fact, B states, "meaning / Pierces in any given point / And in the texture of the sea," sharply poking through A's inclusive moment. The parallelism refuses to let us choose between the phenomenological moment or the deconstructive moment; they exist together, they depend upon opposition: "Dialogism replaces these concepts by absorbing them within the concept of relation. It does not strive towards transcendence but rather toward harmony, all the while implying an idea of rupture (of opposition and analogy) as a modality of transformation" (*DL* 88–89). The transformation, as we have seen, occurs within the reader-author, who constructs his own third column, a time, a pace of interpretation. What Ashbery is interpreted in for this poem is not this or that theory of Time, but the very temporality of thought about Time, a temporality that exists, as we will further see, outside the text itself.

In part II, A continues his analysis of otherness with a synecdochic view of Time ("only parts / Are what is actually seen, and these supply / The rest" (20). A's tendency here is to try to include the Other in the present, for "now the now is what matters" (21). He does this by suggesting the notion of recurrence that B, we saw, brought up in section I, but A does so in a more sophisticated way: everything is "horizontal, without / Beginning or end, and seamless / At the horizon it bends / Into a past which has already begun" (44). The next step is to suggest something like the archive: "the garment falling around you is history, / Someone's anyway." While A seems to have benefited from B's deconstructive approach in section I, B slips into a quasi-transcendental vision in order to overcome his nostalgia. But the vision, for B, fails, "since eternity / Is an eye, and some things elude the eye," since there are always, as we have seen, remainders; it is the notion of the remainder, the possibility of a new chapter in the Yellow River script, that allows B to achieve some balance by the end of the section. Section II, then, marks a divergence and reversal;

in fact, this process implicitly questions the very notion of parallelism which contains within it, as Derrida has shown, the Husserlian "parallelism" that is none other than a closure, a hermeneutical boundary, an overlapping principle to contain multiplicity and free play. That is, Derrida questions the notion as a simple form of dualism, a disguised Platonism (*WD* 161–65). For Ashbery, then, the whole notion of the parallel, and so the related notions of horizon or margin, must be continually disturbed. The parallel is essentially a graphic mark, a possibility of dissemination beyond its own margins:

> beware the right margin
> Which is unjustified; the left
> Is justified and can take care of itself
> But what is in between expands and flaps
> The end sometimes past the print
> Of conscious inquiry, noodling in the near
> Infinite, off-limits.
>
> [42, B]

And it is in section II that the two columns or margins seem more frequently to lag behind each other in their discussions of various ostensible subjects, further calling into question a phenomenological or orderly relational pattern.

In section III, A, after posing several questions concerning Time's double nature as form and / or content, achieves a futural vision, a mood of preparedness, for "the future is right" and the present is a "not-knowing." B continues with its nostalgia for "the place / We started out from" (63). Paradoxically, it is A who enacts this return, for its closing lines, with their description of a city, windows, a dangerous future, return us to the substance of B's opening lines in section I. And B's nostalgia is a failed version of A's opening—"Like me the time flows round again / With things I did in it" (3, A). What are we to make, then, of this cyclic pattern in a poem of parallel columns that, to use the geometric analogy, ought to continue to infinity, like railroad tracks? Is A, which has the last twenty lines or so when B stops early, indecisively, doomed now to follow B's course? Will A retain its self-assuredness? Will B's endless self-questioning provide a richer course if it begins as an A column? But can those courses be repeated? How will the problems be redefined on a second and later readings? What are we to make of this poem of endless displacements, not only in the mirroring of terms, the parallel but out-of-"synch" pacings, but of the very perspectives, positions of the text itself? Does not all this suggest an irreducible alterity, an essential exteriority of Time to itself? Does not history, Time, now become the utter play of position—as Derrida would say, an impossible parallelism of differences, a concept ridiculed by the hint of sarcasm in our opening question, "But, what is time, anyway?"

So persistently does "Litany" secure its playful exteriorizing of each of its parts within the (w)hole, however one decides to divide or mirror that text, so endless is this invaginating of (w)hole and part, that, even confining ourselves to an oral presentation of the poem, far from enforcing the simple presence of the voice, only intensifies the problematic we have been discussing: the questioning of the temporality of Time we saw in section I, of the very notion of parallelism we saw in section II, of the formal strategy of the poem itself we saw in section III. An oral presentation—if that word can be used at all, after Derrida's critique at the beginning of "La Dissemination"—would require a simultaneous voicing that would direct the author's attention to drift between the columns, as in some contemporary music; the result is to preclude the presence of any external referent, to underscore the text's self-referential features, to dismantle any linearity whatsoever that can be associated with clock time. "Litany" is a deconstructive text that not only, as we have seen in Ashbery's career, develops a textuality of Time and existence through an emphasis on writing, but actually allows, insists, that language be spoken, pronounced as he said in *Three Poems*, so that it and understanding may be fully undone. Time, as an emulsion that suspends otherness, an abyssing of origins, ceaselessly disseminating itself despite a radical discontinuity between parts, fragmentary moments, creating fables for itself, mirroring its own parts, always remains an unquestionable remainder, a rebus, a word not pronounced by what we designate as "Time." Such a self-referential Time, paradoxically, absorbs and excludes us:

> There comes a time when the moment
> Is full of, knows only itself.
> Like a moment when a tree
> Is seen to tower above everything else,
> To know itself, and to know everything else
> As well, but only in terms of itself
> Without knowing or having a clear concept
> Of itself. This is a moment
> Of fast growing, of compounding myths
> As fast as they can be thrown off,
> Trampled under, forgotten. The moment
> Not made of itself or any other
> Substance we know of, reflecting
> Only itself. Then there are two moments,
> How can I explain?

How, indeed, does one explain? How can one, in the shadow of an infinite text, still continue to inscribe time? Ashbery begins *Shadow Train* with an oblique glance back to "Litany," particularly to its critique of parallelism and the problematic of exclusiveness:

> It came about that there was no way of passing
> Between the twin partitions that presented
> A unified facade, that of a suburban shopping mall
> In April.

Does this "passing between" signify the negotiation of the third column of interpretation as a compromise in the space between columns or the sideways play between columns? And why are we suddenly excluded? Part of the problem, I think, rests with the very question of the question, "What is Time?" The question itself excludes us. Wittgenstein is helpful here. In his *Blue Book* he writes: "It is the grammar of the word 'time' which puzzles us. We are only expressing puzzlement by asking a slightly misleading question, the question: 'What is . . . ?' " (*BBB* 26). We can no more answer the question, he says, than answer what constitutes blueness. What we must examine is the common use of the expression "Time," not to focus upon a definition, but to uncover rules of usage. We cannot pass between, in Ashbery's phrase, because Time is the ultimate paradox, a trap.

Shadow Train, which was originally to be titled *Paradoxes and Ox-ymorons,* attempts to put into play the temporality encrypted within paradoxical figures of speech, within a microcosmic parallelism that is "A path decorated with our comings and goings" ("The Vegetarians"). And there is a great risk here, for paradox is not a wild play of signifiers but a critique of the signified as well as its logical form. There is a more direct treatment, for example, of the relationship between ordinary expressions for Time which reveal a pattern, a history, an archive, and unique expressions which rupture the history of that discourse (though a dramatic juxtaposition of dictions has always been a signature for Ashbery). In the lines quoted at the opening of this paragraph, for example, the biblical "It came about" clashes against the reductive metaphor of the last clause, but they are paradoxically linked, under the title "The Pursuit of Happiness," as a religious materialism or materialistic religion, a history of bourgeois discourse.

We can explore this problematic of history further by turning to the title poem. There, some pattern of events may constitute a "violence" that carries us along, suspended between a "desire" and a "want," within the "truth inside that meaning" of their relationship. What is at issue here is the difference between a temporality of desire and a temporality of want. Desire carries within it the polite distance of an absence, the meaning: "to desire it / And not want it is to chew its name like a rag." Now the two words suggest two different temporalities, not just the difference between a graphic and a phenomenological Time, but by a certain quality, an intensity, a subjectivity barely revealed by the tension of paradox, but hinted at in its unravellings through a poem. Thus, in the end of "Shadow Train," Ashbery writes: "it is clear / That history merely stretches today into one's private guignol."

As we might suspect, any "stretching," any sense of duration, is also paradoxical. "Indelible, Inedible" *(Sh Tr)* is a title that suggests both a lack of erasure and an inability to consume, a play between textuality and body, word and world, held together by the fact that both words oddly relate to their own kinds of "enduring," as the poem suggests, but are also split apart by the fact that one suggests a monumentality, the other a poisonousness, etc. Duration is also tempered by the form of the poems—four quatrains of irregular line length that loosely suggest the logical pace of the sonnet and which complement the intensity of these poems, as opposed to the extensiveness of poems like "Litany" or "Syringa." The parallelism of stanzaic form imposes the trace of an inherited pace upon these poems, sets arbitrary "frames" that must always be exposed as such by that most traditional of figures, paradox, which now asserts its own fable for Time. "For it seems that all / Moments are like this: Thin, unsatisfactory / As gruel, worn away more each time you return to them," Ashbery writes in "Drunken Americans." Unsatisfactory, that is, "Until one day you rip the canvas from its frame," only to discover that it is, paradoxically, "the reflection in the mirror," the paradox of a self-referentiality of form.

Ashbery's vision of Time, then, always involves, as Nietzsche says in the epigraph for this section, the way "two senses stand side by side," whether within the emulsion, the coined word, the (w)hole, the play between crypt and supplement, recurrence and difference, archive and word, author and reader, column A and column B, the graphic and the phenomenological, timing and content, etc. Ashbery's Time is like Nietzsche's "*Dionysian* world of the eternally self-creating, the eternally self-destroying, this mystery world of the twofold voluptuous delight" (*WP* 1067). It is a world, as Ashbery says in "Here Everything Is Still Floating" *(Sh Tr)*, of the paradox, the "singular / Un-wholeness," and yet also of the "simultaneous." That poem, in fact, provides both a conceptual conclusion and a fitting dramatization of Ashbery's problematic of Time:

> I must concentrate on how disappointing
> It all has to be while rejoicing in my singular
> Un-wholeness that keeps it an event to me. These, these young guys
> Taking a shower with the truth, living off the interest of their
> Sublime receptivity to anything, can disentangle the whole
> Lining of fabricating living from the instantaneous
> Pocket it explodes in, enters the limelight of history from,
> To be gilded and regilded, waning as its legend waxes.
>
> [*Sh Tr* 18]

For Ashbery, then, time is not only a Derridian double inscription, where time must be reinscribed over its old forms, but a process in which inscription and reinscription, as concepts themselves, are subject to the very thing, Time, that they create. Time becomes the infinite inscription, the explosion of history, "waning as its legend waxes," dissolving in the very poems that create it.

Ashbery's poetry, then, becomes truly dialogic in the sense Bakhtin explains: language constitutes an other with whom the author converses and so converses with other times and places, the language being always a form of "verbal decentering" (Bakhtin, *Dialogic*, 302, 367). In this way, Ashbery's poetry becomes, finally, novelistic, but, dialogically, a novel whose character, places, even plots, emerge from a collision of languages and parodies of languages. This explains, I think, the increasing allusions to plot and character, the increasing flirtation with narrative in his work. "The Path to the White Moon," for instance, in *The Wave* (31–32), tells a story, originating (so to speak) in something that "Looked like farmhouses yes," and proceeds to tell not a story *per se* but a narrative of the speaker's attempts to discover a story, a series of propositions, possibilities with references to probable pasts. The poem then ends in the midst of this dialogue:

> We know what is coming, that we are moving
> Dangerously and gracefully
> Toward the resolution of time
> Blurred but alive with many separate meanings
> Inside the conversation.
>
> [32]

And the very next poem picks up the glove, punning on "still" and deconstructing the tone by a dialogic undercutting of language: "and still time / Is draped around your shoulders. The weather report / Didn't mention rain, and you're ass-deep in it, so?" ("Ditto, Kiddo," 33).

In some poems the overt desire for dialogue becomes the main subject, as the narrator talks to himself as other (or other as himself), not across columns but within the doubling carnivalistic nature of languages:

> I keep thinking if I could get through you
> I'd get back to me at a further stage
> Of this journey, but the tent flaps fall,

The parachute won't land, only drift sideways.
The carnival never ends; the apples,
The land, are duly tucked away
And we are left with only sensations of ourselves
And the dry otherness, like a clenched fist
Around the throttle as we go down, sideways and down.

[W 52]

In the end, Ashbery intends the poems to remain "Potentially out of focus, some of it too near, the middle distant / A haven of security and unreachable," as he says in the long poem "A Wave" (68). Ideas become part of the ongoing dialogue—"a luminous backdrop to ever-repeated / Features, having no life of their own, but only echoing / The suspicions of their possessor" (69). So we are "set free on an ocean of language that comes to be / Part of us" and in time becomes "a sculpture / Of moments, thoughts added on" (71). The search extends for newness, novelty—"a new weather / Nobody can imagine" (74). Thus he asks—"Is there something new to see, to speculate on?" Finally, the dialogue in Ashbery is with the future, an attempt to avoid the levelings of the past. What "A Wave" fights against—and its dramatic, narrative power comes from its novelistic plot of triumphs and failures, hopes and despairs—is the simple repetition that has threatened his narrators since the beginning—"And then it all happens blendingly, over and over / In a continuous, vivid present that wasn't there before" (84). He must avoid simple ends "Dreamed into their beginnings" (85). At the end of the poem, he regains a faith that things will change, but the reason lies not in things themselves, rather in the narrator's language—"it is finally we who break it off," call it, the poem, closed, though "We'll / Stay in touch" (89). The narrator's "thirst" remains the same, but "the walls, like veils, are never the same" (89) because he sees them differently, as the history of his unfolding double consciousness. Also, at the end, the dialogic principle is the essential procedure:

I feel at peace with the parts of myself
That questioned this other, easygoing side, chafed it
To a knotted rope of guesswork looming out of storms
And darkness and proceeding on its way into nowhere
Barely muttering.

[W, 88–89]

5

A Common Time

The Poetry of Denise Levertov

I

The Echo of Nothingness

Thus time appears through *trajectories*. But just as spatial trajectories decompose and collapse into pure static spatiality, so the temporal trajectory collapses as soon as it is not simply lived as that which objectively implies our expectation of ourselves. In fact the problems which are revealed to me tend naturally to be isolated as in-itself *probables* and to occupy a strictly separated fraction of objective time. Then the *lapse* of time disappears, and time is revealed as the shimmer of nothingness on the surface of a strictly atemporal being.

—Sartre, *Being and Nothingness*

In an early poem, "Interim" (*CEP* 4), Denise Levertov confronts the "black page of night," the silent pain and fear associated with isolation and loss, in hopes of hearing "some intimation, echo, emanation" of Being by maintaining an "attitude more listening than longing," an attitude, really, that derives from Heidegger's "listening" to the "saying" of Being (*OWL* 57–108). This connection to Heidegger, which Levertov acknowledges, is as crucial as the connection to another student of Heidegger, Sartre, who expresses the intimacy between Being and Nothingness, position and negation. Thus Levertov's poem, structured by negatives ("Not more alone / waking than sleeping, in darkness than in light"), positions itself in an "interim," or rather refuses to position itself, for it takes place in a moment already so "dispersed," to use Sartre's term, that the moment itself has negated its own parameters, is already transforming itself:

> Not less alone
> in city than in solitude, at least
> this time—an hour or minute?—left between
> dreaming and action, where the only glitter
> is the soft gleam of words, affording
> intimacy with each submerged regret,
> awakes a new lucidity in pain,
> so that with day we meet
> familiar angels that were lately tears
> and smile to know them only fears transformed.
>
> [*CEP* 4]

The poem initiates a dialectic between "dreaming" and "action," between the "gleam" of words and the substantiality of things, between the "intimacy" of pure presence and an absence that is "submerged," between memory and transformations, between the "minute" and its context, the "hour"—in short, the major terms that will develop in Levertov's work.

In the long run, the key word of Levertov here will be "action," especially in the light of her struggle to make poetry a means of political action, a form of history. The moment, then, will not rest "between / dreaming and action." Always in the process of negating itself, time becomes a sort of "Anteroom," as the title of one poem describes it, where moments seem temporarily cut off from the meaning of history. The poet must move "out of this season of uprooted hours, / where time, that should grow round as hanging fruit, / rushes like showers of dry and shrivelled leaves, / and no hour quickens into truth," and must allow her dreams a "transformation into life," into acts (*CEP* 5). The difficulty, though, is "to write / of the real image, real hand," to "clarify / all the context of a simple phrase / —the hour, the shadow, the fire, / the loaf on a bare table" ("Too Easy," *CEP* 10). Now it is this movement to contexts, to other times, that invades the original moment of pure presence, that "deconstructs" it, Jacques Derrida would say—it is this movement that has drawn the most criticism for Levertov. Alvin Rosenfield, for example, has suggested that Levertov's poems fail, "erode," just at that point where she commits to action, to politics, where the Heideggerian and Orphic tradition of a language of pure Being becomes concerned with the everyday, the "inauthentic." This conclusion may be appropriate from a "naive" Heideggerian perspective. And we should note, with Christopher Fynsk, that Heidegger's poetics often does not sustain itself well in encounters with the Other: Heidegger's "analysis of Dasein in *Being and Time* leads back insistently to the solitary self" (Rosenfield 195 and Fynsk 185). But Levertov's Heidegger is not the philosopher of a "naive" self-presence; indeed, she first mentions him, in "The Poet in the World," as a poet of what Sartre would call the "for-itself," the actor who initiates exterior encounters. She writes: "Heidegger, interpreting Holderlin, says that 'to be human is to *be a conversation*'— a strange and striking way of saying that communion is the very basis of human living, of *living humanly*" (*PIW* III). Conversation, Levertov explains, involves a dialogue, a dialectic with everything in the world, with the self as it is projected. Thus, on a more ontological level, Sartre's notions of the way the self flees from itself, the way its world is dispersed, its time constantly negated, the way a Heideggerian presence is always qualified, become crucial contexts for understanding the way Levertov's moment "transforms" itself into a complex dialectic of presence and absence, Being and Nothingness. But we have gotten ahead of ourselves; before we can understand the movements to action and the transformations that characterize the middle and later poems, we need to focus upon the development of her sense of the moment itself in the early poems.

"All awareness," Levertov writes, "is an awareness of time" (*PIW* 111). Just what this awareness involves is perhaps nowhere more clear than in her poem "The Instant." The poem, whose origin is certainly the Snowdon episode of Wordsworth's *Prelude* (1850), describes a daughter and mother searching for mushrooms. For a while the focus is on particular, nearby impressions, founded by the confinements of a simple, pure, moment of presence: "Mushrooms firm, cold; / . . . clouds about our knees, tendrils / of cloud in our hair" (*CEP* 65–66). The moment is suffused with physical sensations, until "suddenly" the mist lifts and the mother points out in the distance "—It's Snow-

don, fifty / miles away!—the voice / a wave rising to Eryri, / falling."
Snowdon, then, "resting place of / Merlin, Core of Wales," provides
a context that disrupts the pure presence of the moment in several
ways. For one, the geography of the scene shifts the emphasis from
the "lower" senses to sight, to vision and imagination, to a time not
defined by such things as the instantaneousness of touch, to a consciousness of absence; and yet the narrator maintains a sense of
inclusive presence in having her mother's voice travel towards the
mountain, even out into the mythical context when the poet names
"Eryri" as the point of destination. For another, the mythical and
historical dimensions both disrupt the simple consciousness, and
indeed are seen to be almost interchangeable, thus redefining each
other. Because the mountain is seen as a "core," a religious or at least
metaphysical dimension enters, and this is reinforced by the Wordsworthian literary context. Each of these contexts, besides suddenly
exploding the instant into a visionary moment, brings an increased
awareness of the time of the vision itself, the fact that: "Light / graces
the mountainhead / for a lifetime's look, before the mist / draws in
again."

But even more crucial is the awareness that the moment contains
a radical Otherness, an absence in the presence emphasized by the
distant mountain; and the awareness of this absence informs succeeding moments. Now on the one hand this can be interpreted as a
Heideggerian "projection" of Being. In "The Presence," for example,
Levertov anticipates that "Before I enter the rooms of your solitude /
in my living form, trailing my shadow, // I shall have come unseen"
(*JL* 51). The addressee here will sense the presence of the speaker in,
variously, the flight of a bird past the window, the wandering of a bee
in a hallway. As Heidegger says: "The widest orbit of beings becomes
present in the heart's inner space" (PLT 128). On the other hand, the
projected Being takes on a special character. In "The Lagoon," for
example, there is "the presence of a rippling quiet" ("ripple" is one of
Levertov's favorite words for this expanding motion of consciousness)
that

> draws the mind
> down to its own depths
> where the imagination swims,

shining dark-scaled fish,
swims and waits, flashes, waits and
wavers, shining of its own light.

[*CEP* 90]

What does imagination wait for here? The waiting itself, a typically Heideggerian stance that describes the way Being is filled with anticipation in time, suggests something to come, an absence that defines this seemingly pure presence of the self in itself (*CEP* 6). The imagination, Being, the self, do not, as it first appears, slip into the solipsism of their "own depths," their own phenomenologically bracketed moments. Indeed, we could just as easily deconstruct or negate the presence in "The Presence," hollow it with absence, for it is, for both the speaker and the addressee, an essential absence of each other that has already defined the way they are present to each other.

This is a concept that persists throughout Levertov's work. Later, in "Dialogue" (*RA* 91), she will describe "Absence / an absolute / presence / calling forth / the person [the poet] / into desperate continuance, toward / fragments of light." And her lead note to "Relearning the Alphabet," taken from Heinrich Zimmer, describes the Other as distant: "he who reveals to us the meaning of our . . . inward pilgrimage must be himself a stranger" (110). And the poems are filled with detailed perspectives: seeing gulls inland, she can "smell the / green, dank, amber, soft / undersides of an old pier in their cries" (*F* 17). The nothing, the absent, as Heidegger would say, calls the poet forward: the *Dasein*, he says, is already outside itself, already a "here-there" (7).

A useful context for seeing the complexity of Levertov's poetic here is provided by Sartre. He writes: "Nothingness lies coiled in the heart of being—like a worm" (56 and Altieri, 224–44). This occurs because man "makes himself known to himself from the other side of the world and he looks from the horizon toward himself to recover his inner being. Man is 'a being of distance' " (51). That is, because of this Heideggerian projection, any "presence of being to itself implies a detachment on the part of being in relation to itself" (124). Thus, Sartre notes, "Presence to self . . . supposes that an impalpable fissure has slipped into being. If being is present to itself, it is because it is not wholly itself" (120). Now this fissure is the way the for-itself, consciousness and Otherness, differentiates itself from the in-itself, unconscious presence; it is the mark of an essential act of Being— "Thus nothingness is the hole in being, this fall of the in-itself toward the self, the fall by which the for-itself is constituted. But this nothingness can only 'be made-to-be' if its borrowed existence is correlative with a nihilating act on the part of being. This perpetual act by which the in-itself degenerates into presence to itself we shall call an ontological act. Nothingness is the putting into question of being by being" (126). Now this putting into question, which is a "fall," constitutes, for Sartre, a kind of dispersal, an exteriority. Ultimately, what is put into question is not only Being, but time itself, not just our ordinary conception of it. Thus, says Sartre in the epigraph I cited above, time seems to be separated from itself and "is revealed in the shimmer of nothingness on the surface of a strictly atemporal being" (294). That is, time becomes a matter of "abolitions" and "apparitions," illusions that the for-itself, consciousness, generates on a basically non-temporal environment (282). Temporality is a unity, a vision, that disperses itself from any moment, or instant, just as the self diversifies itself. This dispersal of illusions is given in the phenomenon of the "shimmer of nothingness." This, then, is the "shining" of Being as it "waits" in Levertov's "Lagoon," the "light" that breaks the mist in "The Instant," the "flicker" of fire in "Too Easy," the "glitter" and "soft gleam of words" we began with in "Interim."

How, then, does this "shimmer of nothingness" define the temporality of Levertov's early poems? How does one write poems, use a language, to give a fullness and Being to nothingness? What does it mean, after all, to write poems that contain the desire "to fly off on the whirlwind into / the great nothingness"? ("The Whirlwind," *CEP* 79). It means that the poet, on a metaphysical level, focuses on a "sense of the present" that is defined as "a delight / that what is passing // is here" ("The Coming Fall," *OT* 39); Being, that is, is nothingness, and the poet has to find a way to "let be / what is gone" ("The Charge," *CEP* 87), in both senses of "Letting be"—allowing to exist (as nothingness) and taking a passive stance (waiting). "There's nothing less real / than the present" (*LF* 41), Levertov will later say. So the poet must make " 'every step an arrival' " ("Overland to the

Islands," *CEP* 55), but must realize that the shimmer of Being, of constant arrival, constitutes an "ephemeral eternity" (*CEP* 26). The arrival is into an elsewhere, as she suggests in "Seems Like We Must Be Somewhere Else" (*CEP* 92). Sartre, too, writes: "Nothingness is always an elsewhere" (126). Now, for Sartre, as for Heidegger, this arrival elsewhere is accomplished only through language, which is a being we are (not). As one critic explains, the absent and elsewhere given in language itself derive from the concealedness, the mystery of the unsaid, within authentic language; it is a sort of silence within language that addresses itself to *Dasein* (Marx, 240–44). It is, as Derrida would explain, an always absent source from which all Being derives. Or, as Levertov explains, using by chance Heidegger's metaphor of the stream of saying, a musicality: "the downstream / play of sound lifts away from / the present, drifts you / off your feet" ("The Hands," *CEP* 38).

The problematic of language and time is treated more directly in "Illustrious Ancestors" (*CEP* 77), where she describes how her ancestors used "what was at hand," itself a peculiarly Heideggerian expression suggesting presence, and how she herself hopes to write—

> poems direct as what the birds said,
> hard as a floor, sound as a bench,
> mysterious as the silence when the tailor
> would pause with his needle in the air.

> [*CEP* 78]

We can see here the movement from physical things and sounds through mystery and into silence. And it is not simply that the distance described in "The Hands" is illustrated here again; the language itself is seen to embody the movement. Literally, the more one talks, the more one's language becomes a meta-language, moving beyond things and into the inexpressible. Language loses its purely referential quality, if indeed it was ever pure. Thus, for Levertov, language projects its shimmer because it is, in some ways, non-referential. It reflects the elsewhere that is a nothingness, at least as far as the ontology of the poem is concerned. In *The Poet in the World*, for example, she cites Creeley's admonition: "A poetry denies its end in any *descriptive* act, I mean any act which leaves the attention outside the poem."

What she herself calls for is "a poetry of hieroglyphics, of embodiment, incarnation" (*PIW* 58, 61).

Language, then, becomes the set of empty signifiers Derrida and Lacan have described for contemporary philosophy and psychology. It marks an absence, or refers to a time that cannot exist because no language can refer to it and yet which every language embodies in creating its own meanings. Where does this confused situation leave us? What is this silence of a time that is and is not? What is suggested by all this is an epistemological problem. The movement elsewhere, into silence, promises not just a questioning of Being but a profound doubt, Heidegger's "dread," an uncertainty that goes beyond illusion. We can begin to see how these problems are solved by looking at "Night On Hatchet Cove." The poem begins by describing several disconnected observations, then an "interval" punctuated by the "squawk of a gull," and then a "pause / while silence poises for the breaking / bark of a seal." But the bark never comes; it remains perpetually absent, eternally ephemeral—

> Then
> only your breathing. I'll
> be quiet too. Out
> stove, out lamp, let
> night cut the question with profound
> unanswer, sustained
> echo of our unknowing.

[*JL* 13]

What is important here is the way that what we have seen as characteristic negations, and the unanswering, the unknowing, are actually what "sustain" the moment. "Night" here "cuts" the question in the sense that it puts a stop to questioning, and in the sense that it "cuts into" the question, discovers any answer to the question of Being and presence in silence itself. And we should note that, on an everyday poetic level, silence is used not only to describe the ontological phenomenon I described above, the listening and waiting, but also certain technical features that cut across the pure flow of sound. Levertov, for instance, follows Olson and Duncan in their understanding of the pauses and breaths created by syntax and lineation. These mark the hesitations, the doubts and re-beginnings, within language itself: the points which pace, time, measure out the temporality of words, distinguishing them from a continuous and therefore timeless sounding. Even the line breaks here, which Levertov refers to as "half comma pauses," suggest this undercutting of certainty and simple presence; the hesitation after a word like "profound" not only emphasizes the fact of the "unanswer," but focuses on the idea of profundity, in the context of the silent spaces of night, as an immense emptiness. At the same time, the lineation helps link "your breath" and the "I" of the speaker, the Other and the self, "quiet" and the "out" (elsewhere, outside, as well as "to end")— bringing together, finally, the sustaining and nothing (the "unanswer") in the second-last line. The "then" then, which governs this last paragraph in the poem is thus a complex and indecisive time— punctuated at a certain "then" yet "sustained," "profound" but "unknowing," a time when night is both approaching and already there as it projects its uncertain status.

The uncertainty here is at the (empty) core of Levertov's poetic. What is the status of a text that carries itself elsewhere and negates itself? Does the poem, in speaking the unspoken, deny its own possibility? Is the poem nothing? Is it a dialectics of negation? The negation of a negation? The figure of the "echo" which ends the poem helps us to begin answering these questions. The echo is what calls to the absent, and from it. It is a return from elsewhere, the nothing that is itself something, or, to put it another way, that constitutes presence, Being, language, poetry, the self. It has a double origin—it is not an echo until it returns, but the motion of return denies a point of origin elsewhere. What is the original, the sound or its echo? Even this analysis suggests an origin plus repetitions, but an echo is never purely a repetition because both its pitch and frequency are always falling off, like the Husserlian structure of time. The echo is, in a sense, then, self-referential, originating nowhere, or everywhere, or elsewhere. It establishes a dialogue, a dialectic; it is the mark of ourselves as a conversation, a calling back and forth. A conversation about nothing, made up of nothing; that is, a conversation where everything else, elsewhere, is possible.

Levertov's "A Common Ground" begins characteristically by invoking a "here," the "grit" and physicality of words (section 1), then shifts to a "time of blossoming," of surpassing the thresholds of the present (section 2), and finally (section 3) describes

> A language
> excelling itself to be itself,
>
> speech akin to the light
> with which at day's end and day's
> renewal, mountains
> sing to each other across the cold valleys.
>
> [*JL* 3]

Here the echoing song is a now-song, the muteness of the mountains, a song that is "light" (the shine), a song visible and invisible at once, a song that marks ends and beginnings, that excels itself in echoes that are and are not part of an original. And the dialogue here, like the notion of an echo itself, marks also an enclosure, a limit to the possible, the points from which things return—the enclosure of mountainsides. And yet, as elsewhere, aren't these limits, in some sense, nothing at all?

"The Abyss of Being," Heidegger would say to describe our predicament (*PLT* 96–97). The moment of the poem, as echo, suggests, as Levertov says in "To the Muse," something like "A becoming aware a door is swinging, as if / someone has passed through the room a moment ago" (*OT* 27). The subject of the poem is like a Magritte space that, when the surface presence is broken, reveals a "profound" space behind it, something that was absent and suggests other absences. In "Say the Word," Levertov writes:

> They gazed through and beyond the space the poplar had occupied. There to the northeast, in the scooped-out hollow of the pass, was an area of unclouded sky still pale with the last of daylight, and against it the far mountains were ranged, a wistful blue, remote and austere [*OT* 47].

Not only are the distant mountains presenced, but the absent tree is itself redefined in terms of that far scene; it becomes defined not only by what it was and the space it occupied, but what it hid. So "truth" or certainty becomes, in Levertov's world, a kind of Heideggerian "hidden," what the poet has to "unconceal." Time itself, Heidegger says, is such a "hidden" presence:

> However hidden temporality may be, and above all with regard to its Temporality, and however little the Dasein explicitly knows about it, however distant it has lain from all thematic apprehension, its temporalizing holds sway throughout the Dasein in a way even more elemental than the light of day as the basic condition of everyday circumspective seeing with our eyes, toward which we do not turn when engaged in everyday commerce with things [*Problems*, 307].

This hiddenness of time, then, like the absent tree, still exerts a force; in fact, the absence of the tree is what opens up the possibility of seeing something else that was hidden, another time frame. And that other time frame, hidden while the tree was there, was yet part of the tree's definition, what it acted upon, what it hid. It is curious that neither the tree nor the hidden landscape, in the scheme, asserts priority; even memory tends to suggest only the echoing possibility of the power of each. This is why Heidegger links the "hidden" and "possibility"; and for him, as for Levertov, "within the ontological sphere the possible is higher than everything actual" (*Problems*, 308).

Possibility, then, replaces certainty, and a pattern of echoes, marked more by difference than repetition, replaces a simple structure of presences. "The Springtime" is a good poem in which to watch this process enacted:

> The red eyes of rabbits
> aren't sad. No one passes
> the sad golden village in a barge
> any more. The sunset
> will leave it alone. If the
> curtains hang askew
> it is no one's fault.
> Around and around and around
> everywhere the same sound
> of wheels going, and things
> growing older, growing
> silent. If the dogs

        bark to each other
        all night, and their eyes
        flash red, that's
        nobody's business. They have
        a great space of dark to
        bark across. The rabbits
        will bare their teeth at
        the spring moon.

                                    [*CEP* 82]

The basic pattern of echoes here can be seen in the red of rabbits and dogs' eyes, the repetition of days in a winding-down process, the silence of old age and the silence of dark spaces, the light of the moon risen and the sunset. And we never see things directly or bracketed, but from the side, "askew," from the chance or minor point of view—decentered. And further, in addition to the negative structure, the poem moves by supposition, possibility; "if" anything happens, another "will," the "will" here having the force of "may." Time becomes a matter of relativistic, open perspectives. There are hints, too, of other time frames: "golden village" suggests perhaps an Arcadian vision; the curtain image suggests an abandoned town, another age; the barge suggests the flow of time in the river; and, of course, the time of sunset to moonrise and the projection towards "all night" is contained in the lines. But it is almost as if these times refuse to be spoken; in fact, "Springtime," the time of the "spring moon," is only spoken, framed, by the title and by the last line in this poem that could refer to summer or fall just as well.

    Described by the hidden, the Other, the shine, the illusory, the silent, the unknown, the originless echo, Time itself seems to take on the character of possibility. Time is what is possible. The alterity and the presence of the moment mark, in conventional terms, an impossibility, however. And this is why Jacques Derrida, for example, in his critique of Aristotelian and Heideggerian conception of time, writes: "Time is a name for this impossible possibility" (*Margins*, 55). In Levertov's poetry, it gives rise to a haunting poem like "With Eyes at the Back of Our Heads," a poem built entirely on supposition. The speaker and others see a mountain "with eyes at the back of our heads," then doors "before us in a facade / that perhaps has no house

                                    199

in back of it." The situation, the speaker says, is like needing a
garment to step into, and so, strangely, a knitter is called for. The
characters want

> to enter the house, if there is a house,
> to pass through the doors at least
> into whatever lies beyond them,
>
> we want to enter the arms
> of the knitted garment.

[CEP 86]

Finally, when the "doors widen" and "the sleeves admit us," then "the
way to the mountain will clear" and the mountain will be seen more
specifically, more imaginatively, "echoing / with hidden rivers, mountain / of short grass and subtle shadows." What echoes here, then, is
not even an actuality, only the possibility of such. To think anything
more concrete, and permanent, is to limit the very idea of time. The
question of whether the "hidden rivers" or "subtle shadows" exist, or
are part of the imagination, or whether one leads to another, becomes
irrelevant. What becomes important is a movement of mind, a mode
of action, a way of thinking the possible about the impossible. What
is negated, finally, is impossibility itself.

Now the political implications of this critique of Aristotelian and
phenomenological time are enormous. Where no "time" has a priority
as governing origin, where tradition becomes a receding series of
echoes, where time is the possible, there is a certain freedom, a certain
mode of "action" I referred to with respect to "Interim." In "Kingdoms
of Heaven," for example, Levertov starts to describe "Paradise, an /
endless movie." It suggests endless details, and, like a film, can be re-
started anywhere—

> Stir of time, the sequence
> returning upon itself, branching
> a new way. To suffer, pains, hope.
> The attention
> lives in it as a poem lives or a song
> going under the skin of memory.

[OT 12]

So the realization also comes that time is what you carry within you, unrealized, the "dream" of "Interim"—

> Or, to believe it's there
> within you
> though the key's missing
> makes it enough? As if
> golden pollen were falling
> onto your hair from dark trees.
>
> [*OT* 12–13]

Here even the paradisiacal image of "golden pollen," of full potentiality, returns; time is the myth we make about ourselves, the history. And when the "key," the answer, is missing we found that the discovery is not a problem, but a proof of that faith as the moment is revealed in the golden shine of nothing. When we branch "a new way" we make new selves in making a new history. And it is in the context of the poem, as a mode of "action," that this vision is accomplished.

For Levertov, there is always something that transcends the particular, however absent that something is, however elsewhere, however much of an echo. This sense of absence and transcendence is the basis for historical change as Levertov says in a recent interview:

> I'm interested in Jung's ideas about synchronicity. We might think of our lives and our choices as a field of intersecting roads that we sometimes wander away from and sometimes return to. You have to be able to find ways back, but you also have to be able to feel you are on your own road, whatever happens. You have to be able to feel that you're not a character who has strayed into the wrong tale, the wrong play. There's a significance and appropriateness to what has happened; it is significantly linked to another thing, and what is called coincidence is occurring all the time. This is not in any way a form of determinism, but rather the sense that there is a large pattern we get glimpses of now and then [*Acts* 64–65].

And so, she writes in "Another Journey," our subject should be

> Not history, but our own histories,
> a brutal dream drenched with our lives,
> intemperate, open, illusory,

> to which we wake, sweating to make
> substance of it, grip it, turn
> its face to us, unwilling, and see the
> snowflakes glitter there, and melt.
>
> > [*CEP* 95]

In addition to noting here the key words in Levertov's move from ontology to politics—illusory, dream, the nothing we must "make substance of," the glitter—we should notice the way history is internalized and projected at once. The moment is both personal and the experience of others, the "our." Our relation to others must parallel the moment's relation to the elsewhere. That is why, for instance, she projects herself in "Three Meditations" as: "I, I, I, I. / I multitude, I tyrant, I / I angel, I you, you / world, battlefield, stirring" (*JL* 30). And it is why, in "During the Eichmann Trial" (*JL* 61–67), she can, in its three sections, move from the problematic of "Here is a mystery, // a person, an / other, an I" where she recognizes "We are members // of one another" to the memory of a particular killing, and finally to the way the experience spreads through time, creating mirror echoes of things we hardly want to hear. In the final lines—the glitter and shimmer that is the for-itself's consciousness of others, of what becomes, in history, our responsibility for others—suddenly becomes the shattering and scattering of a revolutionary sense of time. Here, as well as anywhere, the move from an interim to a larger political consciousness, from dream to action, and the link between her personal, metaphysical poems and later political poems are manifest:

> it is Crystal Night
> these spikes which are not
> pitched in the range of common hearing
> whistle through time
>
> smashing the windows of sleep and dream
> smashing the windows of history
> a whiteness scattering
> in hailstones
> each a mirror
> for man's eyes.
>
> > [*JL* 67]

An absent whistle sound, the elsewhere that we can't or won't listen to, the political voices that we delegate to distant places, now become the subjects of Levertov's poems. And it is the ontological structure she has established, the vision of time she has formulated, that will be the basis of those poems.

II

A Revolutionary Time

> Time *is* someone, . . . temporal dimensions, in so
> far as they perpetually overlap, bear each other out
> and ever confine themselves to making explicit what
> was implied in each, being expressive of that one
> single explosion or thrust which is subjectivity itself.
> —Merleau-Ponty, *The Phenomenology*
> *of Perception*

How does the absent, the originless echo, the nothing, structure our lives? What is the ontological power of nothingness? In other words, what is the force, as Levertov asks in "Travels," of the elsewhere? In this poem

> the unremembered
> makes itself into a granite-hued
> nylon scarf, tight at the throat—
> flies out
> backwards, a drifting
> banner, tangles
> the wheel.

[*SD* 49–50]

The movement of overlapping times tends to push towards a future like the car in the poem, but the absent, the unremembered, forces a focus on the present. Shifting to another, overlapping metaphor, Levertov suggests that the "shadow / not of a bird, not of a cloud, / draws a dark stroke over / the hills, the mind." This shadow, in typically negated terms, and linking inner and outer, hills and mind, is what causes the characters in the car to "shift gears, grind / up into the present in first, stop, / look out, look down." Looking down, they see "the lace designs incised / by feet of beetles," and looking up towards the "horizon" they seem to hear "flowers / vaster than cathedrals." This echo that consciousness imposed by the "shadow" of the "unremembered" allows Levertov to take the first step towards a political poetry. For example, in "Life at War" she describes how

> burned human flesh
> is smelling in Viet Nam as I write.
>
> Yes, this is the knowledge that jostles for space
> in our bodies along with all we
> go on knowing of joy, of love;
>
> our nerve filaments twitch with its presence
> day and night,
> nothing we say has not the husky phlegm of it in the saying. . . .
>
> [*SD* 80]

It is a consciousness that is also apparent in a poem like "A Marigold from North Vietnam," which describes the gift of the flower that "to the root-threads cling still / some crumbs of Vietnam" (*RA* 67). Analogously, in "Modes of Being" (*FD* 98–99), the time of jailed protesters against the conflict in Vietnam is broken, interrupted, by a second column of text describing events in that country.

It is an echo consciousness, then, that allows the poet to move from the "implied" to the "explicit," to borrow from Merleau-Ponty's epigraph to this section. For Merleau-Ponty, whom Levertov refers to in a couple of poems, "time is someone"—the consciousness of others in a political sphere. In the same way, Sartre, in the section "Concrete Relations with Others" in *Being and Nothingness*, says "the profound

meaning of my being is outside me, imprisoned in an absence" (473).
It is certainly appropriate, then, that one of Levertov's first forays into
directly "political" poetry occurs in a sequence, "The Olga Poems"
(*SD* 53–60), that is structured by the echoing consciousnesses of
herself and her sister. The sequence itself has six main sections whose
concerns gradually expand—a sort of rippling out of consciousness
within a structure that dialectically opposes the personal and the
political. The first section is very personal and brackets a particular
memory, and leads to the memory of Olga's growing political consciousness in section two. Section three, in three parts, analyzes the
concepts of history and time from a phenomenological perspective.
The fourth section questions larger patterns of history, as opposed to
individual awareness; beside Olga's deathbed is a candle—"all history," she says, "burned out, down / to the sick bone, save for //
that kind candle" (*SD* 57). The fifth section continues the critique of
history, attempting to substitute a personal mythology of memories,
as the narrator says—"A fairy tale existence." The last section counterpoints this mythic past against the present and a larger history to
attempt a dialectic synthesis.

The critical point in the sequence is section three. It begins with a
conventional view of time "from the hymnbook" through which the
narrator and her sister were "linked to words we loved"—"*Time like
an ever-rolling stream / bears all its sons away.*" Through memory
she is able to "inhale a sense of her [sister's] livingness in that instant,"
and a sense of the way her sister attempted to extend beyond the
childhood confinements of their garden wall, their way of life. For her
sister, this was a matter of revolutionary restructuring—"To change, /
to change the course of the river! What rage for order / disordered her
pilgrimage." The flow of the river implied fate, acceptance; now
Levertov can understand time in its historical movement, in its consciousness of "dream," absence, the "unremembered," "as unfolding,
not flowing, the pilgrim years." Unfolding implies choice, openness;
it is a notion that she will refer to later in "Staying Alive"—"I want
the world to go on unfolding" (*SA* 29)—with a more political, day-to-
day consciousness. Here in the Olga poems, unfolding suggests the
way Olga's life and political perspective "winds in me." The climax
of the poem in the last section is a kind of encomium on Olga's eyes,

the way they provoke and are the focal point of memories; what the narrator sees in those eyes, beyond the associations of what the narrator herself sees and how her sister could "sightread" Beethoven, is fear: "I think of your eyes in that photo, six years before I was born, / the fear in them." It is as if Olga could foresee the failures and tortures of her own life, the failed political movements of her time. The sequence ends with the narrator attempting to decipher the memory of her sister's gaze; while there is an "echo of our unknowing there," as there is in "Night on Hatchet Cove," there is also a faith that Olga's eyes knew, and that the narrator might learn from them. The glitter of the elsewhere, the nothing, becomes, here, the possible light of vision:

> I cross
> so many brooks in the world, there is so much light
> dancing on so many stones, so many questions my eyes
> smart to ask of your eyes, gold brown eyes,
> the lashes short but the lids
> arched as if carved out of olivewood, eyes with some vision
> of festive goodness in back of their hard, or veiled, or shining,
> unknowable gaze. . . .
>
> [SD 60]

Behind the gaze of the surface, then, and into the depths—what the narrator attempts to do, as she says in "Who Is at My Window" (*OT* 50), is to "move deeper into today," to ignore the fears that plague thoughts about the future, that plague Olga, or that plague the narrator in "Travels." And the method is to let time unfold, to keep a journal, what Levertov calls a notebook poem, "Staying Alive," which describes her experiences with the anti-war movement in the '60s and '70s. The journal provides a way, even when the object is "somewhere else," even in the presence-absence of a "black moon" that "turns away," of finding a "grasp" between the self and the Other (*CEP* 43–44). As Levertov says in an interview:

It's a question of structuring or grasping, of making intelligible to oneself by some mode or another. I mean, an abstraction like time, when it *is* an abstraction and not a phenomenon grasped by the senses, is something we can only have a partial sense of. One intellectually knows that there is sequence, cause and effect, but that doesn't mean very much until one can find images with which to flesh it out. More than restructuring, then, a sense of time seems to involve finding ways to grasp it. Time telescopes—some periods seem more full of emotion, intensity, realization than others which seem more lax [*Acts* 66].

The notebook, then, provides a vehicle to grasp time and history in both their intense and their lax modes, the poetic and the prosaic, the presence charged by the absent and the simple present. It provides a way to echo self and Other, consciousness and the objects of consciousness. As Heidegger says: "Self and world are not two beings, like subject and object, or like I and thou, but self and world are the basic determination of the Dasein itself in the unity of the structure of being-in-the-world" (*Problems*, 297). The notebook attempts to give the very process, almost as in drafts, through which the self appropriates its world on a day-to-day basis.

But there is also a curious problematic involved with the form. Maurice Blanchot writes, in "The Essential Solitude," that a "Journal represents the series of reference points that a writer establishes as a way of recognizing himself, when he anticipates the dangerous metamorphosis he is vulnerable to" (71)—the metamorphosis into the Other, the absent, that is, into Nothing at all. In other words, the function of a journal is not to record the nearness and presence of experience—or in Levertov's case, of action—but to assert this possibility, to somehow ensure it when it seems most tenuous. And yet, the text inevitably falsifies; it excludes, selects, supplements; it cannot help but condense or expand "actual" time, and so, in a sense, denies, deconstructs that time. The writer is in an impossible bind. Blanchot, again, says: "The Journal shows that already the person writing is no longer capable of belonging to time through ordinary firmness of action. . . . Already he does not really belong to history anymore, but he does not want to lose time, either, and since he no longer knows how to do anything but write, at least he writes at the demand of his day-to-day story and in keeping with his everyday preoccupations" (72). And what of the poet who stands on the protest lines, who is intimately involved with the Berkeley People's Park? Throughout Levertov's poem there is a tragic sense of isolation, marked by the difference, say, from the protester de Courcy Squire and from the others she mentions. The poem is an "act / of passionate attention" to try to touch Others: "Whom I would touch / I may not, / whom I may / I would / but often do not" (*SA* 34–35). We can refer to Blanchot, who places the journal in a larger context of what it means to write: "To write is to surrender oneself to the fascination of the absence of time. Here we are undoubtedly approaching the essence of solitude. The absence of time is not a purely negative mode. It is the time in which nothing begins. . . . Rather than a purely negative mode, it is a time without negation, without decision, when *here* is also *nowhere*. . . . The time of the absence of time is without a present, without a presence" (72–73). A contradiction, then—the very mode of writing that would seem to assert itself as a mode of action, a way to grasp history, also suggests a timelessness, a solitude, an essential absence. But this does not mean that Levertov has fallen back into the same dualities that mark the earlier poems. Indeed, as Blanchot writes, there is no dialectic structure here, especially in a notebook which does not exclude contradictions but includes them, though somewhat randomly in comparison to dialectics. And the shadow of a present—the elsewhere—is something the present poem "carries and hides" in its own moments; from isolation where the Other is "faceless," from the absence of time, the notebook writer understands, by the "intimacy" of such losses, precisely what is lost. And more—the paradoxical stance of the writer, an "I" and a fiction, faceless, both involved and detached, allows for what Blanchot calls "fascination," the "gaze of solitude," but a gaze that monopolizes the gazer, that allows the world to touch her more fully, allows the Other to become "Someone." Action in the notebooks, then, is always an indication that finds, at a distance, its own directions.

Even Levertov's preface for *To Stay Alive* reveals the problematic of the notebook form; she wants it to describe "an experience which is shared by so many and transcends the peculiar details of each life, though it can only be expressed in and through such details" (*SA* ix). Time has a rhythm akin to, but separate from, the sense of history one receives of an era: the dailiness of time is, she says in the poem,

> a substance that expands and contracts, a rhythm
> different from the rhythm of history,
> though history is made of the same
> minutes and hours.

> [*SA* 75]

That shared experience, the history that is a trace, suggests something of an overall structure despite the occasional format. The poem begins with "Prologue: An Interim," which sets the basic issues, and this is followed by four main sections, describing various events and separated by three sections, each entitled "Entr'acte," which analyze, provide transitions, and reevaluate metaphors. In fact, the overall structure is related to that of the Olga poems. That is, it moves from personal and political experiences to considerations of larger metaphysical and historical patterns, then turns towards myth or to the idyllic, and finally attempts a synthesis of these various contexts. The texture of the poem, though, is far more complex than such a schema suggests. Levertov's poem works in a way analogous to Marquez's *One Hundred Years of Solitude* with respect to the temporal rhythm and the problem of isolation. Cesare Serge describes Marquez's novel as a chronicle of circular time, a wheel that is continually moved forward or backward, out of pace, to crucial events as memory and imagination present them (67). The result is a curvature of time; for Levertov, the poem makes not a complete record, not even a confirmation of hopes, but an honest critique of the self's progress as it tries, incompletely, to return to an ever changing image, to echo itself.

"An Interim" initiates a comparison, in the context of de Courcy Squire's hunger strike in 1968, between the breakdown of language and the breakdown of temporal order and of history. Near the opening there is a description of children in a laundromat who say "yes" when they mean "no," or the opposite—a prelude to the language problems to follow, the "gross fiction" of official war accounts, the euphemisms for various horrors. Language, then, is a form of time, an accrual of history that time can also destroy:

> Language, coral island
> accrued from human comprehensions,
> human dreams,
>
> you are eroded as war erodes us.
>
> [SA 22]

Accrual is a luxury in a sense, as is time; Levertov as a poet has an "interim before the trial" for protesting that can be filled by the text of the poem, a luxury the jailed resisters don't have, for they "have

no interim / in which to come and go" (27). To emphasize this difference, Levertov juxtaposes the analysis with fragments from Ms.
Squire's account, reportage, prose diary, and idyllic interims about her
youth, a farm, the seashore. The aim is, as she says later, to "Knit /
idiom with idiom" (83), which is also a way of knitting time frames.
The first main section, in fact, analyzes the slogan from Olga, "Revolution or death," which becomes a refrain that is further explored
throughout the poem in several contexts. As an outsider, an other
herself, the speaker realizes that "Without a terrain in which, to
which, I belong / language itself is my one home, my Jerusalem, //yet
time and the straddled ocean / undo me" (*SA* 34). Her language, she
feels, is out of place, does not consolidate or project history: "My
diction marks me / untrue to my time." In other words, she says: "I
choose / revolution but my words / often already don't reach forward"
(*SA* 34–35). There is no sense of transcendence, power, otherness.
That is why, at the end of the second main section, she emphasizes
her "communion" in a new terrain—the Berkeley People's Park, and
inserts a set of directions for the protestors, as a way of ensuring that
the time and "the words hang on." By the end of the poem, she will
understand the "difficulty of what resonance has the language, for
you, for me,—I need to take up but the push and shove of events
[that's a telling phrase of Merleau-Ponty's!] has me, and meanwhile I
go on writing poems sometimes like shouting down a deep well" (76).
And sometimes she is reminded how powerless we are: "If you would
write me a poem / I could live forever," a girl named Judy writes, the
night she dies, to the narrator (77). And so, the narrator says, in lines
that fairly describe the tone of the poem: "Is there anything / I write
anymore that is not / elegy?" (33). And then, the larger consciousness
of a more sinister time sense—"There is no suicide in our time /
unrelated to history" (81). The language of the poem provides a
limited consolation, a vision that still must be enacted; the journal
form separates the writer, by the very act of writing, as much as it
links her with her subject.

The basic intellectual issue of the poem, then, is what constitutes
"revolution" as a temporal structure. On the one hand, the speaker
wants to retain the sense of "unfolding" time she has developed, but
on the other hand she understands that revolution means new begin-

ning, a hope. The danger is that it might be taken to mean repetition, circularity:

> Robert reminds me *revolution*
> implies the circular: an exchange
> of position, the high
> brought low, the low
> ascending, a revolving,
> an endless rolling of the wheel. The wrong word.
> We use the wrong word. A new life
> isn't the old life in reverse, negative of the same photo.
> But it's the only
> word we have . . .
>
> [41]

Revolution, as a re-beginning, also implies redefinition, and "Staying Alive" is in many ways a poem of redefinitions. Revolution must be redefined in terms of its ultimate aims, not as mere "exchange / of position." So, too, in the context of the struggle against tyrannies, "There comes / a time / when only anger / is love" (81). In this way, too, she can reinterpret Gandhi's pacifism to allow for activism, even provoked violence. The most comprehensive redefinition or revolutionary way of thinking, however, appears in section II, where the ideas of unfolding and revolving begin to coalesce. Time becomes

> not a sequence,
> as man's simplicity thinks, but radiates
> out from a center
>
> every direction,
> all
>
> dimensions
> (pulsations, as from living cells
> radiant—
>
> [43]

In these lines, with their open parenthesis, the relation between the individual and the other, the moment and history, dream and action, can be structured. The lives provide an imaginative way of touching, and of creating change, from single individuals outward; this personal vision thus becomes the most important meaning of revolutionary time.

Now later in the poem, Levertov will begin to radiate, in a sense, too far out; in section III, she visits Europe and views the difficulties in America from a privileged, almost pastoral perspective. She lives "A sense of stolen time" (69) as a result, but the detailed perspective, this extreme of her own Otherness, what Ponty and Sartre would call a "flight out of the self," at least gives "the tragic, fearful / knowledge of *present history,* / of doom" (66). She becomes haunted by sensations of the pastoral turning into a wasteland:

> I don't know
> how to be mute, or deaf, or blind,
> for long, but
> wake and plunge into next day
> talking, even if I say *yesterday* when I mean *tomorrow,*
> listening, even if what I'm hearing
> has the *approaching* sound of terror,
> seeing, even if the morning light
> and all it reveals appear
> pathetic in ignorance,
>   like unconscious heroes trapped on film,
> raised shadows about to descend and smash their skulls.
>
> [64]

The irony she begins to understand is that in the midst of a revolutionary history, her own language, her own time sense, may also deteriorate. What she must avoid is the pastoral tendency to create an unchanging vision, a "tunnel" vision that brackets off the world, a vision that would suggest not "endurance" but passivity. The narrator understands, finally, that the luxury of her own position is itself a pastoral gesture that must be challenged. Thus she says, "we can't wait: time is not on our side." Though time becomes, here, a radical Otherness, it is also something that she temporalizes—as she does in "A Figure of Time" (*OT* 29–30), where an old man, a father time who holds Levertov potentially in memory, is himself in danger of extinction. To temporalize time in "Staying Alive" is to think that unthinkable, the end of time, the extinction of the self.

This sense of urgency is stated more bluntly in an interview: "More imperative, what we must feel today is the unprecedented degree of likelihood that life on this planet may come to an end. We're on the edge of time in that respect. It's impossible to have a conversation about one's sense of time, of history, right now, without dealing with this threat" (*Acts* 66). In *The Sorrow Dance* there is a haunting poem, called "Living." This poem starts out as a pastoral, but the ending forces a re-reading, a revolution, so that the images of "fire," "wind blowing," "shivering," and "red" take on a more apocalyptic accent, especially in the context of the book's political thrust—

> The fire in leaf and grass
> so green it seems
> each summer the last summer.
>
> The wind blowing, the leaves
> shivering in the sun,
> each day the last day.
>
> A red salamander
> so cold and so
> easy to catch, dreamily
>
> moves his delicate feet
> and long tail. I hold
> my hand open for him to go.
>
> Each minute the last minute.

[*SD* 90]

The resonance of the poem here is the result of the perfect and "delicate" balance of pastoral and, say, nuclear wars, even as the time in the refrain gradually contracts. Living, staying alive—the terms of Levertov's poetic of time—have become words for survival. The notion of grasping, of holding, becomes all the more intense and essential. Time now becomes redefined as potentially futureless, and even "Staying Alive" ends on the word "possible," itself couched in a subjunctive construction. So the danger is in our vision of the future: "Blink of an eyelid, / nothing, / obsolete future" (*RA* 8). Without a teleology, even the loose structure of the notebook form would fall apart.

The whole question of time and language, then, must be rethought. The poet must, as Levertov suggests in the title of one book, "relearn the alphabet, / relearn the world" (*RA* 119). "Wanting the Moon" enacts a process of redefinition, based upon the negative structure we have seen earlier, which leads to an oxymoronic vision. The speaker in the poem sees something that is "not" moon, flower, bird, or whatever, but a jester, an image almost of her own self: "The music rings from his bells, / gravely, a tune of sorrow, // I dance to it on my riverbank" (*RA* 42). What she listens to is not the context but the energy; what she celebrates is not sorrow but music itself. And yet, she dances sorrowfully. So too, the poet's stance becomes increasingly elegiac through her career. And the dance, the dance is the dialectic process that the poem enacts; what she learns in the daily workings of the notebook poem is that process becomes as important, at least, as event, climax, idea. The process involves not only an unveiling, as Heidegger would have it (*PLT* 187–210), but also a reveiling, or as Freud would say, the erecting of screen images. In other words, there is a further flight out of the self. Take, for example, the dramatic associative shifts in "Craving":

> Wring the swan's neck, seeking
> a little language of drops of blood.
>
> How can we speak of blood, the sky
> is drenched with it.
>
> A little language
> of dew, then.
>
> It dries.
>
> A language
> of leaves underfoot.
> Leaves on the tree, trembling

in speech. Poplars
        tremble and speak
if you draw near them.

[*RA* 45]

We can see, here, the links to the earlier poetry of absence, and how sometimes Levertov's poetics of absence can be taken for a poetics of presence. What we seem to be left with in the last few lines is the trembling, saying, and nearness of the poplars, but behind the voice is the "language / or leaves underfoot." The leaves, in turn, originate in association with "drenched," which originally referred to the swan's neck, which may have originated—where? Thus originless, proceeding by association, the first, violent image is muted, supplemented, by a sense of presence given by the language of dew, leaves, and poplars, by the progressively redefined and refined language of the poem itself. The poem, in other words, enacts the move away from historical or everyday accounts towards a mythic mode, a move that occurs in the Olga poems and "Staying Alive," but which is the more successful because more complete, more self-contained.

The mythic impulse is important in Levertov as a means of relearning an alphabet for the world, whether the basis for the myth is in a simple transcendent gesture, a personal past, or traditional myths. But it is important to remember that for Levertov a simple mythic poetry is inadequate. As she says in *Poet in the World*, "Myth related metaphor . . . is static; it shares with myth a deeper than merely descriptive meaning, but reveals only one instant, one fixed aspect, of such meaning" (*PIW* 68). For her, the mythological must be a process that occurs within the poem, not as a result of it, or referred to by it. Thus, the "truly mythic must *be* genuinely forceful and . . . it therefore must partake in some degree of the dramatic" (*PIW* 68). The truly mythic, then, is itself a temporalized structure which reminds us that learning its terms, its language, its dramatic relationships is a gradual, never-ending process of reevaluation of ourselves. "A Tree Telling of Orpheus" has as its subject precisely this process (Rosenfield, 195–97). The poem, told from the point of view of the tree, recounts the passing of Orpheus, whose song "ripples" a sense of being, so that, the tree says, "language / came into my roots" and there is a birth of consciousness. Orpheus tells of journeys, dreams,

215

desires—in short, absences which are themselves culminated when
Orpheus dies. The trees, which have followed him, miraculously, wait.
But rather than remain passive, the tree realizes that

> what we have lived
> comes back to us.
> We see more.
> We feel as our rings increase,
> something that lifts our branches, that stretches our furthest
> leaf-tips
> further.

> [*RA* 85]

The dramatic context in myth gets translated into a metamorphic
vision, a vision that will be further developed in *Life in the Forest*. In
the context of the poems we have been discussing, however, the poem
is important, first, as an indicator that the diary vision of "Staying
Alive" may prove insufficient by itself and, second, that language *per
se* has a mythic-dramatic origin that can be explored in order to
dialectically reevaluate a position, to enact change.

But can a language be transformed? Surmounted? Revolutionized?
On the one hand, Levertov would agree with Derrida, who writes that
all discourse is governed by the constraints of language, "a reserve of
language, the systematic reserve of a lexicology, a grammar, a set of
signs and values" (*Margins*, 177). These limit what can be thought
and expressed and as Levertov discovers in "Staying Alive," there is
no escaping this language we inherit; one must use language schemes
against language. Levertov's strategy, which recalls Mallarmé's and,
more recently, Sollers' *Nombres*, is to deconstruct language at the
level of the alphabet, the basis of structure itself. It is a strategy that
combines her search for originless origins with the need to revolu-
tionize. So "Relearning the Alphabet" is structured in sections headed
by letters of the alphabet, but the activity takes place between that
text of associations based on the alphabet, not meaning, and the
meanings actually derived by those associations. The text, then, exists
in a non-place, and it almost appears authorless in its reliance on
language to structure it ("Transmutation is not / under the will's
rule," *RA* 119). It is, in a sense, the ultimate mythic text, a text whose

time is without grounding; or it is grounded in its own process, "lost, refound, exiled— / revealed again / in the palm of / mind's hand, moonstone / of wax and wane" (*RA* 120).

The text itself is in some ways indecipherable, without a key, in the sense that its mesh of interconnections could go on forever, the poem's text marking, as it says, a "beginning," and in the sense that it begins again everywhere. It is a poem more occasional and yet, within the linguistic parameters of the alphabet, more controlled than "Staying Alive." Let us begin, then, at the beginning:

> A
> Joy—a beginning. Anguish, ardor.
> To relearn the ah! of knowing in unthinking
> joy: the beloved stranger lives.
> Sweep up anguish as with a wing-tip,
> brushing the ashes back to the fire's core.
>
> B
> To be. To love an other only for being.
>
> C
> Clear, cool? Not those evasions. The seeing
> that burns through, comes through to
> the fire's core.
>
> D
> In the beginning was delight. A depth
> stirred as one stirs fire unthinking.
> Dark   dark   dark   .   And the blaze illumines
> dream.
>
> [*RA* 110–11]

First, it is not the beginning, but "a" beginning. In fact, "In the beginning was delight" suggests that the biblical text is itself a pretext, but that even it, beginning with light, is preceded by an absence of light, a delimiting of it, a de-light that is no light, nothing, what cannot be spoken. This is confirmed in the opening lines. Before the alphabet, before "A," there is an "ah!" an "unthinking / joy," a pre-consciousness that yet redefines the "ardor" and "anguish" of any

217

search. That is why what has to be learned, spoken, thought, is something to "relearn." Process, then; what is the nature of this beginning, if not the "to be" of "being," which must, as we already know, contain the notion of the "other," the "evasions" of the self, but "evasions" that "shine" to the "core," presence. "Core," in turn, suggests "depth," "delight," the "dark" "dream" language shines on, "illumines." So the embers are rekindled; the poem discovers a critical symbol in the flame as a sign of revolution:

> E
> Endless
> returning, endless
> revolution of dream to ember, ember to anguish,
> anguish to flame, flame to delight,
> delight to dark and dream, dream to ember
>
> F
> that the mind's fire may not fail.
>
> [*RA* 111]

What occurs, then, is a continual pulsation of light and dark, presence and absence, mind and world. As "F" goes on to suggest, the transformation in the poem is from "farewell" to simply "faring." It is a poem that constantly puts into play the trace of one word in another, the trace of letters in different words; it marks a constant process, then, of erasing and tracing, and "endless / revolution" of language and its meaning, of the temporality of language. The trace, or origin, like the teleology, is a play of evasions (36). Thus (not) going back to the origin is a form of "faring," of endurance, the "grace of transformed / continuance" ("G"), "of continuance, to find / I-who-I-am again" ("I," "J"). In the poem, then,

> All utterance
> takes me step by hesitant step towards
>
> T
> —yes, to continuance: into
>   that life beyond the dead-end where
> (in a desert time of
> dry strange heat, of dust

that tinged mountain clouds with copper,
turn of the year impending unnoticed,
the cactus shadows brittle thornstars,
time of
desolation)   I was lost.

[*RA* 118]

The quest that is the poem leads inevitably to absence. In the "time
of desolation," the narrator says, "Absence has not become / a presence" ("L"). The very fact of language, its "presence," prevents such
an occurrence: "Lost in the alphabet / I was looking for / the word I
can't now say," that word being "(love)." The absence of the word,
bracketed in parentheses, like the "time of desolation," does not,
except in the language that denies it, exist. The word is always a
"secret" ("S") that the "vain will" ("Y") tries to uncover and name,
finally, coldly; "will," in this poem, is associated with ash, cinder,
darkness. This absence is what allows for a new temporal order, a
new sense of the anteriority of the elsewhere:

Vision sets out
journeying somewhere,
walking the dreamwaters:
arrives
not on the far shore but upriver,
a place not evoked, discovered.

[*RA* 119]

In attempting to return to the time before the first time, the poem
returns, as the alphabet does, to its own mysteries. The origin of time
is "a place not evoked, discovered." The ambiguity of the meaning
here is itself a mark of the endless ambiguity of language, of the way
time itself must be, as Derrida says, something different. For Levertov,
the elsewhere, this endless echo, is given in the closing lines:

Z
Sweep up
anguish as with a wing-tip:

the blaze addresses
a different darkness:

absence has not become
the transformed presence the will
looked for
but other: the present,

that which was poised already in the ah! of praise.

[*RA* 120]

What is present is not the letter but the evasive sound, the "ah!" the echoed origin of "A." And "Z"—there is no "Z" word here, but it is in a sense everywhere and nowhere. It is hidden in the shimmer of being, of nothingness, in the midst of blaze, that word that contains at its cave the "a" and "z" that echo each other, transform each other. And the "present" already there; as Derrida says, "It can no longer be named 'present' except through indirect discourse, in the quotation marks of citation, storytelling, fiction. It can only go out into language by a sort of ricochet. Transformed here into a regular device, this ricochet confers a quality of indirection, a detour or angle upon every so-called simple, natural, obvious evidence of presence in itself" (*Dissemination*, 303). The ricochet, the echo, then structures our lives, not so much in the world of action as in the language we use to understand ourselves. The journey from the early poems to the political poems and into these structures of thought in "Relearning the Alphabet" has been precisely this indirect movement. What Levertov has succeeded in doing is to arrive at a conception of time and history intimately linked with language, the "soft gleam of words" she refers to in "Interim." She has, really, opened up Derrida's dream for a different history and temporality: "Such a *difference* would at once, again, give us to think a writing without presence and without absence, without history, without cause, without *archia*, without *telos*, a writing that absolutely upsets all dialectics, all theology, all teleology, all ontology" (*Margins*, 66). The revolutionary sense of time, then—a time that Levertov discovers in her movement "deeper into today," into the world of Others that populate her journals and others, but an unexpected time, a time found not in direct action, but in the ricochet of language. A new correction, then—Merleau-Ponty's "time is someone"—must be rewritten: "time is someone's language." But whose?

III

The Metamorphosis of Time

> Therefore it is in the very act by which our mind
> wishes and desires that we have to seize the principle
> of duration. Far from being like rational time, a time
> composed of events experienced and gone, to which
> ceaselessly something is added, this time affirms
> itself a living and multiple entity, which from mo-
> ment to moment advances, in metamorphosing it-
> self, into the future.
> —Georges Poulet, *Studies in Human Time*

In her "Introductory Note" to *Life in the Forest*, Levertov explains the changes in style that have been evolving in her poetry. The changes are motivated, she says, by "two forces":

First, a recurring need—dealt with earlier by resort to a diarylike form, a poem long enough to include prose passages and discrete lyrics—to vary a habitual lyric mode; not to abandon it, by any means, but from time to time to explore more expansive means; and second, the decision to try to avoid overuse of the autobiographical, the dominant first-person singular of so much of the American poetry—good and bad—of recent years [vii].

Levertov's avoidance of the "I" is part of a larger project to avoid subjectivist modes, a poetry of pure presence, as we have seen, and so to express a "flight out of the self," to borrow from Sartre. It is, then, part of a larger step towards transcendence she has been making since her concern with the "elsewhere." For Sartre, there is a certain

221

negation of the self through which the world can be known; though it knows itself through the world, the elsewhere, the nothing, it is itself not-other. So, for him, human reality is a process that marks the "unachieved totality of negatives" (251–52). The negative mode, which we have seen at every step in Levertov's career, is the mode of transcendence—denying the self to extend beyond it. For Heidegger, the negative mode, as it is in Hegel, is the only way to correct error and assert the absent-presence (*Problems*, 332). For Levertov, now, though, the transcendent takes on a non-human dimension. Thus, Sartre says: "Man, being transcendence, establishes the meaningful by his very coming into the world, and the meaningful because of the very structure of transcendence is a reference to other transcendents which can be interpreted without recourse to the subjectivity which has established it" (767). So in "Tropic Ritual" (*CB* 50), for instance, the physical world has a consciousness of its own "without recourse" to human consciousness. The moon's "command transforms" the leaves in an "unwitnessed hour" when "humans / have withdrawn."

And yet, who speaks the poem? We can get a sense of the kind of transcendence Levertov is aiming for by looking at the end of "By Rail through the Earthly Paradise, Perhaps Bedfordshire." The title itself suggests, with its "perhaps," the desire not to bound by a single place, and the speaker hopes the train will halt so that

> In the deep aftermath
> of its faded rhythm, I could become
>
> a carved stone
> set in the gates of the earthly paradise,
>
> an angler's fly
> lost in the sedge to watch the centuries.
>
> [*F* 47]

The speaker would become, in a sense, time herself; the transcendent, as Heidegger suggests, is rooted in temporality (*Problems*, 323–24). The whole book, *Footprints*, itself suggests this strange status of the self, speaking, but hardly known, or known by the traces, the footprints it leaves, the footprints, Levertov says, of "someone" (*F* 1).

"Hut," the second poem in the book, is a description without characters, or the character is given in the fact of the hut itself, which is a "Threshold: a writing, / small stones inlaid, footworn" (*F* 1). Yet this temporality contains, holds, the eternal, the transcendental within it, in its own emptiness, literally a hole in the roof: "By night, through smokehole, / the star" (*F* 1).

Where, as Derrida would say, the inner and the outer as categories no longer apply because they enforce each other, where the temporal and the eternal not only echo each other but contain each other, the self is portrayed as fleeing itself towards a transcendental vision beyond "discrete lyrics"—yet finds itself contained in the very temporality of its language (*M* 60–65). This is precisely the situation in "The Life Around Us":

> Poplar and oak awake
> all night. And through
> all weathers of the days of the year.
> There is a consciousness
> undefined.
> Yesterday's twilight, August
> almost over, lasted, slowly changing,
> until daybreak. Human sounds
> were shut behind curtains.
> No human saw the night in this garden,
> sliding blue into morning.
> Only the sightless trees,
> without braincells, lived it
> and wholly knew it.
>
> [*F* 57]

Totally other, beyond consciousness, the world, time, are nothing. And yet, once they are known, once they are echoed or ricocheted, "consciousness / undefined" becomes precisely defined, the transcendental becomes temporal ("August," and the passage of time in the words and given by the words of the poem), and the absence of "Human sounds" becomes the poem itself. The poem is a text both defined and undefined, both spoken and silent. It is a strange metamorphosis of nothing, or something else into anything. As Levertov says in "3 a.m., September 1, 1969," a poem that begins in a way at the opposite pole of "The Life Around Us" and works in the opposite direction, from the specific to the unnamed, the time "could be any age, / four hundred years ago or a time / of post-revolutionary peace" (*F* 17).

What we have here is not, as in "Life at War," an echoing of two times or places, but an echoing of two structures for time, two temporalities, human and non-human. A similar double structure occurs in "A Woman Pacing Her Room . . ." (*LF* 74–75), where the poem's two parts suggest first an apocalyptic vision, where "beauty is balanced upon / the poignance of brevity," and second, a slow, fading of time. In "The Long Way Round," the instant and the time preceding it become a unified double structure; self-consciousness occurs:

> slowly—for though
> it's in a flash we
> know we know,
> yet before the flash there's a long
> slow, dull, movement of fire
> along the well-hidden
> line of the fuse.
>
> [*LF* 53–56]

In "Man Alone" the doubleness becomes a contrast between the time of the sun going down, as it "writes / a secret name in its own blood for remembrance," and the moon's motion: "though it tarries / a moment, it vanishes / without trace" (*F* 51). In all these cases, the two structures of time are always complementary; neither can exist without the other. Levertov succeeds, in this sort of stereoscopic vision, in more fully discovering the links between being and non-being. "The Balance" is a good example:

> At the door, some *never*, some *let be*,
> those pestering halftruths of impatience . . .
>
> Yet the daily bread gets baked,
> a rush of initiative takes the stairs
> three at a time.

> Crippled by their feet,
> two swans waddle to water,
> the first of them already
> slowly and silently has ripped the silk of evening.
>
> [*FD* 48]

Being and nothingness, the human and the non-human, the patient and the impatient, the threshold and continuance—each of these becomes part of a larger structure. It is a structure, as the accumulation of these dualities suggests, of "unachieved totalities"—what Derrida calls the play of possibilities initiated by such double inscriptions of time. And it is not just "polysemy," as Derrida reminds us, but something more radical, more revolutionary—"dissemination" (*Dissemination*, 303). In "Split Second," Levertov describes the "flimsy shred of the world" she holds the edge of, the "tribes of [her] years passing" and conscious of so many other lives, "And each other dreamer / clutching (wideawake) a different frayed / scrap of fabric" (*LF* 48). Time itself, then, becomes fragmentary, a half-truth, a partial concept.

But more—the fragments are always in the process of being reconstituted. Time becomes metamorphic, extending the impulse we saw back in "Interim," where fears could be "transformed," and later, in the day-to-day evolution of the notebook. A metamorphic time is a perfect solution for Levertov's double writing. Mikhail Bakhtin, for example, says: "Metamorphosis or transformation is a mythological sheath for the idea of development—but one that unfolds not so much in a straight line as spasmodically, a line with 'knots' in it, one that therefore constitutes a distinctive type of *temporal sequence*" (*Dialogic Imagination*, 113). Double writing is a form that allows Levertov to give equal emphasis both to moments of transcendental "glitter" and to the everyday, political acts within a structure more coherent than that of "Staying Alive." That structure itself is the "more expansive means" she refers to in the "Introductory Note," cited above. Without this expansive form that combines a conversational tone with lyric intensity, the vision of the poems would remain bounded, like a "quivering cocoon," as Levertov writes in "Emblem, II":

> The world
> is made of days, and is itself
> a shrouded day.
> It stifles. It's our world, and we
> its dreams, its creased
> compacted wings.
>
> [*LF* 46]

In the more expansive mode, almost anything can happen—"A brown oakleaf, left over from last year, / turns into a bird and flies off singing" ("Run Aground," *LF* 50). But this does not mean that the dualistic tensions in Levertov's poetry suddenly disappear, for, as she says a few lines later, the moon fills the empty space of the leaf, in a gesture we've seen before, and she is left "looking sullenly back at it, / human, thrown / back on my own resources." Similarly, in "Letter," the wind and rain transform her house into an island where "I'm alone / silent within the gusting weather" (*LF* 120). What is curious in both of these last citations, though, is that despite the underscored difference of their humanity, which separates them from the non-human, there is nonetheless a sense of participation—the looking back at the moon, the existence "within" the weather—that does not occur in the earlier poem which stressed a radical otherness. Her muse becomes "The Dragonfly Mother," as the title of a poem in *Candles in Babylon* suggests: "Her children / are swimmers, nymphs and newts, metamorphic" (*CB* 14). But the change is always a version of the self: "When she tells / her stories she listens; when she listens / she tells you the story you utter" (*CB* 14). What she provides are "Journeys over the fathomless waters."

The most directly metamorphic poem is "Metamorphic Journal," the title itself suggesting the way the poem fits within Levertov's development. The poem is a "dance" of "instants," of "moments of absolute sureness" that express, finally, the "act of the mind / to act." In this poem of three parts, fire and water interpenetrate:

> where you are
> is within the envisioning fire
> inside the cave of the mind
> where Images ride to the hunt on the creviced walls
> as the flame struggles out of the smoke.

All about you is watery, within lies the dark
cave, and the fire.

[*LF* 134]

In this poem, where the narrative is "present, but / not present" (133),
other existences, other selves emerge from within—or rather the
within and without, as in the cave image above, continue to be problematic. "I wanted to know / the river's riveriness with my self" (127),
she says early in the poem, only to reveal later: "let me say / it is I
who am a river" (128). The whole sequence of water images begins,
really, with the idea of "ocean of thoughts," with a figure of speech,
language itself, and with the way the poem makes a symbol of the
figure, internalizing and externalizing it at once:

> If I came to a brook, off came my shoes,
> looking could not be enough—
> or my hands at least must be boats or fish for a minute
> to know the purling water at palm and wrist.
> My mind would sink like a stone
> and shine underwater,
> dry dull brown
>   turned to an amber glow.

[*LF* 126]

Now this sort of movement we have traced, from mention to symbol
to metamorphosis, extends to include relationships with others. In
the middle section, the narrator says—

> I met a friend
> as I walked by the river that runs
> through my mind
>
> Or he himself
> was the river,
> for this river
>
> rises in metamorphosis
> when some confluence
> of wills occurs far-off.

[*LF* 129]

The elsewhere, the "far off," is actually not so detailed; there is, after all, a "confluence / of wills," and both are, or are part of, or hold, the river itself. The emphasis is on blending, not echoing. The metamorphosis of river to fire is accomplished when the swirling movement of the water is used to describe the way wind "eddies" (131) through the leaves and the imagination is described as a burning tree. The process could go on forever, with further, far-off confluences. What the poem begins to question, finally, is once again the question of origins. While the metamorphic vision takes the narrator out of herself and inside herself, she asks what the relationship is, far back, between the world and imagination, act and dream. It is the question that never leaves Levertov:

> What is the counterpart, then,
> in these or myself,
> to imagined, retrieved, pines and oaks of the past
> uttering ocean on inland gusts of autumnal wind?
>
> [130]

The "answer" is in the last line of the poem: "they enter the dance" (134). The point is that, in the metamorphic mode, the past, origins, are not so much absent as multiple: the present could be derived from anywhere, any point in the dance, any echo.

In a way, the hope is that, by entering the dance, the ravages of external, daily time can be transcended. This is what "Life in the Forest" examines. The poem describes a woman whose house is "mumbled by termites" and yet "her desire / fixed on a chrysalis" as she ignores everyday time. The poem as a whole counterpoints these two sorts of time—one historical, the other the work of "Eternity's / silver blade." When the butterfly comes forth, it looks at her and her imagination transforms it: "It was a man / her own size, / and it touched her everywhere." The result of all this is that, "when time, later, / once the Eternal had left to go wandering / knocked on her door, she smiled, / and would not open" (118). Her eternal lover gone, the leaves around her change, the termites continue, but "She was marked / by the smile within her. Its teeth / bit and bit at her sense of loss." Once initiated, the process of change continues until, ironically, an ideal state is subverted, eternity deconstructed. Metamorphosis is itself metamorphosed into a dead end, stasis, loss; the future becomes an elegy, absence. What the metamorphic vision discovers, then, is that the play of language, the play of possibilities is limited. It occurs within the echo structure, in that blank space between the two mountains. If there is an advance in the sense that time becomes more coherent and that more possibilities are revealed and realized, there is also a greater "sense of loss," a greater pain.

Those limits structure the present of the opening sequence, "Homage to Pavese," Levertov's strongest single group of poems, in *Life in the Forest*, probably her strongest book. Behind the metamorphic mode and its echo structure is the dialectic pattern we have seen operate in the "Olga Poems" and "Staying Alive," and which operates in "Relearning the Alphabet" in a different way: an initial problem, accompanied by some forays from a personal perspective; a mythic and autobiographical swerve into a past to search new structures, to re-examine the present; a return in which the initial temporal structure is redefined in more expansive terms. The first poem, "Human Being," a coda of sorts, establishes the problem—the limits of transformation:

> Always the mind
> walking, working, stopping sometimes to kneel
> in awe of beauty, sometimes leaping, filled with the energy
> of delight, but never able to pass
> the wall, the wall
> of brick that crumbles and is replaced.
>
> [*LF* 3]

The wall becomes, literally, a wall of ignorance; those who cannot learn "suffer, are tortured, die." What is at stake, and here Levertov's metamorphic sense of unity has advanced her vision, is the way the mind and the world, dream and action—to use her original terms—are linked. The way one overcomes the wall is to metamorphose time itself, to restructure it. Thus in the next poem the narrator argues "which beginning / to begin with?" ("Writing to Aaron"). She could "echo / the sound of facts, their weather," and create a symbolic time, or she could try "chronological narrative," which seems only to participate in the temporal passage it records, "and that would be nothing, / dust, parchment dried up, invisible ink" (5). Perhaps, she suggests, "I'll leave the whole story / for you to imagine" and tell only a mythic tale about a tree. Finally, she realizes, in a Heideggerian way, that it is not so much the myth but language itself, the "Word," with all its transformations, that she will "always hear, each leaf / imprinted, syllables in our lives" (6).

Implicit in "Writing to Aaron" and in its concern with the structures initiated by different beginnings, and also in the two short narratives that follow it, is the function of memory. Precisely how origins and memory work is counterpointed in two poems, "Chekov on the West Heath" (10–14) and "A Mystery (Oaxaca, Mexico)," themselves separated by a sequence of poems that examine the ways men and women deal with the changes of time and with each other's temporalities, pasts, and hopes. The Chekov poem deals with the confluence of times suggested by the "Metamorphic Journal." The narrator begins with memories and dreams about the different characters in her life, seeing herself as an Other, and about the story by Chekov, which seems to provide the time with a coherent structure. In addition, the land itself seems to persist as a presence:

> What has the Heath,
> Which Bet has lived close to always, and I,
> though decades away, never quite lost sight of,
> meant in our lives? A place of origin
> gives and gives, as we return to it,
> bringing our needs.
>
> [13]

And because they always bring their needs, which change, and because memory changes, what the land means, the past, what Chekov "has meant / and goes on meaning, can't be trapped / into close definition." Like one of the characters in the story, who carries in him "the seed of change," their "little hill / in time, in history," they can constantly redefine their whole temporal structure. Chekov, who provided the coherent vision, "looked over our shoulders" as they glanced back at the hill, the past—

> half of our lifetime gone by, or more,
> till we turn to see

who you were, who you are, everpresent, vivid,
luminous dust.

[14]

But while the past as origin, however redefined by fiction, by illusion, allows a regenerative vision in the Chekov poem, it is almost non-existent in "A Mystery." The poem concerns a street vendor: "Decades he has passed / back and forth and around and back and forth / in the square." But it is the very repetition, the worst sense of revolution, that marks the origin as inaccessible:

> When he was young there was
> something he wanted badly,
> some desire that flamed in his eyes once,
> like a spiralling saint's day star it was,
> rising from the heart when someone, something,
> put a match to it . . . What was it? He's calm but
> there's something
> he can't remember.

[22]

But the past does exist as a trace, and so a possibility. The vendor, then, seems to live in two worlds: "The bells of two unsynchronized / clocks are ringing: eleven-midnight" (23). And he carried a woven woollen blanket "through the years," a burden he won't put down. The burden is precisely the lack of a past that can be metamorphosed and so regenerated. And yet there is a certain strength, a faith, that even the narrator ("I'll lie down / as if in the snow") can't understand. If metamorphosis ultimately means the metamorphosis of metamorphosis itself into the wall, perhaps simple endurance, the poem seems to argue, will provoke memory, initiate change.

The final three poems in the sequence deal with the relationship between a character and her dying mother. It is important to note that the narrative voice in the sequence gradually metamorphoses itself into a sort of double consciousness. The character becomes a voice for the narrator, who has, in Sartre's sense, taken flight out of the pure, bracketed self (*BN* 51); a metamorphosis has occurred as the self flies from its cocoon, to use Levertov's imagery. But the flight is also one of anguish, as Sartre so carefully analyzes it; the self seems always separated, even in the midst of the metamorphic process. As the self rises into the elsewhere, the nothing, "it is from the point of view of beyond the world that being is organized into the world, which means on the one hand that human reality rises up as an emergence of being in non-being and on the other hand that the world is "suspended" in nothingness. Anguish is the discovery of this double, perpetual nihilation" (51). This, at least, explains the melancholy tone that so marks *Life in the Forest* and *Candles in Babylon*. More specifically, in the last part of the sequence, it is manifest in the feelings associated with the mother's death, the passing of a past.

The first problem to be confronted, in "A Daughter (I)," is that of language: "a terminal wall; / there would be words to deal with: funeral, burial, / disposal of effects" (26). In fact, it seems as if the death will not be real, only the words. And it is precisely this strange sense of detachment that allows the daughter to project herself into the consciousness of her mother ("will her mother now / ever rise from bed, walk out of her room, see if her yellow rose / has bloomed again?") (26), even into her past "to the London garden, forty, fifty years ago / her mother younger than *she* is now" (26). This projection prepares for the metamorphic climax of the sequence:

> Now mother is child, helpless; her mind
> is clear, her spirit proud, she can even laugh—
> but half-blind, half-deaf, and struck down
> in body, she's a child in being at the mercy
> of looming figures who have the power
> to move her, feed her, wash her, leave or stay
> at will. And the daughter feels, with horror
> metamorphosed: *she's* such a looming figure.
>
> [27]

What she fears here is her own death, her own end projected by the metamorphosis. Although the mother gives her a blessing, she leaves, and though "she wants / to hear it again and again," her fear stops her: "she does not go back." Instead, seeing herself as a "monstrous" figure of time and death, she tries to avoid time altogether:

> She imagines herself
> entering a dark cathedral to pray, and blessedly

falling asleep there, and not wakening
for a year, for seven years, for a century.

[28]

Such fear, or dread, says Heidegger, is always a projection, and so acts
as a powerful structuring device for our lives. The reaction is often to
distance oneself, to make the other more radically other, thus to
subvert the metamorphic mode and attempt to establish an idyllic
setting. It results, Heidegger suggests, in precisely the same lack of
understanding that the narrator warned about in "Human Being"
(*BT* H141–42). And so, in "A Daughter (II)," the daughter has fled not
herself towards the other, but the other back into herself, into stasis:
"Southward, deathward, time inside the jet / pauses" (29). When she
does return, she hopes a while for a stop to time—

> This tide that does not ebb, this persistence
> stuck like a plane in mournful clouds,
> what can it signify?
>
>   is any vision
>
> an entrance into a garden
> of recognitions and revelations, Eden
> of radiant comprehensions, taking
> timeless place in the wounded head, behind
> the closed, or glazed half-open, eyes?

[30]

The hope that the mother might transcend death, though, is abandoned when she realizes that what would be expressed by the mother
has to occur in "words" that counterpoint "joy" and "pain," that is,
when the daughter re-enters a dialectical frame of mind. Finally, she
realizes, all dialectic, all metamorphosis is incomplete: "something /
went unsaid. And there's no place / to put whatever it was, now, / no
more chance" (31).

The unsaid is a more radical notion than the silence we discovered
earlier: what the narrator discovers is that the past has never been
present. It is an illusion, striven for by the same metamorphic process
that projects forward in time. Everything is transition and trace; the
only way for metamorphosis to continue is to transform the concepts
of beginning and ending. It must aim towards transcendence, but

since it cannot stop, it cannot achieve such transcendence and so exists, after all, within the echoes of beginning and ending. This, then, is the basis of all the double inscriptions that have marked Levertov's work from the beginning. And the poem "Death in Mexico," which ends the Pavese sequence, summarizes this. When the mother dies, so does the garden—"each day / less sign of the ordered, / thought-out oasis, a squared circle her mind / constructed for rose and lily" (32). And this confluence of mind and world, a perfect metamorphosis, ends ironically with a "gaze" that announces death— "An obdurate, blind, all-seeing gaze: I had seen it before, in the museums, / in stone masks of the gods and victims" (33). It is a metamorphosis, then, that leads to the past as stasis, preserved by death, and a gesture towards the future that is a "smirk of denial facing eternity." The transcendence here, into the historical past, provides the terms of both the triumph and the defeat of any metamorphic vision.

The historical past, though it cannot provide a point of origin, can at least provide a point of reference from which a metamorphic vision may proceed. In one of the most haunting images in all of Levertov's work, the past literally becomes a trace, a shadow that extends to the future:

> But the shadow,
> the human shadowgraph sinking itself
> indelibly upon stone at Hiroshima
> as a man, woman or child was consumed
> in unearthly fire—
> > that shadow
> already had been for three days
> imprinted upon our lives.
> Three decades now we have lived
> with its fingers outstretched in horror clinging
> to our future, our children's future,
> into history or the void.
>
> > > > [*LF* 58]

And the shadow speaks—or rather the shadow, as trace, is supplemented by the narrator, who also interprets, echoes the shadow in its own voice, a voice of "redemption" that is reinforced by the symbolism of three days cited above. The final metamorphosis of metamorphosis, then, needn't be an end, but a prophecy: time becomes prophetic. The wall itself, the wall in "Human Being" that blocked progress, is a wall on which time itself is written: it is not the end. In "Time Past," Levertov says that an "instant" from earlier in a marriage "is what twines itself / in my head and body across the slabs of wood / that were warm, ancient, and now / wait somewhere to be burnt" (*FD* 15). Even disappearing or lost, even as traces, as the vague sense of the Mexican street vendor, the past persists, not to be assimilated, but to provoke, as prophecy. So she says in "Unresolved," "we know no synthesis" (*CB* 105). In the metamorphic vision moments exist, as Bakhtin says, as crises: each "knot" is a crisis "for showing how an individual becomes other than he was" (115).

It is precisely this counterpointing of crisis and prophecy that informs *Candles in Babylon*. The moment as crisis occurs early, both in the work and in a life:

> at the marrow of all this joy, the child
> is swept by a sudden
> chill of patience: notices wearily
> the abyss that Time
> opens before it.
>
> [*CB* 5]

On a more political level, Levertov wonders, in "An English Field in the Nuclear Age," how "to render it!—*this* moment" (*CB* 79). The wall is transformed; metamorphosis, now with religious overtones, suggesting a possible resurrection, allows an uncanny perspective that sees the potential end as a past, already metamorphosed. One holds, literally, a candle in Babylon:

> (gold mirrors of buttercup satin
> assert eternity as they reflect
> nothing, everything, absolute instant,
> and dread
>
> holds its breath, for

this minute at least was
not the last).

[*CB* 79–80]

It is curious that these lives are put in parentheses, as a sort of whispered hope against the fear that "there is no sharing save in the furnace, / the transubstantiate" (*CB* 79). It is no wonder, then, that every potential last moment in the book is transformed; like the "Old People Dozing" (*CB* 55), what visions we have, what "night gulls" we view are "always at [the] vanishing point," but always "memory / moving again through the closed door" (*CB* 55), the wall. In *Oblique Prayers,* her most recent book, the sense of apocalyptic urgency is perhaps greater, as in the poem "The Cry"—a cry that can be that of the end of the world, the cry for peace, perhaps the surprising call of "hellbird / in branches of / snowrose / blossoming," an angelic cry of hope (45–46).

We are, then, always already inscribed with time, as Derrida would say. We are written by our own selves, our own texts for our pasts and futures, and by the Other, what transcends us. We become orphans of time:

no one
has known us always,
we are ancient orphans,
parchment skins stretched upon crutches,
inscribed with epitaphs.

[*CB* 11]

And when we see our own breath, it is that we "See / for an instant the arc of / our vanishing" (12). We live, then, in the midst of an enormous doubt. In fact, the headnote to this section is from Poulet's account of Pascalian time, it is a time of wish and desire, an elegiac time, always frustrated in its attempts to keep pace with metamorphoses, with states always already just vanishing. The metamorphosis out of the self, the echo of the elsewhere, the absent, the glitter of nothingness, all these remain glimpsed in the arc of vanishing. Levertov, like Pascal, has a mind that "never gives up the hope of overtaking, by means of new exercises, this movement out of the self which outstrips the self: tentative, complex, in which are combined the patience of a premeditated design, the violence of the effort, and a kind of physical suppleness of mind" (Poulet, 83). It never gives up hope because, beneath the doubt, there is a certainty, not the "vicious certainty" Levertov says we look for in history (*CB* 77), but the certainty that comes from trusting language itself, writing. But a language whose prophetic and metamorphic impulses have become religious in tone, a language now with increased ability to convert itself to action, to enter worldly time (*Oblique Prayers* includes several overtly religious poems). Thus, for example, the narrator asks, in "Mass for the Day of St. Thomas Didymus": "can the name / utter itself / in the downspin of time? / Can it enter / the void?" (*CB* 113). It is precisely the void that it enters, here in the word incarnate: "The word / chose to become / flesh" (*CB* 113). Time is someone's language, we said earlier—the transcendent's, anyone's. Levertov's poetry in *Life in the Forest, Candles in Babylon,* and *Oblique Prayers* becomes the kind of poetry she hoped for early in her career—a poetry, a word, of incarnation, action. There is a sense of religious community, of communal time, a common time of writing that finally defines the temporality of Levertov's vision, her mode of "action":

> Keep writing in the dark:
> a record of the night, or
> words that pulled you from depths of unknowing,
> words that flew through your mind, strange birds
> crying their urgency with human voices,
>
> or opened
> as flowers of a tree that blooms
> only once in a lifetime:
>
> words that may have the power
> to make the sun rise again.
>
> [*CB* 101]

The "unknowing"—what must always remain unknown within words—will always be at the center of her vision. In "Of Being" (*OP* 86) she says: "I know this happiness / is provisional." Yet this is not a pessimism, as we have seen, but an imaginative triumph. The unknown, as she says in "Oblique Prayers" (*OP* 82), is "not the profound *dark / night of the soul //* and not the austere desert," but rather "gray / a place / without clear outlines." It is a place, a poetry, where one seems to "remember"

> the blessed light that caressed the world
> before I stumbled into
> this place of mere
> not-darkness.
>
> [*OP* 83]

6

An Anonymous Time

Charles Simic's Mythologies

I

The Summoning

> That which is said before all else by this first source
> of *leitmotifs* of thinking gives voice to a bond that
> binds all thinking, providing that thinking submits
> to the call of what must be thought.
> —Heidegger, *Time and Being*

In the beginning, always, a myth of origins of the poetic act. A longing to lower oneself one notch below language, to scoop out the bottom—that place of 'original action and desire,' to recover our mute existence, to recreate what is unspoken and enduring in words, and thus live twice as it were." So writes Charles Simic in "Composition," in a sentence that contains much of his poetics, a poetics based upon the desire to repeat what is "authentic" in language, "recall" what is "primordial," "veiled," "silent"—our "origins." And so, says Simic, extending his characteristically Heidegerrian language, "the poem is the place where origins are allowed to think" (*NLH* 149–51). (The quoted words in the previous sentence are common to Simic and Heidegger, whom the poet has studied.) For Simic, as for Heidegger, the origin is a phenomenological construct given by the very language that paradoxically veils it: language's "saying," writes Heidegger, is an "inner recalling" that concerns "the invisible of the world's inner space" (*PLT* 133).

There are, in effect, two basic causes for this paradox of language, for the mythic nature of origins. First, says Simic, "Out of the simultaneity of experience, the event of Language is an emergence into

240

linear time." The reason is that the "paradox of this original experience is that it doesn't have Time. All its elements are simultaneous.
It is a totality—the whole psychic weight of a single human being.
Only in telling does time enter" (*NLH* 149). That is, the experience
is made up of such a network of instantaneous and overlapping
impressions and impulses that it overloads language with associations
that get lost in mere words. "Any verbal act includes a selection, a
conceptualization, a narrowing down" (*Acts* 21), he says, of what seem
infinitely complex, endlessly modulated sensations. But, of course, it
is only in telling itself that an origin, however falsified, can be re-
called; language is bound to a lie, and the poet must remain constantly
"suspicious" of it (*PP* 109–20, 134–48). But not only is the overall
structure of language inadequate to accurately recall origins, its very
elements name origins wrongly. In an interview, Simic says: "The
problem is then with a language that is larger than [the poet's] uses
for it. On the one hand it's not specific enough to carry all of his
experiences, but on the other hand it contains echoes and resonances
he never suspected before he began to write about the experiences"
(*Acts* 66). That is, our "words want to bring back more," Simic says
in "Ballad" (*RPLGM* 52).

Yet it is this second problem, the overplus—what Derrida calls
supplementarity—that, ironically, provides the poet with a way to
find origins within, or "below," language. The poet must find a way
to let language's secrets speak to him, summon him. This occurs, as
Heidegger says, "when we cannot find the right word for something
that concerns us, carries us away, oppresses or encourages us. Then
we leave unspoken what we have in mind and, without rightly giving
it thought, undergo moments in which language itself has distantly
and fleetingly touched us with its essential being" (*OWL* 59). Language in poetic form "thinks," in other words, by "provoking
thought" about its own nature, its origins in relation to original
experience. This thought, for Simic, takes the form of myth as an
uncovering of the archetypes of language. Thus, he says, "It occurred
to me that mythological consciousness, the kind that is still present
in our world, is to be found in language," in, he goes on, riddles,
metaphors, dismantled images, idiomatic expressions, surrealistic
structures, any language element that will, with a little play, unfold

plots. What happens, he asks, what plot evolves, if we literalize an expression like "counting bats in his belfry"? Language, then, can act as an instrument of discovery—"I follow the logic of the algebraic equation of words on the page which is unfolding, moving in some direction" (*Acts* 20–21). The language of the poem, then, "restores strangeness to the ordinary," discovers as origin "a realm where magic is possible, where chance reigns, where metaphors have their supreme logic," where time is a "manipulation" of the poem, a product of language in its search for the timelessness of origins (*NLH* 149–50).

The language of the poem recalls the realm of origins precisely by what Heidegger calls a "summoning." The nature of poetic language is that it "calls" or "summons" the self's "own-most potentiality-for-Being" (*BT* 314, 318). The summons is therefore a "challenge" or "appeal" to a higher level of being, performance, perception. Yet, as a potentiality, what is called remains volatile; in "Nursery Rhyme" (*CC*), the narrator sees this potentiality as "a blur, a speck, meagre, receding / Our lives trailing in its wake." So, Heidegger explains, "Language speaks in that it, as showing, reaching into all regions of presences, summons from them whatever is present to appear and to fade" (*OWL* 124). For Simic, the paradigmatic poem that illustrates what we have been saying is "Eraser" (*CC* 30):

> A summons because the marvelous prey is fleeing
> Something to rub out the woods
> From the blackboard sound of wind and rain
> A device to recover a state of pure expectancy
>
> Only the rubbings only the ending patience
> As the clearing appears the clearing which is there
> Without my even having to look
> The domain of the marvelous prey
>
> This emptiness which gets larger and larger
> As the eraser works and wears out
> As my mother shakes her apron full of little erasers
> For me to peck like breadcrumbs

The flight of the marvelous prey provides a reason to summon, yet a summons to "erase," a term Derrida deploys in similar contexts, to clear away our usual conceptions that project a traditional world view—a summons to begin again, "to recover a state of pure expectancy." Thus the prey itself will always escape, and the language of its hiding places in old words, old woods, must be replaced by new language, new signifiers, new metaphors as the old "wear out." The summons that the poet hears leads him back toward the origin, the mythical presence of Being revealed by recalling its absence, presencing it, in language, in the absent mother veiled behind the apron of always more erasers. For Simic, this quest is endless, the region of absence or "emptiness" getting paradoxically "larger and larger" as more discoveries are made. Yet if the past cannot be simply returned to, something new can be originated within the folds of language's apron. In "The Time Before the First," Jacques Derrida suggests that "Far from being erased," the origin's "oppositions" are "thrown back into play," become the constantly-being-revised subtext—the poem itself (*D* 330).

Language, then, acts as an originator when the poet follows the "logic of the algebraic equation of words" as if they contained their own self-referential reality. This leads, eventually, to certain contradictions which Simic sees as the heart of a poem's dramatic power, to what Keats described as "negative capability," the ability to deal with "uncertainties," "mysteries," "doubts" (Simic, "Negative Capability," 15). In "Erasers" the essence, the "domain of the marvelous prey," is described as an "emptiness," but this word is a specific modulation of "clearing," which, with respect to "woods," suggests something of a grassy, not a barren, field. In addition, "clearing" itself derives from Heidegger's discussion in *Discourse on Thinking* of the regioning of Being, the clearing of Being, using the same woods and field metaphor. In this case, the clearing is a mark of the fullness of Being that can only be felt by "bracketing" off the word, by emptying oneself of preconceptions. In a way, then, the clearing is both empty and full. Heidegger describes the situation in his "On the Origins of the Work of Art"—

And yet—beyond what is, not away from it but before it, there is still something else that happens. In the midst of beings as a whole an open place occurs. There is a clearing, a lighting. Thought of in reference to what is, to beings, this clearing is in a greater degree than are beings.

> This open center is therefore not surrounded by what is: rather, the
> lighting center itself encircles all that is, like the Nothing which we
> scarcely know [*OWL* 53].

Time here becomes manifest in spatial terms—beyond and before are
co-ordinate terms here—in an attempt to reduplicate the simultaneity of the origin. Similarly, in Simic's poem, the spatial metaphor is
complicated by the idea that the clearing seems to "appear" within
the time frame of the poem's saying—and indeed this would be a
corollary to the connection between language and Being that under-
lines Heidegger's and Simic's poetic—yet also "is there," *always already,* as Derrida would say. This, of course, is also accounted for in
the Derridian notion of traces, erasures, ghosts of a lost presence;
there is a sort of two-handed writing and erasing going on. In a poem
that recalls origins, "pure expectancy" can only be a myth, an ideal
subverted by traces, marks against the purity of origins, holdovers
from past words (woods). So, then, the poem blurs kinds of Being,
pure presence and the absence of presence, prophecy and memory,
perception and imagination, hope and history. And this is why the
poem, emphasizing a linear structure leading back to the mother, also
bases its movement on "endless" activity, deferral—that is, on the
"possible." And that is why, finally, the texture of this "domain"
touches both a real and a surreal world, words and woods, why its
domain exists in the relation between present and origin and between
present and future. The poem in itself, that is, is its own starting
place for a new inquiry into Being, its own origin, a "device to recover
a state of pure expectancy." As with Heidegger, the "clearing" or
"region" denotes a highly problematic place, a "state" as much as a
place, something subject to the temporalities of the physical world
and the mind, however conflicting these may become.

Because it is a state, a frame of mind as much as a place, that region
to which we are summoned and which we create in being summoned,
and because it is an emptiness, the region is always isolated—and
always dangerous. The hunt for the marvelous prey is after all a hunt,
but a hunt where prey and predator may change places. "This is the
last summoning. / Solitude—as in the beginning," Simic says in
White (23). Yet this book-length poem also describes, in the words of

one critic, "a realm of pure possibility, new selves, new words, and new names" (Schmidt, 528). White appears in the poem as a prey under many guises, both benevolent and malevolent, as various parts of speech, spoken or unspoken in connection with objects, places, notions. Paradoxically, the closer it gets, the less it is seen: "All that is new, / I no longer give it a name," the speaker says. Associated with everything and nothing, white becomes the subject and the lack of a subject is the poet's inquiry; from its lack of color come colors in the traditional rhetorical sense—metaphors, narratives, figures of speech. "Out of poetry / To begin again," the poem opens, emphasizing not only its originating intent, but the fact that it has been attempted before. It is a beginning and an end. And yet, though this opening and the associative progression subvert a linear structure, there is a sort of plot by metaphor, especially with reference to the idea of weddings. White is "the color of the bride," associated with "light" and the ability to "linger / on the threshold" of Being and non-Being, or in sexual terms, virginity and its loss, barrenness or emptiness and fertility. It is a poem, that is, which is a marriage of opposites in Blake's sense, a poem of reversals and subversions of itself, a poem of erasures.

The poem, then, is also about itself—white is also the blank page, what the poet starts with, and what his words, as erasures, leave him with, the nearly empty clearing. "If I didn't err, there wouldn't be these smudges," he writes, after a litany of mistakes about what he can or can't be called. In the end, on two facing pages beginning with the same line, and using similar phrases and structures, White gives its duplistic response to the poet's failed attempts. "I thought of you long before you thought of me," White teases:

> You've invented name after name for me,
> Mixed the riddles, garbled the proverbs,
> Shook your loaded dice in a tin cup,
> But I do not answer back even to your curses,
> For I am nearer to you than your breath.

Wherever he is, White insists, whatever he thinks, "the sea in which you are sinking, / And even this night above it, is myself." On the second page, White takes a more consoling attitude (the dialectic is between teasing and consolation, and between violence and love): "I am the emptiness that tucks you in like a mockingbird's nest" (the bird is one of the most musical but also one of the most vicious). This marriage of opposites, this love of ambiguity, persists as a supreme joy:

> Poems are made of our lusty wedding nights . . .
> The joy of words as they are written.
> The ear that got up at four in the morning
> To hear the grass grow inside a word.
> Still, the most beautiful word has no answer.

What, finally, is the issue of this poem? Where, finally, does it leave us, this "last summoning?" It leaves us and the speaker not with companionship but "loneliness" and fear. White becomes, it says, like the monkey for the organ-grinder-poet's tune, a necessity and a diversion, the subject and the loss of the subject.

> It's as if we had not budged from the beginning.
> Time slopes. We are falling head over heels
> At the speed of night. That milk tooth
> You left under the pillow, it's grinning.

White is finally the muse—language—the mythic Being who is never there, who is always nearing but always absent, who is the origin that returns not to itself but rather spawns new origins throughout the poet's linguistic-sexual acts. It is the origin, the blank page, the empty fullness, the companion who is the sign of the poet's loneliness. "Time slopes" because the origin is always erased, always smudged, and always on the verge of absorbing the speaker within its absolute emptiness. What *White* suggests, in the end, is that the summons as both the call of Being and of non-Being is by that same token an opportunity and a danger. What is at stake is the survival of the poet for whom whiteness can refer to the coldness of death, the white space enclosed by a zero, the terrible blank, brief page of our lives—"who's fast enough / To write his life on it?" Who's fast enough to escape yet heed the call of the single toothed grin of death from the pillow, ironically the only white spot in a black night? Who's fast enough to structure a time for himself that embraces beginnings and ends, who can use the black print of his words to remain on the "threshold" where time seems simultaneous? Who, finally, is fast enough to maintain a version, a myth of the self, even as time slopes away?

II

The Anonymous Voice

> Presence means: the constant abiding that approaches man, reaches him, is extended to him.
> —Heidegger, *Time and Being*

Early on in *White* the narrator declares—"There are words I need. / They are not near men." Besides calling into question the status of a supposedly unspoken, unthought language, a language spoken by language, as we suggested earlier, the statement calls into question the status of its speaker who separates himself off from man. In fact, the danger we discussed at the end of the previous section is acknowledged a few lines later when the speaker meditates on the vowel "O," also a zero—"Little known vowel, / Noose big for us all." Is it *too* big for us, so that we can slip through, on language—or is it big enough for us all, trapping us? The problem is, that the attempt to reach the empty origin is also an attempt to strip away the lenses and presuppositions we see with—our words, the symbols by which we order our lives. "Pure expectancy" has to mean free of any presupposed expectations:

> Perhaps, the time has come again
> To go back into forests and snow fields,

> Live alone killing wolves with our bare hands,
> Until the last word and the last sound
> Of this language I am speaking is forgotten.
>
> ["Hearing Steps," *DS* 30]

Here, certainly, the danger is clear. It is not simply a matter of finding new words and metaphors, but of shucking away the old. The poet has to burn the bridges of his language behind him. What is at risk is a sense of the self, the authority of the narrator, his own sense of Being. He speaks not in his old voice, his old self, but in an anonymous voice, one on the verge of losing everything in order to gain the very origins of the self.

Despite its risks, the desire for anonymity is the only way a larger, mythical version can be embraced. Myth, in fact, mutes, or at least distances the self from dangers. And in a paradoxical way, anonymity undercuts the sense of isolation it is usually associated with:

> I've always felt that inside each of us there is profound anonymity. Sometimes I think that when you go deep inside, you meet everyone else on a sort of common ground—or you meet nobody. But whatever you meet, it is not yours though you enclose it. We are the container and this nothingness is what we enclose. This is where Heidegger is very interesting to me. He describes the division between the world as nothing, as what he calls the "open," and any act of conceptualizing which restores the world in a particular way. Many of his texts are longings to experience that anonymity. The condition where we don't have an "I" yet. It is as if we were in a room from which, paradoxically, we were absent. Everything is seen from the perspective of that absence. I suppose, in some ways, this is a mystical vision that brings to me a sense of the universe as an anonymous presence. The force of that sometimes frightens me, sometimes delights me [*Acts* 22].

This sense of "otherness" produces the strange sensation, in his texts, that the speaker is simultaneously present and absent. He becomes like the narrator in "The Partial Explanation," who experiences, as the basis of the way "I chose myself," "a longing, / Incredible longing / To eavesdrop / On the conversation / Of cooks" (*CC* 3). Or like the narrator in "Position without Magnitude" (*CC* 47), a title that underscores the problematics of any domain, who rises in an empty theater to see for a moment his shadow on the screen "Among the fabulous horsemen," blending for that moment the real and the mythical, the temporal and the eternal. Probably the paradigmatic poem to describe this situation is "The Inner Man" (*DS* 28), where the narrator's body seems inhabited by the Other—"There are women / Who claim to have held him. / A dog follows me about. / It might be his." In the end, unsure of his own status as well as that of the Other, both anonymous to each other, he concludes—

> We cast a single shadow.
> Whose shadow?
> I'd like to say:
> "He was in the beginning
> And he'll be in the end,"
> But one can't be sure.
>
> At night
> As I sit
> Shuffling the cords of our silence,
> I say to him:
>
> "Though you utter
> Every one of my words,
> You are a stranger.
> It's time you spoke."

What this anonymous other speaks, in essence, is the language of the poems. Or, in a sense, the other is language itself, as Jacques Lacan would have it—the originator, the voice of the summons.

This, at least, is the way Heidegger conceives of the situation. "Language *speaks*," he says, "And not man? Are we . . . also going to deny now that man is the being who speaks?" (*PLT* 198). The answer is that the sort of saying we have been describing is a special use of language, a consciousness of its power to name origins precisely where it fails, as we saw earlier, to name certain experiences. In these cases, in poems, language itself, as a sort of character, summons the poet, who remains nearly anonymous, and speaks for him, saying less and more than he could. What does this language summon? asks Heidegger—

This naming does not hand out titles, it does not apply terms, but it calls into the word. The naming calls. Calling brings closer what it calls. However, this bringing closer does not fetch what is called only in order to set it down in closest proximity to what is present, to find a place for it there. The call does indeed call. Thus it brings the presence of what was previously uncalled into a nearness. But the call, in calling it here, has already called out to what it calls. Where to? Into the distance in which what is called remains, still absent [198].

In other words, the silences of language, that aspect, Heidegger suggests, which is beyond simple speech, has a way of establishing Being, and it is linked to the emptiness of place and of self, to a certain anonymity that is the occasion for the origination of a new self. Simic explains:

The aim is to reduce myself to some sort of minimal proposition, and then to work my way out of that. Many of the poems have that sort of predicament: somebody is there as an "it," a geometric point. This is the essence, there's nothing around it except empty space. Here is where he locates himself, and now he has to do something out of that, tell a story, establish a place, a time [*Acts* 25–26].

And so, he goes on, "there is no one 'I.' 'I' is many. 'I' is an organizing principle, a necessary fiction, etc." (*Acts* 25–26). These, then—the problematic domain, the problematic self, a problematic time—constitute the basis of the mythic, the summoning of origins in Simic's work. We now need to examine more closely the various forms this mythology takes, and the implications for the poet's vision of time.

The anonymity of the summons itself, because it cannot be pinned down to a single voice, a single perspective seems "always / on the brink— / as it were / of some deeper utterance" ("The Stream," *CBD* 37). And because the utterance provides a sense of presence and a sense of what is always absent, it is "Summoning me / to be / two places at once," even if, in this marvelous domain, the call is from "Nothing / that comes to nothing." It is in this empty context that the self can be authentically originated. Thus, for example, "The Bird" (*RPLGM* 4) begins: "A bird calls me / From an apple tree / In the midst of sleep," and a few lines later he discovers—"In the throat of that unknown bird / There's a vowel of my name." As the poem continues, the fragment of the name evolves, the unknown bird comes closer to the self, and the narrator becomes more and more enraptured at its sound, until the voice "touches" him and he seems to follow the flight of its "trajectory." The metamorphosis is completed later in the poem—

> Later, I fell
> In a field of nettles
> And dreamt I had
> The eyes of that bird,
>
> Watching from the heights,
> How the roads meet
> And part once again.

Such a metamorphosis is a natural outgrowth for the anonymous narrator: being nothing himself, he can, to paraphrase Stevens, take part in the nothing that *is* as well as the nothing that *isn't*. This sort of metamorphosis that occurs between meetings and partings, nearing and distancing, is precisely the rhythm of the dialectic of summoning; in more philosophic terms, it is the rhythm between Being and non-Being.

This is apparent in a poem such as "Navigator" (*CBD* 36), which begins—"I summoned Christopher Columbus," only to have Columbus, nothing himself as a fictional Being, become the narrator's father, a suitcase-burdened traveler, and a sort of drunken troubadour. The problem for Columbus is that "On this particular voyage / He discovered nothing," and his non-being is further undiscovered by the narrator's tongue-in-cheek tone: "I had forgotten to provide the stars," the narrator self-consciously laments. And yet if the original, historical Columbus is lost, the mythical character is given a certain Being by some of the specifics—"Sitting with a bottle of wine in his hand, / He sang a song from his childhood." And more—Columbus becomes the originator of another reality—

> In the song the day was breaking.
> A barefoot girl

An Anonymous Time

> Stepped over the wet grass
> To pick a sprig of mint.

What the strategy of the poem does is to use various time frames—
the historical, the fictional, the lyrical (of the song within the poem),
and the poetic (the time of the narrator speaking)—to subvert one
another. The idea of a linear time is underscored by the cross-sec-
tioning of numerous times, each denying the primary reality of the
others. The poem's scheme, and indeed the scheme of many of Simic's
poems, resembles that described by Borges in "The Garden of the
Forking Paths," its labyrinth of time that is both a life, an autobiog-
raphy, and a fiction, a book. And within the book there is

> An infinite series of times, in a dizzily growing, ever spreading network
> of diverging, converging and parallel times. This web of time—the
> strands of which approach one another, bifurcate, intersect or ignore
> each other through the centuries—embraces every possibility. We do not
> exist in most of them. In some you exist and not I, while in others I do,
> and you do not, and yet in others both of us exist [Borges 100].

The status of any particular "I," any particular place, idea, event, is
undermined in favor of a sense of direction, of movement—of the
nearing and distancing, the regioning, of Being and non-Being. Columbus is no one and everyone; the poem refers to events and relates
no events except whimsical fancies. Undecidable about these things,
the poem then ends by subverting its own progress just at the moment
the song's content was seeming to project a conventional—though
ideally pastoral—reality. Time, that is, enters, as it must, in the form
of the linear accountability Simic described as undermining simultaneity—

> And then nothing—
> Only the wind rushing off with a high screech
> As if it just remembered,
> Where it's going, where it's been.

And yet the trace, the erasure, remains in memory, and in anticipation—"where it's going"—that summons through the language of the

wind. The "nothing," that is, becomes defined as a future and a past—as the realms, in imagination, of "pure expectancy." And the anonymous voice that summons—the wind's call—summons us towards a time that, in Borges' terms, "embraces every possibility," a time we can hardly imagine, an anonymous general time where "origins are allowed to think."

This anonymous time is what governs a poem like "Rural Delivery" (*A* 24), where the speaker tells his lover: "it's subtraction / And the art of erasure we study." In order to locate themselves, he says,

> I had to stick my bare hand
> All the way to nothing and no one
> To make absolutely sure
> This is where we live.

But the poem also moves in conventional time frames, emphasized by temporal references such as "end up," "this week," "one more time." And it is also a movement towards the origin—"We retraced our footsteps homeward" through a snowy land where origins and ends, and bits of past, all intersect. A certain temporality begins to develop in Simic's poems, then—a time linked by its specifics to everyday time, but a time that is "dizzily growing" in the language that speaks it. This is the case, too, in "The Frontier" (*B & L*), where the summons comes from an inanimate object—"the hills multiplying / and some clairvoyant wheat / Summons me from a great distance / To harvest it." Here the summons is refused because it brings frightening associations—the far frontier, "the guard-towers and their sentries," and the poet remains isolated. In other cases, the summons can come at the most unlikely places, as the call at the end of "Butcher Shop" (*DS* 24). Here the poem's references to altars, religious images, magic, the blood on the butcher's apron like a map, and the light in the shop like that in a convict's tunnel, suggest a calling from a primitive, dark, vaguely prehistoric source—a call, as it were, from the anonymous reptilian brain within us. Even a poem which literalizes the ideas of the summons as a legal document provides a sort of mythic dimension: "The robes of the judges are magnificent / when they enter among the assembled / The one with a head of a lamb will be mine" ("The Summons," *CC* 9). As it ends out, they address each other in the "gutted" courtroom that is so "vast" it has the feel of a universe—"A little snow beginning to fall through the cracks / Stretches of emptiness over which we / Address each other." And yet the anonymity is countered, in the end, by the "cleaning women" who sweep up the flakes and "know each one by its suffering and name," though the names are only known by the women, themselves anonymous. If they seem to provide a link to the everyday world, it is only a momentary and vague link, so that they end up reinforcing the anonymity of events, of history, of time.

The anonymity of Time must be linked to what might be called an anonymity of Being. This does not deny the self, as we have seen, but rather considers it under a more general aspect. That is, it deals with existence on an ontological rather than an outer level, is concerned with *Dasein*, with the origins and possibilities of Being, rather than specific entities themselves—to borrow again from Heidegger. It is this sense that Simic explores; *Dasein* is ontologically prior to the self, a condition for it (*BT* sections 1–8). So, for example, Heidegger will use convoluted expressions to suggest how language cannot really reach this originating condition, and how language also reveals it. In *Time and Being*, for example, he discusses this originating force as the "there is, It gives, Being," to signify the state (is), the act (gives), and the vagueness (It) of Being. The statement, for Heidegger, remains open to suggest the openness of this vague origin, its "approach" towards us, its nearness that is also a withholding, a distance, as we have seen (*TB* 8). Now Simic uses one remarkably similar strategy. For Heidegger, the "meaning" of the "it" is a range that "extends from the irrelevant to the demonic" (*TB* 18–19). More specifically, *it* suggests "what is already present." But since *it* always points—towards something else—*it* "names a presence of absence." For Heidegger, then, *it* names the way Being is sent, names Being as an "extension of time." For Simic, *it* leads us away from the self, names the lost, erased origin, makes the presence of another, bifurcated time. *It* refers, in other words, to the truly anonymous time.

In "Like Whippoorwills" (*CBD* 63), he opens with—

> It—it—it!
> That's what the strange bird said,

254

and another answered,
likewise,

without identifying the agent,
some animal or thing.

Actually, the subversion of reference is not only to what the birds
call, but also to the birds themselves, the origins. In fact, later the
narrator asks—"it looks like it, / and acts like it, / but who's to say?"
and then follows this with a playful—

they are here this evening,

in the vicinity of,
in the dizzying nearness of,

which is why they proclaim
that is so.

Here the object-less prepositions underscore the ambiguity—the non-
entity, really, of the reference. But the poem ends severely, the narrator
becoming a sort of St. Francis amongst these mythical birds and "very
anxious / to have it be thus." That the "it" is never defined, that it
becomes, as Simic says in "Elegy" (*CBD* 44), "disengaged / from reference," does not weaken the authority of the voice, however; in fact,
by gradually letting the "it" accumulate any number of references,
the voice becomes larger than life, as it were, mythic, ontological. A
similar sort of subversion of referentiality occurs in "A Day Marked
with a Small White Stone" (*CC* 36)—here an animal—perhaps—is
caught in a trap, hurt, but also vaguely on the margins of possible
existence,

In a ring
Of magnanimous coyotes,
In a ring of
Compassionate, melancholy
Something or other . . .

The reference is deferred, and the associations, one imagines, could
go on indefinitely past the three dots that technically end the poem.

In attempting to get to origins, the "It gives, Being," language does not define but rather extends and mythologizes time.

In two poems in *Return to a Place Lit by a Glass of Milk*, "Two Riddles" (26) and "Solving the Riddle" (28), the use of the "it" is combined, as the titles suggest, with the literary form where "the word truly becomes *mythos*, becomes the place of origins." The riddle, Simic says, "asks a question which is never completely answered . . . There's a gap, and there's potential for dialectics" (*NLH* 10). In "Two Riddles," the thing hangs "Between the earth and sky. / I, it says. I. I." It is, in a sense, the last self, rhyming with sky, picking upon the immensity, the loss of selfhood implicit in the expanse, the distance of sky. The word denotes not only the pronoun, but a scream, a terror of suspension, of the very anonymity of its own voice. And this is extended in the second half of the poem, the second riddle, which begins: "It goes without saying . . . / What does? No one knows." And so, the speaker goes on,

> No use trying to pin it down.
> It's elusive, of a retiring habit,
> In a hurry, of course, scurrying—
> A blink of an eye and it's gone.
>
> All that's known about it,
> Is that it goes
> Without saying.

Now as the second poem, "Solving the Riddle," answers itself by the playfulness of the mythic tone—"the comic and mythic strategies are similar, if not identical," says Simic; "the trick is to be literal-minded in the world of multiple metaphors, and fabulous in the face of the literal" (*NLH* 7). Following this reading strategy suggests that the "it" referred to is self-referential; it is it. It goes without saying, without revealing its reference, and so "It will be here tomorrow, / Disguised, hard to recognize." "It" eternally appears and disappears. "It" makes a time where beginnings and ends are reversible, the closest thing Simic is able to get to the simultaneity of origins. And it truly constitutes a world, gives Being—

256

Around a riddle
Which yields no answer
We made our nest
Of straw and matches.

A nest of beginnings and potential ends, of Being and Nothingness. For "it" is just as much nothing as anything. In fact, the poem between these two poems in *Return* that we have been discussing is "Nothing" (27), whose opening line is: "I want to see it face to face." This poem, that is, at the heart between the two riddles poems, provides the absolute origin for whatever something it can refer to—nothing, the perfectly anonymous.

This sort of playfulness, and it helps to distance the sense of danger we discussed earlier, is extended in other poems that find mythic qualities, as Simic suggested in a passage quoted earlier, in idiomatic expressions. For instance, the little poem, "Theoretical" (*WFUV* 36), takes off from the expression about having a mote in your eye—

She's got something in her left eye.
It's a step ladder.
Very tiny. Very interesting.
There's a bucket too, and a man
In white overalls. He's got a brush.
He's going to paint her eye black.

I make kiss-like noises
To scare him off.

It begins with the actual—a speck in her eye. But then it becomes a metaphor, literalized. For what? What's in her mind? What she sees? What's in the scene behind them? Maybe the possible black eye is an expression of the narrator's anger, frustration, which he solves in the last two lines, perhaps out of guilt. Maybe he's jealous. With every possibility comes a new narrative, a new time scheme, one of the strands of time Borges described. Or Ariadne's thread, as Simic refers to it several times, especially in "In Midsummer Quiet," a thread "Resuming, farther on, / Intermittently," a "phantom" that is "Talking to my own conundrums, / Mazes" (*WFUV* 37).

Other poems develop the mythic possibilities within language by quick references that literalize figures of speech, such as: "This is a tale with a kernal. / You'll have to use your own teeth to crack it" ("Chorus for One Voice," *DS* 16). The poem "Nowhere" (*CBD* 57 is literally an investigation of the Being that the word ironically contains: "That's where No lives, / Happily ever after." This is a place, the narrator mythologizes, where "Its sky has no stars / No morning or evening," a timeless place that is a true origin in that, in typical dialectic fashion, it must include its opposite, "Yes," which is desire and a beginning. The contradictory logic of the language here has already set the terms of the poem, has already provided the condition for Being and for Time.

Language encounters its greatest challenge, that point where the "right word," Heidegger said, cannot be found, in poems about geometric figures. Here the reference is ghostly, a perfect trace, perfectly anonymous. After all, apart from the object it is connected with. A poem about a geometric figure is a poem about that figure, a perfect tautology which also says it is a poem about nothing. So, for example, in "The Point" (*RPLGM* 32), the narrator describes it as "the story / afraid to go on," as a dream, as the "shadow of its beginning" and the "madness of this / Single burnt consonant." The playfulness—what is the point of "The Point"?—gives way, in this poem that mythologizes its point as a biography, to a somber conclusion—"after its death / They opened the story / Afraid to go on. / And found nothing." Or inside they found "a slip / of the tongue," a "loose hair," whatever—"Whatever / Is destroyed / Each time / It is named." Suddenly the mythological and philosophic stakes shift—the poem is, after all, and like all Simic's poems, about survival, about ways of structuring a life that can go on. What the linear structure of the poem about the most instantaneous, simultaneous marking we can give a page reveals, is a life, a dialectic of birth and death—the way even what seems remote and distant is linked to us, summons us.

"Euclid Avenue" (*CC* 44) attempts to link remote and near in a most radical way by hoping to extend the domain of its concern beyond the finite dimensions of our Euclidean space-time. It begins in a conventional manner—"All my dark thoughts / laid out / in a straight line." They are given in a "Language / as old as rain," whose

origin seems in a primitive past, literally an animal past for the
narrator, who is momentarily metamorphosed as a dog. What the
secret leads to is "A place / known as infinity / toward which that old
self advances." Now what is curious here is the way it is not infinity,
but the name "infinity" that is approached, and what approaches is
the past, time. The attempt is to include all time, future and past, in
the infinite moment, endless. And yet, as we can imagine, time enters—the narrator is the "son of poor parents" at "a late hour," as he
speaks. The narrator, finally, is caught between time and eternity in
world beyond language, a world that evokes a primordial cry and the
screeching of some futural, endlessly deferred time—

> A place known
> as infinity,
> its screendoor screeching,
> endlessly screeching.

What begins to happen, after a while, in Simic's poems, is a strange
reversal—referents and language not only attempt to summon origins
and call from the origin, but the timelessness of the origin begins to
modify the way we look at objects, giving them a certain aura, a sense
of mystery. Language, in effect, begins to re-orient our world, our
histories, within its anonymous structure.

III

The Mythology of the Thing

> In everything that speaks to us, in everything that
> touches us by being spoken and spoken about, in
> everything that gives itself to us in speaking, or
> waits for us unspoken, but also in the speaking that
> we do *ourselves,* there prevails Showing which
> causes to appear what is present, and to fade from
> appearance what is absent. Saying is in no way the
> linguistic expression added to the phenomena after
> they have appeared.
> —Heidegger, *"The Way to Language"*

The dialectic pattern that emerges in Simic's mythological language begins to suggest not a self-referential poetics, but rather a
radically different, originating way of looking at the world. This
poetics owes, as he says in the Introduction to *Another Republic,* a
debt to surrealism as a means of "uncovering and using archetypal
imagery. It restored to the familiar world its strangeness and gave
back to the poet his role as myth maker" (17). The aim, finally, is to
look at objects, at the world, as if for the first time, as if one could
return to the original experience of anything. The dialectic between
present and origin, then, is essential to the surrealistic tendency.
Poetry, for Simic, is a way "of keeping allegiance to the soil, to our
everydayness in the same instant as we experience the transcendental" (*Acts* 23). Joseph Halpern, in "Describing the Surreal," suggests
that there is a double structure consisting of the projective push of
language, as we have discussed it in the previous section, and a

"second system," unspoken, behind the language. Thus, in a riddle whose answer is, say, "brooms," it is the only word that can't be spoken, that must be silent, an invisible referent. Yet it has an existence, and a time, separate if related to the language of the poem. For Simic, then, the anonymous voice of language and the anonymous things it generates ultimately connect to named things, to objects, to images.

In "Description" (*CC* 16), Simic confronts the relation between words and things directly. It begins with a characteristic gesture towards the unnamed "it" and then begins to worry about "its" identity, "its" origin:

> That which brings it
> about. The agent.
>
> The old sweet temptation
> to find an equivalent
>
> for the ineffable.

The problem is that to describe anything requires that the narrator describe many things: the thing itself is not simply an object or place but carries a context.

> Among all the images
> that come to mind,
>
> where to begin?
> Contortions, infinite shapes
>
> pain assumes. Some old woman,
> for instance,
> a lame child
> passing me by
> with incredible exertions
> for each step.

The poem, as it describes its problem, begins also to evolve a plot through a series of images related to pain. The ineffable spawns images because no one thing is exactly "equivalent" to another, as we saw in the case of words about the origin, and so each image must be supplemented, to use Derrida's term. The "for instance" becomes the actual, central plot as the poem mentions, in sequence, the street where she walks, the narrator's separation from her and himself, his consequent two selves "limping," the confinement of infirmary and prison, and finally a doctor who "won't use any anaesthetic." What, then, is it a description of? What is the unspoken referent? Besides itself, its own activity of describing, perhaps separation or the narrator himself. Whatever the answer, each one imposes its own structure on the reading of the poem — philosophical, autobiographical, biographical, and hence its own time.

This function of the "image" as a possible equivalent for the ineffable as well as for the object it refers to is a central one for Simic. In his essay "Image and 'Images,' " he begins: "Image: to make visible . . . What?" Imagism, as such, expressed, he says, "the faith that this complex event ["the act of attention"] can be transcribed to the page without appreciable loss," a faith we have already seen held in great suspicion. The result is a deconstruction of the event: "The nagging sense that the object is 'concealed' by its appearance. The possibility that I am participating in a meaning to which this act is only a clue" (Simic, "Images," 24). So, for example, the chair in "For the Victims" (*DS* 37) reveals, in Stevens' phrase, "unexpected magnitudes," a second world: "And this chair will reveal itself / As the exact shadow of someone / Who stood here all this time." So, too, for Heidegger, a "vessel's thingness does not lie at all in the material of which it consists, but in the void that holds" (*PLT* 169), to the emptiness that is a clearing. The "thing," then, or the "image" of the thing, is something that gathers, collects, presences what seems distant, invisible. It is the image, then, that gives language its power to summon, that speaks with the anonymous voice. Language summons, the image summons, says Heidegger, because it "rescues" objects from their distance and brings them near-to-hand, names them things. Poetry is thus

the rescue of things from mere objectness. The rescue consists in this, that things, within the widest orbit of the whole draft, can be at rest within themselves, which means that they can rest without restriction within one another. Indeed, it may well be that the turning point of our unshieldedness into worldly existence within the world's inner space must begin with this, that we turn the transient and therefore preliminary character of object-things away from the inner and invisible region of the merely producing consciousness and toward the time interior of the heart's space, and there allow it to arise invisibly [*PLT* 130].

This interiorization is the source of the movement in poems like "Stone" and "Stone Inside a Stone" (*DS* 59–61). "From the outside," the narrator says, "the stone is a riddle." The deconstruction of separate inner and outer worlds occurs as the narrator realizes how "cool and quiet" it must be inside, and as a boy throws the stone into a river. Then, recalling the way sparks fly when two stones are rubbed, he suggests it may not be dark inside, and, in fact,

> Perhaps there is a moon shining
> From somewhere, as though behind a hill—
> Just enough light to make out
> The strange writings, the star-charts
> On the inner walls.

Here a whole possible world blossoms, a tendency that is furthered in "Stone Inside a Stone," so much so that the situation of observer and observed is reversed: "A stone among us is taking notes." Now, almost literally inside the narrator, the stone suggests, as an image, a word-thing, other word-things, another time—

> I hear the steps of the stone.
> I lift them with my tongue
> To keep myself in shape
> For an unknown time.

This "inner recalling" is the poem's way of possessing, interiorizing, or, as Heidegger would say, "appropriating" its reference. It is not a specific time that concerns the narrator in the context of such interpenetration, nor even the bifurcation of time we saw earlier, but the very possibility of any time at all, of a time different from any—

in terms of events and of its very nature—that has gone before. The time of the word-thing is a new possibility, hardly explored.

So, says Heidegger, the word for anything "not only stands in a relation to the thing," but "is what first brings that given thing, as the being that is, into this 'is,' " and therefore "holds the thing there and relates it and so to speak provides its maintenance with which to be a thing" (*OWL* 82). This maintenance is the function of language as time and overtime, bestowing time on the thing, giving it a history and a future. In a way, language and thing are inseparable, as suggested in the relation between "words" and "woods" in "Erasers," the poem we began with. But now we see the ontological nature and the reason for that relationship. And more: as Heidegger says—"if the word is to endow the thing with being, it too must be before anything is— thus inescapably be itself a thing" (*OWL* 86). This is why, in Simic's poems, things can speak; they speak the silence and invisibility of origins, paradoxically sustained over time by the very language that hides them. In "Explorers" (*DS* 66–67), for example, the narrator describes a journey into the interior of an object: "They arrive inside / The object at evening." But what they see is within them—"The lamps they carry / Cast their shadows / Back into themselves." And yet, they write, "make notations" on what is not there, which is, in a sense, everything. What they hear in the end is "a faint voice" which could belong "Either to one of them / Or to someone who came before." In a way, their own writing provides the language and is the origin of the voice they hear, a further underscoring of the merger of presence and origin, and the voice itself, the calling, the summons from the object-word defines them, and the reader who has entered the textuality of the setting, as what the object is missing—"You are all / That has eluded me." The line break here emphasizes the dialec- tic between presence and absence, the self and its other, author and reader, "you" and "me." The thing reaches out to the "you" and absorbs the you into its own temporal structure. A similar phenom- enon occurs in "Forest" (*DS* 3), where the forest itself speaks—"My time is coming," it begins, recounting its history in images such as "the imprints of strange flowers / . . . in my rocks." Eventually, it, too, summons the reader to complete its time: "Ladies and gentlemen, you will hear a star / Dead a million years, in the throat of a bird."

The poem, then, summons, gathers the reader into its structure, and, in an ontological sense, creates the reader as character, however anonymous the reader remains to the poem itself.

What the image-word-thing does, in addition, is gather, besides the perceiver, a set of perceived properties around it, the region, that distinguishes it from the materiality of objects. Heidegger uses the example of a bridge. As an "object," it is placed at a "site," a "location" (variations on "region"); but that is misleading, for Heidegger says the site comes into existence only as the bridge comes into existence. It is not there before; thing and site are "simultaneous" as experiences, which recalls Simic's use of that word. In fact, Heidegger goes on, "The bridge is a location." Now the reason for this is all those mythic characteristics—the invisible, the empty region, the word as thing, the anonymous author and reader, the void, the unnamed, the language as origin—that constitute the thing, the origin, beyond its materiality. Take, for instance, Simic's "Return to a Place Lit by a Glass of Milk" (*RPLGM*, 61):

> Late at night our hands stop working.
> They lie open with tracks of animals
> Journeying across the fresh snow.
> They need no one. Solitude surrounds them.
>
> As they come closer, as they touch,
> It is like two small streams
> Which upon entering a wide river
> Feel the pull of the distant sea.
>
> The sea is a room far back in time
> Lit by the headlights of a passing car.
> A glass of milk glows on the table.
> Only you can reach it for me now.

The image-object itself, reached for, summoning the reader (or the other within the narrator), is what centers this world. The poem marks a movement from a passive to a more active participation, from a specific setting which feels entropic to an originating past time. In other words, the poem enacts the coming-to-be it calls for. Even the act of touch reveals this distant summons, as from the sea, the origin of us all. But even that timeless origin is ironically defined in terms of a specific, datable image, the automobile, and the central image, the glass of milk. The glass of milk lights the place and indeed the time, establishes the setting as a "region" and a "location" because to grasp it—to gather it and to be gathered by it—would be to begin again, to complete the return to an authentic origin.

But how, more specifically, can we image this location-thing, find more readily available terms for its mythology? Heidegger says: the thing "originates in that distance where earth and sky, the god and man reach one another" (*OWL* 104). Here, then, is that region to which the "marvelous prey" was fleeing, from which we are summoned. So, for instance, Heidegger says, that the "bridge is a thing— and, indeed, it is such *as* the gathering of the fourfold." What, precisely is this fourfold, then, given by the words earth, sky, god, and man? They are, we might begin, categories through which the object becomes thing, in other words, categories of the summons given implicitly in language. In describing them, Heidegger suggests that they derive from ancient Greek thinking about the nature of Being, and that the Latin names for these categories, translated as substance, accident, subject, object, are literalizations and reductions from the Greek that cover over the truth of the experience (*PLT* 22–23). It is in this way that language covers origins. Not to understand the function of this fourfold, not to understand the resonance it gives to poetry, moving it away from a simple materialism and towards the mythic, is to write a static poetry, Simic has himself declared in conversation. It is to write a poetry of the dead rather than the originating image, an apocalyptic rather than a prophetic poetry.

This fourfold that is gathered around the image-thing involves, as the title of one of Heidegger's essays suggests, "Building Dwelling Thinking" as one originating act. The fourfold is what frees the object, sustains it; to say one of the four is also to think of the other three. By *Earth*, Heidegger means the object in its relation to the physical, changeable nature of experiences, to the particular muck of experience. Its temporality is merely that of the clock. When we are conscious, how close we are to rocks, plants, animals. In "Poem" (*DS* 5), Simic describes how in the morning he forgets this, until "I remember

my shoes, / How I have to put them on, / How bending over to tie
them up / I will look into the earth." This consciousness leads to a
sense of what might be called natural time, seasonal, cyclic, of larger
patterns, the perspective of *Sky*. It is here that one derives a sense of
what is happening just over the horizon, as in "Drawn to Perspective"
(*A* 61), where the world seems to converge on a "couple about to
embrace / At the vanishing point." Or it is the perspective one arrives
at in "The Work of Shading" (*A* 29), where rain is the "Color of old
erasers," where the scene shifts to a classroom, the graying teacher,
and then suggests a related scene "one sees in the distance." *Divinity*
is the perspective from beyond mere distance, beyond the vanishing
point; it is a sense of the absent, the unreachable, the silent, the
invisible, the timeless. It generates the mystery that seems to endow
existence, a sense of a forgotten or indecipherable meaning, like the
star charts on the inside of the stone. *Man* is the perspective of
mortality, of loss, the end of things—how things are used, appreciated,
culturized. It means the consciousness of death, of danger as we saw
it earlier, that defines the way we live. For Heidegger, and for Simic,
each object, stated as an image, given in language, gathers these
perspectives, avenues, really through which to approach the origin.
Thus, even from a brief poem such as "Theoretical," we get the basic
dramatic setting, a sense of the larger perspective (the world outside
that imaged on the eye) which leads to a sense of mystery (Who's
speaking? Why? What actually happens? What is at stake?) leading
to a sense of mortality, of vulnerability, the breaking off of the relationship—earth, sky, divinity, man.

Ideally, if we could recover original experience, these four would be
an indistinguishable unity acting simultaneously; the fact that we
can discuss them in language, however, emphasizes their temporality.
We have discussed the originating coalescence of word and think, but
now we must consider their conflict. The word-image is an attempt
to grasp the thing in space, devoid of time. Simic writes:

Modern poetics: slowing perception or disrupting reading habits to convert time into space by emphasizing visual elements. Joseph Franks says
of the image that its intent is to "overcome the inherent consecutiveness
of language, frustrating the reader's normal expectation of sequence and

forcing him to perceive the elements of the poem as juxtaposed in space rather than unfolding in time." In short, what the image does is convert time into space. Thus, you have time-logic of language versus space-logic of images. [Simic to Jackson, correspondence]

But we do not speak in nouns, and even that part of speech is volatile, shifting definitions. We follow what Heidegger calls the "path of saying," a temporal meandering. What an image means changes, and from this a narrative emerges. In "Dear Isaac Newton" (*A* 55), for example, the narrator begins: "Your famous apple / Is still falling." That is because Newton's "Old Testament apple" is not an object alone, even as an image, but a fourfold, and we have come to understand matter (earth), nature (sky), the origins of the universe (divinity), and ourselves differently from Newton's age. Newton's laws of gravity structured a whole way of looking at the universe that has now been called into question. So, the poem ends:

> O she's falling lawfully,
> But isn't she now
> Perhaps even more mysterious
> Than when she first started?
>
> And wasn't that one of her
> Prize worms
> We saw crawling off
> Into the unthinkable?

There is always a conflict, Heidegger says, between "world" and "earth," between things as we structure them in images, and things as they remain "closed" and beyond our knowledge, "unthinkable" (*OWL* 179–81).

This translates, for Simic, into a conflict between the stasis of images and the push of narrative, a source, really, for much of the dramatic tension in his poems; the world seems constantly to be extrapolating itself beyond him. It is a conflict between timelessness and time, simultaneity and sequence, origin and words about the origin. Ultimately, this suggests an unresolvable problem at the heart of Simic's poetics, a conflict between myth and its object or language, and between image and narrative. Yet it is in the struggle between these two that we find our place, our region, our things. To dramatize the problem is to dramatize the question of origins, and that, in poems, is to approach origins. Such a conflict/solution is at the heart of "The Tale" (*DS* 75). The first part of the poem begins a description of a stillness after the writer has stopped—

> The only movement now
> is the slow unfolding of a tale
> like a white cloth
> over the bare, carefully scrubbed
> table of the night.

And then, as the tale, whatever it is, unfolds, the narrator projects another moment—"that moment / in every tale when only / the shadows linger behind." This trace, fast becoming the lost origin, ends the poem—sort of. What follows are four sub-texts, poems with titles in typeface that suggests they are appendices, four "invention" poems about the knife, the invisible, the place, color, the hat, nothing—images spawned by the original story. About the invisible, for instance,

> when we go looking for them
> there's only his empty chair
> around which the old ant,
> now barely able to move
> has almost made a circle.

It soon becomes clear that such possibilities continually clash: the "place" is inhabited by mobsters, the "color," in fact, "doesn't exist, / like the steady dripping of a faucet / which, all of a sudden, has ceased." The narratives that emerge from the images, then, go their separate ways in the tale. But the images have derived from the larger tale. In other words, the tale, unable to clarify its origins, turns to originating images, to the ways they are "invented," originate, in the author's mind and in "earth," yet they themselves spawn narratives that conflict with each other and the original tale with its "shadow" moment. And the images in those narratives could spawn other narratives. The only thing that temporarily halts this geometric progression is the final section-poem, "errata," which redefines the spoken and unspoken images of the sequence and the book. All images, it seems, are mistakes. They fail to arrive at the origin in the same way we saw the language of non-things fail.

In a way, the narrator, the characters, the reader, all things themselves, anonymous as they are, begin to exist "inconspicuous, / To exist almost without an image," as Simic says in "The Guest" (*CBD* 47). The guest in the poem lives such a marginal existence that he has lost all sense of origins, "trying to remember / How he got there." He is surrounded, it seems, by nothing, by

> No one at all. An eye in a world
> That would otherwise remain dark.
> Improbable sky. His two hands.
> The austere exhibits of his two hands.
>
> They are not there. No matter. Voices
> Of children on the street. Distant.
> Games of another country, another age.
> A hush. Breeze at the end
>
> Of a long hot dusk. Voices. Purple clouds
> That must be hurrying over the rooftops.
> No one at all. Grimy pillow.
> The lamps lit by the stooped widows.

In this imagistic narrative, if we can call it that, a narrative suggested by the "shadows" of images, the images tend to dissolve almost as soon as they are imagined, and yet they leave a narrative bit or fragment in their wakes which the push of the language takes up. The tension between physical things such as the "hands," the "pillow," the "rooftops," are counterbalanced by the "Distant," by "another age," by what is "not there." The desire to stay time, evident not only in the images but by the choppy syntax and by the repetition, say, of "No one at all," is counterbalanced by the incredibly fast paced sense of narrative. Out of the shadows of things, the images, emerges a sense of narrative that, with a change in perspective in the last section, begins to provide a history, a new origin for the guest:

Things and their shadows.
Their vast powers of persuasion.
It is still light outside.
The breeze parting the curtains.

The house by the river, for instance.
This house seen from a great distance
With its dark windows
Toward which the guest travels.

A deadman's hat raised in greeting.
Further on a door opening.
Empty sky.
A nightbird indigenous to these regions.

At the end, the emptiness is also an "opening"; the new beginning recalls what is indigenous to the regions, recalls its origins. The story of the guest, however anonymous he remains, begins to be a possibility. It is a story, a mythology, really, that evolves out of images; it is as if the anonymity of the guest and the nothingness of the images cancelled each other out as a double negative, or at least that seems to be the point of the poem's "persuasion." The timelessness of image generates and defines the temporality of the story. And like all good myth, it is a communal affair, the shift in perspective, "seen from a great distance," recalling the inclusion of the reader. It only remains now to see how this mythology, how the proliferation of myths, constitutes for this anonymous community of words, things and people, a history—"Games of another country, another age." History, we might say, is the dialectic of relationships between image and narrative, perspective and thing, language and origin.

IV

History and Myth, Things and Images

> Whenever art happens—that is, whenever there is a
> beginning—a thrust enters history, history either
> begins or starts over again.
>   —Heidegger, "The Origin of the Work of Art"

The fourfold cannot be thought of as a sequence, but rather as a simultaneous bestowing. Yet it is a history. For Heidegger, history is "not a sequence in time of events of whatever sort, however important. History is the transporting of a people into its appointed task as entrance into that people's endowment" (*OWL* 77). In the terms we have been using, it is a handing down of the mythos of origins. But what can this mythic history say to us? How does it summon us? How does it escape mere time? What temporality does it possess? For Simic, as for Heidegger, the problem is to avoid a Nietzschean history, "Eternal recurrence and its nibble" ("Nursery Rhyme," *CC* 10). In this sort of a vision, everything fits neatly, but is fated—"The little pig goes to market. / Historical necessity. I like to recite / And you prefer to write on the blackboard." The sing-song quality, the neat balance of opposites, the quick cast-off given the phrase "historical necessity," all suggest an inherent problem with the mythic vision— a simplicity that threatens to reduce everything to nursery ditties. The end can only be an utter loss of self—

> Give me another cigarette, quickly.
> Misery. Its wedding photograph.
> I see a blur, a speck, meagre, receding
> Or lines trailing in its wake.

Simple "eternal recurrence," in the way Simic defines the term, would be a return, absolutely, to origins, something we have already seen as impossible. Or it would be a belief in the return to absolute origins which leads to frustration, failed lives and empires, "rubble." It is because we can't return, that history arises, not as a necessity, but as a freedom. It is important to remember, in this respect, Simic's images of prisons, border guards, infirmaries, squalid environments— so many forms of confinement—that must be transcended, even as the object, the simple piece of matter, must be transcended. The aim of the fourfold is to transcend, then, poetically to inscribe and circum- scribe the "misery" that results from visions of "historical necessity."

But how, exactly, can a poetics of origins, a poetics that searches for the simultaneous and the timeless, avoid stasis, or eternal recur- rence in its worst senses? How does it project a history? We can begin to answer by taking up again the question of the thing. For Simic, an historical consciousness includes both the objects of history and the history of objects, and it is this second that provides our key. Take, for instance, almost any of the numerous object poems in Simic's work. "Fork" (*DS* 55) describes that utensil in terms of a bird that "must have crept / Right out of hell"—everything has a mythological history. And as we saw earlier, it involves the reader implicitly or explicitly, blending object, reader, and mythic referent in a complex entanglement of histories: "It is possible to imagine the rest of the bird: / Its head which like your fist / Is large, bold, beakless and blind." And "Ax" (*DS* 63) ends, after describing the object in terms of its "usage," one of the functions of the fourfold category "man" ("The Thing," *PLT*)—

> These dark prophecies were gathered,
> Unknown to myself, by my body
> Which understands historical probabilities,
> Lacking itself, in its essence, a future.

What is curious here is the split between self and body, as if the body itself, as earth, can witness and contrive histories. And it does suggest that the darker histories, the ones of earth, need to be qualified by those of sky, man, and divinity. The thing, when it is qualified by the fourfold, can be a supplement for history, a writing of it as image that,

Simic says in "The Spoon" (*DS* 54), can "be passed on / To the little one / Just barely / Beginning to walk." In the poem "Brooms" (*RPLGM* 21–24), the object is associated with scarecrows, trees, the devil, dreams, a martyr's arrows, a woman, and whatever it sweeps. Finally—

> And then finally there's your grandmother
> Sweeping the dust of the nineteenth century
> Into the twentieth, and your grandfather plucking
> A straw out of the broom to pick his teeth.

So historicized has the object become we do not want to forget that it retains a sense, a trace as we saw earlier, of the timeless, its depthless origin; "Long winter nights. / Dawns a thousand years deep," Simic remarks a few lines later. And the image can itself project other imaginative, associative histories that seem in the context of the poem to become present. For example, the "neat pyramids" of dust swept into shape by the brooms become literalized, images for a history "always already there," as Derrida would say—they "have tombs in them, / Already sacked by robbers, / Once, long ago." The images of history derived from other images, given such particular attention in the poem, seem to become more real. The paradox is that the deeper you go into the poem, the further outside, into the referential world, you also go. At the heart of the poem, at the heart of its timeless origin, in other words, seems to be an historical span— a subject we will return to in a few minutes.

Even the most insignificant object can generate a history. In "History" (*A* 13), for example, it is an apple—

> On a gray evening
> Of a gray century,
> I ate an apple
> While no one was looking.
>
> A small, sour apple
> The color of woodfire,
> Which I first wiped
> On my sleeve.

274

Then I stretched my legs
As far as they'd go.
Said to myself
Why not close my eyes now

Before the Late
World News and Weather.

What begins as a vague, nearly anonymous account in the opening
two lines turns into a very specific, if isolated, event. And the event,
crazily minute and insignificant, is given incredible attention, as it
turns out in the end, to the exclusion of any attention on history. The
counterpointing between the particular object and the general, but
detached passage of events on the news and the weather, and the
exclusion of each to the other, suggests just how important the link
between the fourfold and the object, centered on the object, must be—
without it, both objects and histories become insignificant.

History demands, in Simic's view, a focus on the present as, first,
the site upon which the fourfold acts and, second, as a trace of all that
is absent. The focus is not upon a dead past, but upon a mythic past
where all times are blended, that is just as much a mythic future or
present. Heidegger says in *Being and Time:* " 'history' signifies a
'context' of events and 'effects,' which draws on through the 'past,'
the 'Present,' and the 'future.' On this view, the past has no special
priority" (*H* 432). History, then, becomes a "totality" of specific
changes. This view leads to haunting images as in "My Widow" (*CBD*
26), where the narrator takes a "photograph of a woman in black" out
of a "history book," talks to her "like a lover," tries "to cheer her up."
She becomes like a real figure, sitting at the supper table. He even
supplies her history—"She comes from Poznan. / One of her feet is
shorter than the other." But when the lights are off, when he can
imaginatively see and hear her, the vision becomes disturbing—

Now she's walking through the snow.
She's coming my way,
But there's a wolf-headed dog behind her,
And a soldier with high squeaky boots.

275

The situation is reversed: his summons to her becomes a summons from her, from her age. And so time becomes reversed also; the object becomes a meeting point for times, the picture not only records the past but also the evolving present. In some other poems the time is truly undecidable. "Second Avenue Winter" (*RPLGM* 9) describes a time

> When the horses were no longer found in dreams,
> And the country virgins ceased riding them naked.
> When their manes ceased to resemble sea-foam,
> And the twitching of their ears no longer prophesied
> > great battles.

It is a time when a horse, "pulling a wagon / Piled up high with old mattresses, / Bent under a grey army blanket," makes its way, suggesting perhaps one of the war-refugee carts from old pictures. The picture suggests a couple of other things—"Partly a ghost, partly a poor man's burial." Yet the "wagon wheels whined their ancient lineage / Of country roads, of drunks left lying in the mud— / A million years of shivering and coughing." In other words, the "when" of the opening lines becomes at best ambiguous, a no time, a time that borrows from several mythic dimensions. In the last few lines, when the narrator follows the cart "like a bearded pilgrim," there are references also to New York City and to a more vague, religious context, where he expresses a "wish to be anointed." Here the totality of history also summarizes various kinds of life: the perennial peasant, perennial war, the "million years of shivering" associated with the horse wagon, down to the "old negro driver" who keeps the similar wagon in the modern city. Time, history, becomes all of these—timed certainly, but also harking back to the simultaneity of origins which is always at the heart of Simic's work.

But even times that are more historically delimited still retain this universality. "Baby Pictures of Famous Dictators" (*CBD* 22), for example, convolutes several images—a famine in India, horse-drawn streetcars, Edison, typical turn-of-the-century homes—that suggest the subject is Hitler, Stalin, Mussolini, and their like. Yet the poem creates, in its own words, "a kind of perpetual summer twilight," ominous because the sense of decline, after all, defines baby pictures, and yet also ironically poignant—"Lovable little mugs smiling faintly toward / The new century. Innocent. Why not?" Another poem, "The Little Tear-Gland That Says" (*CBD* 23), begins by describing "Johann, / The carousel horse," who is also, as it turns out in the end, the Johann of "the Viennese Waltz." In a way, the composer as historical entity becomes also the music as it is played in later years, even reductively on the carousel. He becomes also associated with the Wolfian philosophical-linguistic school who "regard / logical necessity and reality as identical." It feels, in many of these poems, as if the characters are unwitting participants in the rush of history about them—

> He stood before the Great Dark Night of History,
> a picture of innocence
> held together by his mother's safety pins—
> lissome, frisky.

And yet the results of such innocence are tragic. Innocence itself is the pure origin, the comically pastoral world Simic ridicules in "My Little Utopia" (*CBD* 53) and "Strictly Bucolic" (*A* 33), but it leads to—

> On his exam he wrote:
> The act of torture consists of various strategies
> meant to increase
> the imagination of the *homo sapiens*.

The point is not to ridicule Strauss, but rather the innocence of his age and his art—eventually, the innocence of us all before history. It is to create a mythological history, a story that tries to know origins without confining itself, as Michel de Certeau notes, to static similitudes, to a dead past (*YFS* 47). History, for Simic, is something produced, not reported; it affirms the beginning, not the end of history, and so ironically affirms its own origins. It is held in the sense, as Heidegger suggests, that tells us of "the-having-been-there" (*BT* 432), a sense of our still possessing, even as an absence, the past in our presences, our images.

This affirmation owes itself to a certain sense of discovery, epiphany, in the consciousness of Simic's narrators. Take, for example, "Prodigy" (*CBD* 21). The poem is spoken by a chess player who begins by recounting a series of disconnected memories—

> I grew up bent over
> a chessboard.

> I loved the word *endgame*.

> All my cousins looked worried.

Later, the line break at "bent over," the notion of "endgame," and the worry came back to haunt him. "That must have been 1944," he says, and

> I'm told but do not believe
> that that summer I witnessed
> men hung from telephone poles.

> I remember my mother
> blindfolding me a lot.

> She had a way of tucking my head
> suddenly under her overcoat.

> In chess, too, the professor told me,
> the masters play blindfolded,
> the great ones on several boards
> at the same time.

Here the simultaneousness of things, what we began with back in "Erasers," achieves its most forceful and most complex treatment. What is required is a certain blindness on the part of the narrator-historian, for history is, after all, a myth whose objects are always absent, and more—always partially invented. What is required is a disinterestedness, a gesture of distance and anonymity that tries to subvert the inescapable biography of the narrator, what he has at stake. What is required, in the context of this blindness and this anonymity, is the spatialization of time into a simultaneous and original unity, the imaging of history through the chess pieces and the fourfold sense the pieces and game as objects themselves, as images or symbols for man's history, as simple counters for the time of any game (or history), and as am image of a plan, chance, or motive beyond the local, beyond the blindfolded vision. All these impulses which we have discussed in detail come together, in the end, to suggest both the vision and the blindness we have towards our histories, towards the ways we order our lives. Here, then, is Heidegger's history, not of a sequence of events in time, but of a handing down, a true history of origins, or rather, a history of originating—an original history.

The final gesture of the poems, then, is towards the infinite; the simultaneity of origins is imaged in the simultaneity of infinite and eternal spaces, and one "only" has to pass through time and history to get from one to the other. More correctly than we imaged earlier, then, history lies not at the heart of the timeless moment, but between two timeless moments. The structure, as we have seen, is the myth, which partakes of the anonymity and the timeless at both beginning and end. This, for example, is the sort of vision that informs poems like "Anatomy Lesson" (*DS* 39), which ends with a "period a careless dot," after which is a "sentence" that is "A void big enough / For the universe / To make its kennel in." Or the vision of the "child crying in the night" in "Unintelligible Terms" (*CC* 27), where the sound becomes part of the "expanding immensity" of references "Simultaneous Oh God, / With all the empty spaces." Or the most encompassing vision of all in Simic's work, that of "Charon's Cosmology" (*CC* 14), that old master of beginnings and ends and all that lies between. With only his feeble lantern, with all those trips, Simic says, "I'd say by now he must be confused / As to which side is which // I'd say it doesn't matter." It is Charon, then, who is our historian-cosmologist, the one who goes through the pockets of all he ferries for the lost objects of history, the mythological ferryman carrying his anonymous passengers on the river of time from the simultaneity of origins to the simultaneity of ends, "the dark river / Swift cold and deep."

In the end, our cosmology is also a teleology, then, and we are, as Simic suggests in the title of a recent poem, at the "Midpoint" (*A* 40).

That poem, divided into two halves, begins: "No sooner had I left A. / Than I started doubting its existence"—even, this anonymous voice says, "Even the back alley where I was born." But then the voice, thinking ahead, goes: "B. at which I am destined / To arrive by and by / Doesn't exist now." What "they" are building for his arrival at B is his history, his past, "Even the schoolhouse where I first / Forged my father's signature . . ." We are always forging our pasts and futures, and for that reason B "will vanish forever / fast as A did." Between two origins—our past origin and its supplement (supplements, really)—we have only dubious traces. But at least the midpoint, the threshold we always find ourselves occupying, as Heidegger says, is what gives us our "connectedness," and so our sense of direction with which to interrogate our fragmented lives (*BT* 425). At the heart of Simic's poetic, if we can ever use that figure again, is an intense questioning, a questioning that leads to the undercutting and mocking we have occasionally seen in Simic. He says in one essay, "The secret ambition of image-making is gnosis—an irreverence which is the result of the most exalted seriousness." The image of history, then, or the history of images, the time of the timeless, provokes an endless questioning—"To know history . . . is to lose innocence and ponder what the 'images' are saying" ("Images," 26). It is to discover the hidden histories of our images, our origins, to create the marvelous prey we search for.

Selected Bibliography

GENERAL

This listing includes the major books of poetry written by each of the poets interviewed (disregarding chapbooks) and, for the reader who wishes to explore further the concerns of the essays, a short selection of critical books or major essays about the poets. As yet, no books or major essays have been written about several poets, especially the younger ones. For them, the reader should refer to reviews in various journals, which are indexed in *Contemporary Poets* (New York: St. Martin's Press); *Contemporary Authors* (Detroit: Gale Research Co.); the excellent bibliographies in *PMLA, Contemporary Literary Criticism, Journal of Modern Literature,* and *An Index to Book Reviews in the Humanities;* and the book-length bibliographies that have been published for several of the poets included here. The reader should also be aware of *American Poets since World War II,* 2 vols. (Detroit: Gale Research Co., 1980), edited by Donald Grenier, which includes excellent introductory essays on many poets and for which a second part is planned to include poets not covered in the first two volumes. The reader may also consult Kirby Congdon's *Contemporary Poets in American Anthologies, 1960–1977* (Metuchen; N.J.: Scarecrow Press, 1978), and the two standard bibliographies of contemporary poetry, Charles Altieri's *Modern Poetry* (Arlington Heights, Ill.: AHM, Goldentree, 1979) and Karl Malkoff's *Crowell's Handbook of Contemporary American Poetry* (New York: Crowell, 1973). In addition, informative essays on several of the poets interviewed appear in Charles Altieri, *Enlarging the Temple: New Directions in American Poetry of the Sixties* (Cranberry, N.J.: Bucknell University Press, 1979); Robert Boyers, ed., *Contemporary Poetry in America: Essays and Interviews* (New York: Schocken Books, 1974); Richard Howard, *Alone with America,* 2d enlarged ed. (New York: Atheneum, 1980); Laurence Lieberman, *Unassigned Frequencies: American Poetry in Review* (Urbana: University of Illinois Press,

1977); Helen Vendler, *Part of Nature, Part of Us* (Cambridge, Mass.: Harvard University Press, 1980); Ralph J. Mills, Jr., *Contemporary American Poetry* (New York: Random House, 1965); and Stephen Stepanchev, *American Poetry since 1945* (New York: Harper and Row, 1965). Finally, Alberta Turner's *50 Contemporary Poets: The Creative Process* (New York: David McKay Co., 1977) contains essays by several poets on their own poems.

MAIN POETS DISCUSSED

John Ashbery, b. 1927, Rochester, New York; taught at Brooklyn College.
POETRY: *Turandot and Other Poems* (New York: Tibor de Nagy, 1953); *Some Trees* (New Haven: Yale University Press, 1956; reprint, New York: Corinth, 1970); *The Tennis Court Oath* (Middletown, Conn.: Wesleyan University Press, 1962); *Rivers and Mountains* (New York: Holt, Rinehart and Winston, 1966; reprint, New York: Ecco, 1977); *The Double Dream of Spring* (New York: Dutton, 1970; reprint, New York: Ecco, 1976); *Three Poems* (New York: Viking, 1972; reprint, New York: Penguin, 1977); *The Vermont Journal* (Los Angeles: Black Sparrow, 1975); *Self-Portrait in a Convex Mirror* (New York: Viking, 1975; reprint, New York: Penguin, 1976); *Houseboat Days* (New York: Viking/Penguin, 1977); *As We Know* (New York: Viking/Penguin, 1979); *Shadow Train* (New York: Viking/Penguin, 1981); *A Wave* (New York: Viking, 1985).
CRITICISM: Gilbert Allen, "When Paraphrase Fails: The Interpretation of Modern American Poetry," *College English,* 1981 Apr., 43(4):363–370; Bonnie Costello, "John Ashbery and the Idea of the Reader," *Contemporary Literature,* 1982 Fall, 23(4):493–514; John W. Erwin, "The Reader Is the Medium: Ashbery and Ammons Ensphered," *Contemporary Literature,* 21:588–609; Cynthia Evans, "A Moment Out of the Dream," *American Poetry Review,* 8, iv, 1979:33–36; Thomas A. Fink, "Here and There: The Locus of Language in John Ashbery's *Self-Portrait in a Convex Mirror,*" *Contemporary Poetry* (now *Poesis*), 1982, 4(3):47–64; David Fite, "John Ashbery: The Effort to Make Sense," *Mississippi Review,* 1979 Spring, 2(2–3):123–130; David Fite, "On the Virtues of Modesty: John Ashbery's Tactics against Transcendence," *Modern Language Quarterly,* 1981 Mar., 42(1):65–84; Jonathan Holden, "Syntax and the Poetry of John Ashbery," *American Poetry Review,* 8, iv, 1979:37–40; David Kalstone, *Five Temperaments* (New York: Oxford University Press, 1977); Lynn Keller, "Thinkers without Final Thoughts: John Ashbery's Evolving Debt to Wallace Stevens," *English Literary History,* 1982 Spring, 49(1):235–261; David K. Kerman, *John Ashbery:*

A Comprehensive Bibliography (New York and London: G. K. Hall, 1976); John Koethe, "An Interview with John Ashbery," *Substance,* 1983, 11–12: 178–186; Laurence Lieberman, "Unassigned Frequencies: Whispers Out of Time," *American Poetry Review,* 1977 Mar.–Apr., 6(2):4–18; William Packard, ed., "The Craft of Poetry Interviews," from *The New York Quarterly* (Garden City: Doubleday, 1961); A. Poulin, Jr., "The Experience: A Conversation with John Ashbery," *Michigan Quarterly Review,* 1981 Summer, 20(3):242–255; Goran Printz-Pahlson, "On John Ashbery," *Artes,* 1981, 6:28–33; Robert Richman, "Our 'Most Important' Living Poet," *Commentary,* 1982 July, 74(1):62–68; Marianne Shapiro, "John Ashbery: The New Spirit," *Water Table: Poetry, Poetics* (Seattle), 1:58–73; David Spurr, "John Ashbery's Poetry of Language," *Centennial Review,* 1981 Spring, 25(2):150–161; Nigel Wheale, "The All, the All in the Poetry of John Ashbery," *Poetry Review,* 69, iii:56–60; Dana Yeaton, "Compliments of a Friend: A Review of John Ashbery's *As We Know,*" *American Poetry Review,* 1981 Jan.–Feb., 10(1):34–36.

OTHER: *The Compromise,* New York, Poet's Theatre, 1955; *The Philosopher,* published in *Art and Literature* (Paris), no. 2 (1964); *Three Plays* (Calais, Vt.: Z Press, 1978).

Denise Levertov, b. 1923, Essex, England, teaches at Tufts and Stanford.
POETRY: *The Double Image* (London: Cresset, 1946); *Here and Now* (San Francisco: City Lights Books, 1956); *Overland to the Islands* (Highlands, N.C.: Jonathan Williams, 1958); *With Eyes at the Back of Our Heads* (New York: New Directions, 1960); *The Jacob's Ladder* (New York: New Directions, 1961; London: Cape, 1965); *O Taste and See* (New York: New Directions, 1964); *The Sorrow Dance* (New York: New Directions, 1967; London: Cape, 1968); *Relearning the Alphabet* (New York: New Directions, 1970; London: Cape, 1970); *To Stay Alive* (New York: New Directions, 1971); *Footprints* (New York: New Directions, 1972); *The Poet in the World* (New York: New Directions, 1974); *Oblique Prayers* (New York: New Directions, 1985); *Candles in Babylon* (New York: New Directions, 1983); *The Freeing of the Dust* (New York: New Directions, 1975); *Life in the Forest* (New York: New Directions, 1978); *Collected Earlier Poems: 1940–1960* (New York: New Directions, 1979).
CRITICISM: William Aiken, "Denise Levertov, Robert Duncan, and Ginsberg: Modes of the Self in Projective Poetry," *Modern Poetry Studies,* 1981, 10(2–3):200–245; Alicia Ostriker, "In Mind: The Divided Self and Women's Poetry," *Midwest Quarterly,* 1983 Summer, 24(4):351–356; Diana Surman, "Inside and Outside in the Poetry of Denise Levertov," *Critical Quarterly,* 22,i:57–70; Linda Wagner, *Denise Levertov* (New York: Twayne Publishers,

1967); Linda Welshimer Wagner, ed., *Denise Levertov: In Her Own Province* (insights, working papers in contemp. crit. 2) (New York: New Directions, 1979), 144 pp.; Robert A. Wilson, *A Bibliography of Denise Levertov* (New York: Phoenix Book Shop, 1972).

John Hollander, b. 1929, New York City; teaches at Yale University.
POETRY: *A Crackling of Thorns* (New Haven: Yale University Press, 1958); *Movie Going* (New York: Atheneum, 1962); *Visions from the Ramble* (New York: Atheneum, 1965); *Types of Shape* (New York: Atheneum, 1969); *The Night Mirror* (New York: Atheneum, 1971); *Tales Told of the Fathers* (New York: Atheneum, 1975); *Reflections on Espionage* (New York: Atheneum, 1976); *Spectral Emanations: New and Selected Poems* (New York: Atheneum, 1978); *Blue Wine and Other Poems* (Baltimore: Johns Hopkins University Press, 1979); *Powers of Thirteen* (New York: Atheneum, 1984).
CRITICISM: Harold Bloom, "The Sorrows of American-Jewish Poetry," *Commentary*, 53 (March 1972):69–74; Harold Bloom, "The White Light of Trope: An Essay on John Hollander's 'Spectral Emanations,' " *Kenyon Review*, new series, 1 (Winter 1979):95–113; J. D. McClatchy, "Speaking of Hollander," *American Poetry Review* (1982 Sept.–Oct.), 11(5):23–26; Philip L. Gerber and Robert J. Gemmett, "The Poem as Silhouette: A Conversation with John Hollander," *Michigan Quarterly Review* 9 (Fall 1970):253–260.
OTHER: *I. A. Richards: Essays in His Honor*, ed. Hollander, Reuben Brower, and Helen Vendler (London: Oxford University Press, 1973); *Modern Poetry Essays in Criticism*, ed. Hollander (London, Oxford, and New York: Oxford University Press, 1968); *The Oxford Anthology of English Literature*, 2 vols., under general editorship of Hollander and Frank Kermode (New York, London, and Toronto: Oxford University Press, 1973); *The Untuning of the Sky: Ideas of Music in English Poetry, 1500–1700* (Princeton: Princeton University Press, 1961; London: Oxford University Press, 1961); *Vision and Resonance: Two Senses of Poetic Form* (New York: Oxford University Press, 1975).

Charles Simic, b. 1938, Belgrade, Yugoslavia; teaches at the University of New Hampshire.
POETRY: *Dismantling the Silence* (New York: George Braziller, 1971); *Return to a Place Lit by a Glass of Milk* (New York: George Braziller, 1974); *Charon's Cosmology* (New York: George Braziller, 1977); *White: A New Version* (Durango, Colo.: Logbridge-Rhodes, 1980); *Austerities* (New York: George Braziller, 1982); *Selected Poems* (New York: George Braziller, 1985); *Classic Ballroom Dances* (New York: George Braziller, 1980); *Weather Re-*

port for Utopia and Vicinity (New York: Station Hill Press, 1983); *Unending Blues* (New York: Harcourt, Brace, 1986).

CRITICISM: Victor Contoski, "Charles Simic: Language at the Stone's Heart," *Chicago Review,* 28, no. 6 (1977):145–157; Richard Jackson, "Charles Simic and Mark Strand: The Presence of Absence," *Contemporary Literature,* 21:136–145; *Manassas Review: Essays on Contemporary American Poetry* 1, no. 2 (Winter 1978): [special issue on Simic].

Other: *The Uncertain Certainty: Interviews, Essays, and Notes on Poetry* (Ann Arbor: University of Michigan, 1985).

Robert Penn Warren, b. 1905, Guthrie, Kentucky; lives in Farmington, Connecticut.

POETRY: *Thirty-Six Poems* (New York: Alcestis Press, 1935); *Eleven Poems on the Same Theme* (New York: New Directions, 1942); *Selected Poems: 1923–1943* (New York: Harcourt Brace, 1944); *Brother to Dragons* (New York: Random House, 1953, revised 1979); *Promises: Poems, 1954–1956* (New York: Random House, 1957); *You, Emperors, and Others: Poems, 1957–1960* (New York: Random House, 1960); *Selected Poems, New and Old: 1923–1966* (New York: Random House, 1966); *Incarnations: Poems, 1966–1968* (New York: Random House, 1968); *Audubon: A Vision* (New York: Random House, 1969); *Or Else: Poem/Poems, 1968–1974* (New York: Random House, 1974); *Selected Poems, 1923–1975* (New York: Random House, 1977); *Now and Then: Poems, 1976–1978* (New York: Random House, 1978); *Being Here: Poetry, 1977–1980* (New York: Random House, 1980); *Rumor Verified: Poems, 1979–1980* (New York: Random House, 1981); *Selected Poems, 1923–1985* (New York: Random House, 1985).

CRITICISM: Calvin Bedient, "Greatness and Robert Penn Warren," *Sewanee Review,* 1981 Summer, 89(3):332–346; Cleanth Brooks, "Episode and Anecdote in the Poetry of Robert Penn Warren," *Yale Review,* 1981 Summer, 70(4):551–567; David Farrell, "Poetry as a Way of Life: An Interview with Robert Penn Warren," *Georgia Review,* 1982 Summer, 36(2):315–331; Frank Graziano, ed. (Hilton Kramer, introd.), *Homage to Robert Penn Warren: A Collection of Critical Essays* (Durango, Colo.: Logbridge-Rhodes, 1981), 92 pp. [introd., 9–16]; T. R. Hummer, "Robert Penn Warren: *Audubon* and the Moral Center," *Southern Review,* 16:799–815; Richard Jackson, "The Generous Time: Robert Penn Warren and the Phenomenology of the Moment," *Boundary 2,* 1981 Winter, 9(2):1–30; Richard Jackson, "The Shards of Time: Robert Penn Warren and the Moment of the Self: A Review Essay," *Southern Humanities Review,* 14:161–167; Laurence Lieberman, "The Glacier's Offspring: A Reading of Robert Penn Warren's New Poetry," *American Poetry*

Review, 1981 Mar.–Apr., 10(2):6–8; Joseph Parisi, "Homing In," *Shenandoah,* 1979, 30(4):99–107; Dave Smith, "He Prayeth Best Who Loveth Best: On Robert Penn Warren's Poetry," *American Poetry Review,* 1979 Jan.–Feb., 8(1):4–8; Victor Strandberg, "*Brother to Dragons* and the Craft of Revision," pp. 200–201 in James A. Grimshaw, Jr., ed., *Robert Penn Warren's Brother to Dragons: A Discussion* (Baton Rouge: Louisiana State University Press, 1983), 309 pp. (So. Lit. Studies); Peter Stitt, "Robert Penn Warren: Life's Instancy and the Astrolabe of Joy," *Georgia Review,* 34:711–731; Victor Strandberg, "Warren's Poetic Vision: A Reading of *Now and Then,*" *Southern Review,* 16:18–45; Floyd C. Watkins, *Then & Now: The Personal Past in the Poetry of Robert Penn Warren* (Lexington: University Press of Kentucky, 1982), xiv, 184 pp.; Max A. Webb, "*Audubon a Vision:* Robert Penn Warren's Response to Eudora Welty's 'A Still Moment,' " *Mississippi Quarterly,* 1981 Fall, 34(4):445–455; Mark Royden Winchell, "Robert Penn Warren's *Brother to Dragons:* Irony and the Image of Man," *Mississippi Quarterly,* 1981–82 Winter, 35(1):15–24; Thomas Daniel Young, "Assessing Robert Penn Warren's Literary Achievement," *Mississippi Quarterly,* 1981–82 Winter, 35(1):41–52.

OTHER: Floyd C. Watkins and John T. Hiers, eds., *Robert Penn Warren Talking: Interviews, 1950–1978* (New York: Random House), 304 pp.

James Wright, b. 1927, Martins Ferry, Ohio; d. 1980.

POETRY: *The Green Wall* (New Haven: Yale University Press, 1957; London: Oxford University Press, 1957); *Saint Judas* (Middletown, Conn.: Wesleyan University Press, 1959); *The Lion's Tail and Eyes: Poems Written Out of Laziness and Silence,* by Wright, Robert Bly, and William Duffy (Madison, Minn.: Sixties Press, 1962); *The Branch Will Not Break* (Middletown, Conn.: Wesleyan University Press, 1963; London: Longmans, 1963); *Shall We Gather at the River* (Middletown, Conn.: Wesleyan University Press, 1968; London: Rapp & Whiting, 1969); *Collected Poems* (Middletown: Wesleyan University Press, 1971); *Two Citizens* (Middletown: Wesleyan University Press, 1973); *To a Blossoming Pear Tree* (New York: Farrar, Straus, and Giroux, 1977); *This Journey* (New York: Random House, Vintage, 1982).

CRITICISM: William V. Davis, " 'A Grave in Blossom': A Note on James Wright," *Contemporary Poetry,* 1982, 4(3):1–3; Peter Stitt, "The Art of Poetry XIX," *Paris Review,* 16 (Summer 1975):34–61; Madeline De Frees, "James Wright's Early Poems: A Study in 'Convulsive' Form," *Modern Poetry Studies,* 2 (1972):241–251; John Ditsky, "James Wright Collected: Alterations on the Monument," *Modern Poetry Studies,* 2 (1979):252–259; Nicholas Gattuccio, "Now My Amenities of Stone Are Done: Some Notes on the Style of

James Wright," *Concerning Poetry,* 1982 Spring, 15 (1):61–76; Michael Graves, "A Look at the Ceremonial Range of James Wright," *Concerning Poetry,* 1983 Fall, 16 (2):43–54; William Heyen and Jerome Mazzaro, "Something to Be Said for the Light: A Conversation with James Wright," ed. Joseph R. McElrath, Jr., *Southern Humanities Review,* 6 (1972):134–153; David Jauss, "Wright's 'Lying in a Hammock at William Duffy's Farm in Pine Island, Minnesota,'" *Explicator,* 1982 Fall, 41(1):54–55; Walter Kalaidjian, "Many of Our Waters: The Poetry of James Wright," *Boundary* 2, 1981 Winter, 9(2):101–121; Edward Lense, "This Is What I Wanted: James Wright and the Other World," *Modern Poetry Studies,* 1982, 11 (1–2);19–32; George S. Lensing and Ronald Moran, *Four Poets and the Emotive Imagination: Robert Bly, James Wright, Louis Simpson, and William Stafford* (Baton Rouge: Louisiana State University Press, 1976), pp. 87–132; William Matthews, "Entering the World," *Shenandoah,* 20(1969):80–93; Jerome Mazzaro, "Dark Water: James Wright's Early Poetry," *Centennial Review,* 1983 Spring, 27 (2):135–155; Charles Molesworth, "James Wright and the Dissolving Self," in *Contemporary Poetry in America: Essays and Interviews,* ed. Robert Boyers (New York: Schocken Books, 1974), pp. 267–268; James Seay, "A World Immeasurably Alive and Good: A Look at James Wright's *Collected Poems,*" *Georgia Review,* 27 (Spring 1973):71–81; Peter Serchuk, "On the Poet, James Wright," *Modern Poetry Studies,* 1981, 10 (2–3):85–90; Dave Smith, "An Interview with James Wright: The Pure, Clear Word," *American Poetry Review,* 9, iii:19–30; Dave Smith, ed., *The Pure Clear Word: Essays on the Poetry of James Wright* (Urbana: University of Illinois Press, 1982); Peter A. Stitt, "The Poetry of James Wright," *Minnesota Review,* 2 (1972):13–32; Paul Zweig, "Making and Unmaking," *Partisan Review,* 40 (1973):269–273.

OTHER· *Collected Prose,* ed. Ralph Mills (Ann Arbor: University of Michigan Press, 1984); *Neruda and Vallejo, Selected Poems,* trans. Wright, Bly, and Knoepfle (Boston: Beacon Press, 1971); George Trakl, *Twenty Poems,* trans. Wright, John Knoepfle, and Robert Bly (Madison, Minn.: Sixties Press, 1961); Cesar Vallejo, *Twenty Poems,* trans. Wright, Bly, and Knoepfle (Madison, Minn.: Sixties Press, 1962); Leslie Smith and James Wright, *The Delicacy and Strength of Lace* [Letters], ed. Anne Wright (St. Paul: Graywolf Press, 1986); *The Shape of Light* (White Pine, 1986).

OTHER TEXTS

Altieri, Charles. "Motives for Metaphor: John Ashbery and the Modernist Long Poem," in *Genre,* XI (1978).

Selected Bibliography

Ashbery, John. "Craft Interview with John Ashbery," in *The Craft of Poetry*. Ed. William Packard. New York: Doubleday, 1974.

Bachelard, Gaston. *The Poetics of Space*. Trans. M. Golas. Boston: Beacon Press, 1969.

Bakhtin, Mikhail. *The Dialogic Imagination*. Trans. Holquist. Austin: University of Texas Press, 1980.

Bell, Marvin. *These Green-Going-To-Yellow*. New York: Atheneum, 1981.

Berger, Charles. "Vision in the Form of a Task," in *Beyond Amazement: New Essays on John Ashbery*. Ed. David Lehmon. Ithaca: Cornell University Press, 1970.

Bergson, Henri. *Time and Free Will*. Trans. F. L. Pogson, 1910; rpt. New York: Harper and Row, 1960.

Bertoldi, Eugene. "Time in the *Phenomenology of Perception*," *Dialogue*, 13 (1974).

Bishop, Elizabeth. *The Complete Poems, 1927–1979*. New York: Farrar, Straus, and Giroux, 1983.

Boman, Thorlief. *Hebrew Thought Compared with Greek*. Trans. Jules Moreau. New York: W. W. Norton, 1960.

Borges, Jorge. *Ficciones*. Ed. Kerrigan. New York: Grove Press, 1962.

Brisman, Susan, and Leslie Hawk. "Lies against Solitude: Symbolic, Imaginary, and Real," in *The Literary Freud: Mechanisms of Defense and the Poetic Will*. Ed. Joseph Smith. New Haven: Yale University Press, 1980.

Coleridge, S. T. *Biographia Literaria*, rev. ed. London: J. M. Dent, 1965.

———. *Collected Letters of Samuel Taylor Coleridge*. Ed. E. L. Griggs. Oxford: Clarendon Press, 1959. 3 (1807–1814), no. 814.

———. *The Collected Works of Samuel Taylor Coleridge*, vol. 4, *The Friend*, I. Ed. by B. Rooke. Princeton University Press, 1969. 430 (Essay IV).

———. *The Notebooks of Samuel Taylor Coleridge*. Ed. Kathleen Raine. New York: Bollingen Foundation, 1961.

Corngold, Stanley, "*Sein* and *Zeit:* Implications for Poetics," in *Martin Heidegger and the Question of Literature*. Ed. William Spanos. Bloomington: Indiana University Press, 1979.

Coward, Rosalind, and John Ellis. *Language and Materialism: Development in Semiology and the Theory of the Subject*. London: Routledge and Kegan Paul, 1977.

Deleuze, Gilles. *Proust and Signs*. Trans. Richard Howard. New York: George Braziller, 1972 (orig. 1964).

Derrida, Jacques. *Dissemination*. Trans. Barbara Johnson. Chicago: University of Chicago Press, 1981.

———. *Margins*. Trans. Barbara Johnson. Chicago: University of Chicago Press, 1981.

———. "Fors." *Georgia Review* (1977). Also in *Margins.*

———. *Of Grammatology.* Trans. G. Spivak. Baltimore: Johns Hopkins, 1976.

———. *Positions.* Trans. Alan Bass. Chicago: University of Chicago Press, 1981.

———. "Scribble Power." *Yale French Studies,* 58 (1979).

———. *Speech and Phenomena, and Other Essays on Husserl's Theory of Signs.* Trans. D. Allison. Evanston: Northwestern University Press, 1976.

———. *Writing and Difference.* Trans. Alan Bass. Chicago: University of Chicago Press, 1981.

———. "Writing On." *Deconstruction and Criticism.* Ed. G. Hartman. New York: Seabury, 1979.

Foucault, Michel. *Language, Counter Memory, Practice.* Trans. D. Bouchard. Ithaca: Cornell University Press, 1977.

———. *The Archaeology of Knowledge.* Trans. Rupert Sawyer. New York: Harper and Row, 1976.

———. *The Order of Things.* New York: Random House, 1970.

Freud, Sigmund. *Collected Papers,* vol. 5. Trans. James Strachey. New York: Basic Books, 1959.

———. "The Relation of the Poet to Daydreaming," in *On Creativity and the Unconscious.* Trans. and ed. Benjamin Nelson. New York: Harper Torchbooks, 1958.

Frost, Robert. *The Poetry of Robert Frost.* New York: Holt, Rinehart and Winston, 1967.

Hall, Donald. *Kicking the Leaves.* New York: Harper and Row, 1977.

Harr, Michael. "Nietzsche and Metaphysical Language," in *The New Nietzsche: Contemporary Styles of Interpretation.* Ed. David Allison. New York: Delat Books, 1977.

Hegel, G. W. F. Preface to *Phenomenology of Mind in Hegel: Texts and Commentary.* Trans. Walter Kaufman, 1965; rpt. New York: Doubleday/Anchor, 1966.

———. *The Phenomenology of Mind.* Trans. J. B. Baille. New York: Harper Torchbooks, 1967.

Heidegger, Martin. *An Introduction to Metaphysics.* Trans. Ralph Monheim. New Haven: Yale University Press, 1959.

———. *Basic Problems of Metaphysics.* Trans. A. Hofstadter. Bloomington: University of Indiana Press, 1982.

———. *Being and Time.* Trans. Maquarrie and Robinson. New York: Harper and Row, 1962.

———. *Discourse on Thinking.* Trans. J. Anderson and E. Freund. New York: Harper and Row, 1966.

———. "Holderlin and the Essence of Poetry." Trans. Douglas Scott.

————. *Existence and Being.* Chicago: Henry Regnery Co., 1949.

————. *Identity and Difference.* Trans. Joan Stambaugh. New York: Harper and Row, 1969.

————. *Kant and the Problem of Metaphysics.* Trans. James Churchill. Bloomington: Indiana University Press, 1962.

————. *Nietzsche,* vol. I: *The Will to Power as Art.* Trans. David Krell. New York: Harper and Row, 1979.

————. *Poetry, Language, Thought.* Trans. Albert Hofstadter. New York: Harper and Row, 1972.

————. "The Nature of Language." Trans. Peter Hertz. *On the Way to Language.* New York: Harper and Row, 1971.

————. *Time and Being.* Trans. Joan Stambaugh. New York: Harper and Row, 1972.

Heyen, William, and Jerome Mazarro. "Something To Be Said for the Light: A Conversation with James Wright," in *Southern Humanities Review.* Ed. J. McElrath. 1975.

Howard, Richard. *Alone with America,* 2d ed. New York: Atheneum, 1979.

Husserl, Edmund. *The Phenomenology of Internal Time-Consciousness.* Trans. James Churchill. Bloomington: Indiana University Press, 1964.

Jabes, Edmond. *The Book of Questions,* vol. 1. Trans. Rosmarie Waldrip. Middletown, Conn.: Wesleyan University Press, 1976.

Jackson, Richard. *Acts of Mind: Conversation With Contemporary Poets.* Tuscaloosa: University of Alabama Press, 1983.

————. "The Deconstructed Moment in Modern Poetry," in *Contemporary Literature,* 23 (1982).

Kant, Immaneul. *Critique of Pure Reason.* Trans. Norman K. Smith, 1929. Rpt. New York: St. Martin's Press, 1965.

Kierkegaard, Søren. *Either/Or,* rev. ed. Trans. Dr. E. L. Swenson. Princeton: Princeton University Press, 1959.

————. *Repetition: An Essay in Experimental Biology.* Trans. Walter Lowrie. New York: Harper Torchbooks, 1964.

————. *The Journals of Kierkegaard.* Trans. A. Dru, 1939. Rpt. New York: Harper Torchbooks, 1959.

Koethe, John. "The Metaphysical Subject of John Ashbery's Poetry," in *Beyond Amazement: New Essays on John Ashbery.* Ed. David Lehman. Ithaca: Cornell University Press, 1980.

Kofman, Sarah. "Metaphor, Symbol Metamorphosis," in *The New Nietzsche: Contemporary Styles of Interpretation.* Ed. David Allison. New York: Delat Books, 1977.

Kristova, Julia. *Desire in Language.* Ed. Roudiez. New York: Columbia University Press, 1980.

Kumin, Maxine. *Our Ground Time Here Will Be Brief.* New York: Penguin Books, 1982.

Kunitz, Stanley. *The Poems of Stanley Kunitz, 1928–1978.* Boston: Atlantic Monthly Press, 1979.

La Planche, J., and J. B. Pontalis. *The Language of Psychoanalysis.* Trans. Donald Nicholson-Smith. New York: W. W. Norton, 1973.

Lacan, Jacques. *Écrits: A Selection.* Trans. Alan Sheridan. New York: W. W. Norton, 1977.

———. *The Four Fundamental Concepts of Psycho-Analysis.* Trans. Alan Sheridan. New York: W. W. Norton, 1978.

———. "Desire and Interpretation of Desire in Hamlet," in *Yale French Studies.* 55/56 (1977).

———. "Of Structure as in Mixing of an Otherness Prerequisite to Any Subject Whatever," in *Structuralist Controversy.* Ed. Macksey and Donato. Baltimore: Johns Hopkins University Press. 1970.

Lehman, David, ed. *Beyond Amazement: New Essays on John Ashbery.* Ithaca: Cornell University Press, 1980.

Levine, Philip. *They Feed They Lion.* New York: Atheneum, 1974.

———. *Ashes.* New York: Atheneum, 1979.

———. *7 Years from Somewhere.* New York: Atheneum, 1979.

Matthews, William. *Flood.* Boston: Atlantic Monthly Press, 1982.

Merleau-Ponty, Maurice. *The Phenomenology of Perception.* Trans. Colin Smith. London: Routledge and Kegan Paul, 1962.

Miller, J. Hillis. "Ariadne's Thread: Repetition and the Narrative Line." In *Critical Inquiry,* 3, no. 1 (1976).

Nietzsche, Friedrich. *The Will to Power.* Trans. Kaufman. New York: Vintage, 1954.

———. *Thus Spake Zarathustra.* Trans. Kaufman, in *The Portable Nietzsche.* New York: Viking, 1954.

———. *On the Genealogy of Morals.* Trans. Kaufman. New York: Vintage Books, 1967.

———. *The Gay Science.* Trans. Kaufman. New York: Vintage, 1974.

Pack, Robert. *Walking to My Name: New and Selected Poems.* Baltimore: Johns Hopkins University Press, 1980.

Plumly, Stanley. *Summer Celestial.* New York: Ecco Press, 1983.

Poulet, Georges. *Studies in Human Time.* Trans. E. Coleman, 1956. Rpt. New York: Harper and Row, 1959.

Quinn, Sr. Bernetta. "Warren and Jarrell: The Remembered Child." In *Southe i Literary Journal,* 8 (1976).

Ricc ur, Paul. *The Rule of Metaphor.* Trans. Robert Czerny. Toronto: University of Toronto Press, 1977.

Riffaterre, Michael. *Semiotics of Poetry.* New York: Columbia University Press, 1978.

Sartre, Jean Paul. *Being and Nothingness.* Trans. Hazel Barnes. New York: Washington Square Press, 1966.

Schiller, Friedrich. *On the Aesthetic Education of Man.* Trans. Reginald Snell. New York: F. Ungar, 1965.

Shapiro, David. *John Ashbery.* Columbia University Press, 1979.

Shelley, P. B. *Complete Works.* Ed. Neville. Boston, Mass.: Cambridge University Press, 1974.

Simic, Charles. "Composition." In *New Literary History* (Fall 1984), pp. 149–151.

———. "Image and Images." In *The Uncertain Certainty,* pp. 105–108. Ann Arbor: University of Michigan Press, 1985.

Spanos, William, ed. *Heidegger and the Question of Literature.* Bloomington: Indiana University Press, 1979.

Spears, Monroe K. "The Latest Poetry of Robert Penn Warren." In *Sewanee Review,* 78 (1970).

St. John, David. *The Shore.* Boston: Houghton Mifflin, 1980.

Stevens, Wallace. *Collected Poems.* New York: Alfred Knopf, 1955.

———. *The Palm at the End of the Mind.* Ed. Holly Stevens. New York: Alfred Knopf, 1971.

Strandberg, Victor. "Warren's Poetic Vision: A Reading of *Now and Then.*" In *The Southern Review,* 16, no. 1 (1980).

Watkins, Floyd, and John Hiers. *Robert Penn Warren Talking: Interviews, 1950–1978.* New York: Random House, 1980.

Wilden, Anthony. "Lacan and the Discourse of the Other," in *The Language of the Self.* Ed. Wilden. New York: Delta Books, 1968.

Wittgenstein, Ludwig. *The Blue and Brown Books.* New York: Harper and Row, 1965.

Index

Index

101; and non-being, 224, 232, 245, 246, 251, 252. *See also Dasein*, Presence, Temporality, Time, Trace
Bell, Marvin: "The Hedgeapple," 17–20
Bergson, Henri, 30, 34, 59; *Time and Free Will*, 30; Bergsonian duration, 153
Bible, 71
Bishop, Elizabeth, 20–21
Blake, William, 3, 245
Blanchot, Maurice, 207–08 ("The Essential Solitude")
Bloom, Harold, 13, 123
Bonaparte, Napoleon, 133
Borges, Jorge Luis, 97, 167, 252, 253, 257; "The Garden of the Forking Paths," 252
Brisman, Susan and Leslie, 117–18
Byron, George Gordon, 6, 136

Center, 88, 92, 95; and circumference, 70. *See also* Expansiveness
Certainty, 125, 198–99. *See also* Meaning
Chance, 22, 73, 97, 135, 169, 242. *See also* Frayings
Closure, 15, 63, 86, 151, 152. *See also* Ends
Coleridge, Samuel Taylor, 2, 3, 6, 9, 28, 105, 106, 108, 109, 137; *The Friend*, 2, 3; *Biographia Literaria*, 28
Columbus, Christopher, 251
Consciousness, 29, 42, 45, 48, 77, 186, 193, 202, 207, 215, 223, 241. *See also* Perception, Phenomenology, Self
Creeley, Robert, 194

Dasein, 26, 45, 190, 192, 194, 207, 254
Death, 107, 114, 246. *See also* Mortality
Decentering, 93, 173, 199. *See also* Deconstruction, Displacement
de Certeau, Michel, 277
Deconstruction, 10, 12, 14, 21, 58, 88, 91, 92, 94, 96, 97, 101, 103, 104, 105, 162, 179. *See also* Decentering, Deferral, Difference, Dissemination, Erasure, Fragmentation, Frayings, Language, Supplement, Trace, Uncertainty
Deferral, 4, 60, 62, 75, 78, 80, 85, 86, 87, 92, 94, 102, 111, 113, 118, 142, 143, 144, 150, 151, 198, 244. *See also* Difference, Duration, Pause, Uncertainty
Deleuze, Charles, 108

DeMan, Paul, 67, 178
Derrida, Jacques, 6, 9, 10, 22, 32, 38, 39, 44, 45, 52, 68, 69, 72, 77, 78, 89, 92, 116, 117, 123, 129, 134, 137, 142, 146, 148, 150, 151, 153, 154, 157, 161, 165, 176, 180, 181, 189, 194, 195, 219, 223, 236, 241, 242, 243, 244, 262, 274; *Writing and Difference*, 39, 111, 113; "Violence and Metaphysics," 39; *Speech and Phenomena*, 68; "Force and Signification," 72; *Of Grammatology*, 77; *La Carte Postale*, 121; "Genesis and Structure," 163; *Margins*, 199, 216, 220; *Dissemination*, 220, 225
Dialectic, 67, 91, 196, 220, 245, 258
Dialogic, 142, 177, 178, 179, 186. *See also* Bakhtin, Mikhail
Difference (and *differance*), 10, 45, 46, 62, 113, 114, 135, 146, 151, 160, 161, 165, 220. *See also* Deconstruction; Derrida, Jacques
Displacement, 88, 147, 181. *See also* Decentering, Frayings
Dissemination, 163, 180
Doublings, 8, 9, 89, 158, 224, 225, 234. *See also* Meaning, Difference
Dreams, 9, 54, 75, 76, 81, 117, 133, 189, 205, 228, 230. *See also* Unconscious
Duncan, Robert, 195
Duration, 32, 68, 73, 130, 149, 152, 160, 163, 183; "perdurance," 33; as "epoch," 97. *See also* Fourfold, Instant, Moment, Pause, Presence, Temporality, Time

Echoes, 55, 91, 114, 125, 176, 181, 196, 197, 198, 199, 200, 201, 202–04, 220, 223, 224, 228, 229. *See also* Repetition
Eliot, T. S.: *Four Quartets*, 14, 152
Elsewhere, 203, 206, 219, 221–22, 228, 236. *See also* Absence, Other
Emptiness, 93, 243, 245, 271. *See also* Nothingness
Encomium, 206
Ends, 105, 146, 186, 247. *See also* Beginnings, Closure, Origins
Epiphany, 278. *See also* Transformation
Erasure, 78, 151, 242–43, 244, 245, 252. *See also* Trace
Eternal recurrence, 95, 104, 146, 159, 161, 175, 272, 273. *See also* History, Repetition, Return
Eternity, 194, 225. *See also* Time

294

Index

Index

About the Author

Richard Jackson is U.C. Foundation Associate Professor of English, University of Tennessee at Chattanooga, and Editor, *The Poetry Miscellany*. He is author of *Acts of Mind: Conversations with Contemporary Poets* (1983), and two books of poems, *Part of the Story* (1983) and *Worlds Apart* (1987).